FAITH

STUDIES IN PRACTICAL THEOLOGY

Series Editors

Don S. Browning

James W. Fowler

Friedrich Schweitzer

Johannes A. van der Ven

FAITH

*A Practical
Theological Reconstruction*

F. Gerrit Immink

Translated by
Reinder Bruinsma

*William B. Eerdmans Publishing Company
Grand Rapids, Michigan / Cambridge, U.K.*

Original Dutch edition published under the title
In God geloven. Een praktisch-theologische reconstructie.
© 2003 Uitgeverij Meinema

Wm. B. Eerdmans Publishing Co.
255 Jefferson Ave. S.E., Grand Rapids, Michigan 49503 /
P.O. Box 163, Cambridge CB3 9PU U.K.

Printed in the United States of America

10 09 08 07 06 05   7 6 5 4 3 2 1

Library of Congress Cataloging-in-Publication Data

Immink, F. Gerrit.
[In God geloven. English]
Faith: a practical theological reconstruction /
F. Gerrit Immink; translated by Reinder Bruinsma.
p.   cm.
Includes bibliographical references and index.
ISBN 0-8028-2793-4 (pbk.)
1. Theology, Practical. 2. Faith. I. Title.

BV3.I45 2005
234'.23 — dc22

2005040483

www.eerdmans.com

Contents

CONTENTS

Preface

Reflecting on the life of faith is a fascinating adventure. To a certain extent, this is what every believer does. We wonder what we actually believe and what meaning this has for our everyday life. Also, the truth of our faith is tested and confirmed during the journey we travel through life, and this also demands repeated reflection. Because our life of faith is such an existential process, we need to evaluate it constantly. Only in so doing will we become aware of the value of our faith.

This book is a result of a systematic reflection on the praxis of faith. Two aspects played a major role in the background while I was writing it: (1) attention to the unique character of faith as it is lived; and (2) the construction and development of a theoretical framework within which we can analyze faith as it is lived. I consider both aspects to be vital to the discipline of practical theology. With regard to faith as it is lived, I am concerned with *praxis* in the Christian tradition, and in the theoretical framework I explore not only fundamental concepts from the faith tradition but also some nontheological concepts

This book is based on theological training and exposure to praxis. My initial interest in systematics received a new depth during my training in analytical philosophy with Alvin Plantinga and Nicholas Wolterstorff. They have inspired me in the conceptual analysis of belief in God. During my years in a Reformed Church parish (1979-1987) I became more intensely aware of the close ties between faith and everyday life. As dean of the Theological Seminary of the Reformed Church (1987-1993), I was involved in the training of ministers and consciously turned toward practical theology. During that period, clinical pastoral training and the practical training of ministers made me increasingly aware of the complexity of interpersonal communication.

Since my appointment as professor of practical theology at the University of Utrecht (The Netherlands), I have concentrated on a theoretical study of the praxis of faith. In teaching theology students I attempt to keep theological content, faith as it is lived, and interpersonal communication together; and in doing so I have put the concept of faith at the center of my analysis. In this book I will focus primarily on the international discussion in the field of practical theology, with a special interest in the foundations of practical theology.

The Theory of Praxis

Faith in Practice

Faith has meaning: it is a source of inspiration, it shapes our lifestyles, and it creates hope and expectation. Faith receives concrete form in human life: it is shaped by the developments we experience, in the crises we face, and in the encounters, relationships, and contexts in which our lives evolve. In this sense, faith has a human measure and a personal face. Faith is lived. The fact that it is lived also means that it is embedded in human life and is something that matters. Faith and life interact closely and are interwoven. At times the facts of life challenge our faith; at other times our faith enables us to keep going. In short, there is a dynamic relationship between everyday life and human faith.

Faith is, as a very part of its nature, a social and communicative event. It presupposes the presence of the Other, of God as well as other human beings. Faith is realized in intersubjective relationships. Having faith not only implies that I have certain opinions, but also that I live in a relationship with God and with other people. This relationship implies a living communion. Significant aspects of our faith, such as love, justice, and faithfulness, express themselves in intersubjective relationships — that is, they are realized in encounter and communion. And our faith is therefore indissolubly linked with the quality of the life of communion. So it will hardly surprise us that the core of the praxis of faith is formed by the interaction between God and human beings, as well as among humans.

Faith implies — at least in the Christian praxis of faith — belief in God, and this dimension of our faith will form an explicit theme of this study. Having faith in God not only means that we have certain opinions about God but that we live in a dynamic relationship, or dialogue, with God. There is a communal relationship with God that we may imagine as a mutual, concrete interaction between subjects. For that reason it is important in our analysis of the praxis of faith to investigate both the human act of faith and the divine activity in the life of human beings. We should never separate these two poles from each other. In our secularized society, most questions arise concerning the pole of the divine presence and action. I will not ignore such questions; rather, I will argue that there is ample justification for a theological analysis of the praxis of faith.

Numerous activities in the praxis of the church, such as worship services, diaconal and pastoral care, catechesis and working with "small groups," indicate that faith is indeed a social and communicative phenomenon. These activities, which contribute to the nurture and development of spiritual life, are embedded in interpersonal communication. We are able to talk about our faith and to share it with one another. And it is precisely this ability to put faith into words and to share these words with others that also helps to frame and build our spiritual life. One of the key questions in this book is how this human interchange is related to the practice of our communion with God.

This study focuses on the praxis of faith. Faith as it is lived by men and women, rather than faith as a system of doctrine, is the central theme. What do we mean by "faith as it is lived"? What role does communication play in the praxis of faith? And how do we name God?

The Uniqueness of the Praxis of Faith

Faith is realized in the concrete acts, convictions, experiences, and expectations of human beings. Practical theology is the theological discipline that deals with faith-under-construction. This makes it both fascinating and problematic: fascinating because we study a dynamic reality, a reality that is constantly changing and is determined by the specific moment and the uniqueness of the situation; problematic because, as in any scientific discipline, we like to work with concepts and models. Scientific understanding is linked to theoretical constructs and systematic reflection: we look at phenomena from our conceptualizations and theoretical constructs, and in so doing we detect what is constant or variable, regular or irregular. We may well ask whether practical theology is at all possible. Shouldn't we stay with the practice that always tends to be at variance with any abstraction? Doesn't this abstraction always do injustice to the existential character of our faith?

In our pursuit of practical theology we attempt to do justice to the peculiar character of our domain of study. But we should always keep the following considerations in mind: (1) We must distinguish between the act of faith and the reflection on faith. In living our faith, we use language in a certain way and are involved in acts that do not occur in our reflection on our faith praxis. In the first instance we are faced with existential language of actual praxis; in the second instance we meet reflective and scientific analysis, which takes place at a different level. Practical theology is, according to Schleiermacher, the theory of praxis.[1] (2) But this requires that, in reflective analysis, we do justice to the language and experience that are peculiar to the exercise of our faith. In some instances it may be advantageous for the researcher himself or herself to participate in the field of inquiry. He or she will then know from experience about this existential dimension and will have an eye for the complexity and the dynamic of praxis. A homiletician who has never preached in a church service or a pastoral theologian who has never worked in a pastoral setting runs the risk of studying praxis solely from a theory-driven perspective, resulting, fairly readily, in an elimination of the complexity and unruliness of praxis. (3) This leaves us with the question of how we can, from the level of the theoretical, truly touch on the praxis of faith. How can we observe faith as it is lived? Is it at all possible to grasp it, since faith by its very nature is not dissolved in the mundane but, in fact, reaches out to a reality beyond the visible? In our practical theological reflection we try to do justice to the mysteriousness of the life of faith, with a view to both the existential character of the human act of faith and the *presentia Dei*.

In the most recent pursuit of practical theology, this awareness of the peculiarity of the praxis of faith has returned. Practical theology,

---

1. "The expression 'praktisch' [practical] is not fully correct, for Practical Theology does not refer to praxis, but to the theory of the praxis." Friedrich Schleiermacher, *Die praktische Theologie nach den Grundsätzen der Evangelischen Kirche im Zusammenhang Dargestellt,* ed. Jacob Frerichs (Berlin, 1850; repr., New York, 1983), p. 12.

3

H. G. Heimbrock affirms, must take note of a power that discloses reality; for humans continue to reach out, through faith, toward a new God-given reality.[2] Heimbrock maintains that a strictly empirical approach to the praxis of faith will not do full justice to the phenomenon of "believing," and he calls for a phenomenological approach. The point at stake is the study of the unique character of faith reality. Albrecht Grözinger calls for a more aesthetic approach from the very same motive. He compares the experience of God with the kind of experience we have when faced with a work of art. Grözinger sees the concept of revelation as a central notion in the praxis of faith. But isn't revelation associated with various negative attitudes, such as subjection and dependence? In his attempt to get some grip on the phenomenon of revelation, Grözinger draws a parallel with the way we look at a painting. How does it have an impact on us? We are moved along, we are impressed, but are we also overpowered by it?

> When we deal with a work of art, we move into a sphere of influences that carry us along. And that has everything to do with power, but nothing with violence.[3]

Both the phenomenological and the aesthetic approaches try to do justice to the peculiar nature of the life of faith. They represent currents of thought that demand attention for "the art of observation," and they warn against a reductionist way of dealing with the reality of faith. But we should not forget that their contribution is limited to the observation of the way in which faith is manifested in daily life. They do not provide us with any method for analysis. In that respect, empirical theology offers better opportunities by describing the reality of faith in empirical documents by means of qualitative and quantitative methods, such as interviews, polls, observations, or protocols, followed by a systematic analysis.

2. Wolf-Eckart Failing and Hans Günther Heimbrock, *Gelebte Religion Wahrnehme. Lebenswelt — Alltagskultur — Religionspraxis* (Stuttgart/Berlin, 1998), pp. 11-36.
3. Albrecht Grözinger, *Praktische Theologie als Kunst der Wahrnehmung* (Gütersloh, 1995), p. 149.

Points of Departure in Practical Theology

The concrete field of religious practice has through the years been charted from various perspectives. I will mention two classical approaches that still retain a certain plausibility. First, there is the ecclesial model, which views religious praxis from the perspective of the church's activities. Naturally, this emphasizes the institutional aspects of religion. We find this line of thinking particularly in the nineteenth-century approaches to practical theology. "The content, the object of practical theology," Theodor Liebner says, "is what the church itself does to itself."[4] In the second half of the twentieth century we see a growing interest in the way the church functions as a whole. "Emphasis has been laid on (a) the *internal* functioning of the congregation . . . and (b) the *external* impact of the church."[5] Don Browning, for instance, offers an intensive description of three congregations before he attempts to answer the question, "In what way do religious communities make sense?"[6] Several good arguments support this attention to the church. The Christian faith expresses itself within the context of the church, and we cannot deny that the activities of the church provide shape and content to the Christian faith. There are numerous church activities — for instance, worship services, catechesis, work in small groups, pastoral and diaconal work — that give expression to faith, while at the same time providing stimulus and nurture to it. Of course, we need to keep in mind that the church does not exist for its own sake. The church is an instrument in the service of the gospel and exists to support the life of faith.

In addition to this ecclesial approach, one may choose leadership in the praxis of faith as the point of departure. We refer to this as the clerical model, for it focuses on the work of pastors, priests, and all those who hold a church office or have a paid job in church work. It is not surprising that those who are involved in practical theology as an academic discipline start from the leadership perspective. The classical

---

4. Theodor Albert Liebner, "Begriff, Gegenstand und Einteilung der praktischen Theologie," in *Praktische Theologie. Texte zum Werden und Selbstverständnis der praktischen Disziplin der Evangelischen Theologie,* ed. Gerhard Krause (Darmstadt, 1972), p. 59.

5. G. D. J. Dingemans, "Practical Theology in the Academy: A Contemporary Overview," *Journal of Religion* 76:1 (1996): 84.

6. Don S. Browning, *A Fundamental Practical Theology: Descriptive and Strategic Proposals* (Minneapolis, 1991), p. 1.

subdisciplines in practical theology — liturgy, homiletics, pastoral work, and catechesis — study the various aspects of the work of the pastor. The connecting link is found in the fact that a faith community is provided with leadership, and that these leaders are supposed to have academic and professional competence. It was Schleiermacher who gave a significant impetus to the development of this all-encompassing view by placing the structure of the academic study of theology in this framework. Even though leadership is embedded in a relationship of reciprocity with the faith community, this does not take away from the distinction between church leadership and the community, according to Schleiermacher. This distinction has to do with the communication of faith that takes places within the faith community; for there is a producing and a receiving element in the communication of the faith.[7] In accordance with this unique character of a faith community, adequate leadership must be developed and, consequently, the cohesion of the theological disciplines is found in the work of the pastor. Even today this approach, which starts with the work of the pastor, plays an important role in pastoral theology. According to Manfred Josuttis, pastors give support to people as they journey through life, and the key aspect of their work is to accompany people in "the hidden zone of the holy."[8]

New Models

In the course of the twentieth century, resistance to the ecclesial and clerical models increased. The 1950s and 1960s brought drastic change in society, which in turn raised the question of the social and political relevance of church and theology. Religion is judged on the basis of its relevance to society and not on the basis of its meaning within the confines of the church. Fully in line with these developments, Alfred Müller writes that the church does not exist "for its own sake, but for the sake of the Kingdom of God, in support of the claim that God has on this world."[9] In the 1960s, in particular, we saw an apostolic,

7. Schleiermacher, *Praktische Theologie*, p. 16.
8. Manfred Josuttis, *Die Einführung in das Leben. Pastoraltheologie zwischen Phaenomenologie und Spiritualität* (Gütersloh, 1996), p. 14.
9. Alfred Dedo Müller, *Grundriss der praktischen Theologie* (Gütersloh, 1950), p. 14.

outward-directed movement: the church exists for the world, and the world plays a role in determining the church's agenda. This resulted in practical theological models that gave priority to the interaction between the church and the world. In addition to the ideology-critical method, James Poling and Donald Miller say that the relationship between church and society provides the second axis in practical theology.[10] At the same time, the social sciences received an independent place within practical theology. Friedrich Schweitzer says that, in those days, the impression was sometimes created "that the social sciences have become the only legitimate access to contemporary culture."[11] This interaction between church and society also is an important theme in the kind of practical theology that developed in the 1980s — with its hermeneutical and empirical orientations. Johannes van der Ven says that the interaction between church and society, not the church as such, forms the object of study of practical theology.

> In this orientation, practical theology is no longer located within the boundaries of the church, but rather within the system of coordinates that is made up of society, Christianity and the church. The task of the church is to trace and to think through the interactions or lack thereof between Christianity inside the church and that outside of it, as well as between religious and non-religious phenomena in society.[12]

As a result of these changes, practical theology not only seeks to give account of the theological character of the Christian faith but also wishes to observe the developments in modern society and to take these into account in the analysis of religious praxis. The modernizing of society, Gerben Heitink says, has changed practical theology into a science of crisis.[13]

---

10. James N. Poling and Donald E. Miller, *Foundations for a Practical Theology of Ministry* (Nashville, 1985), p. 31.

11. Friedrich Schweitzer and Johannes A. van der Ven, eds., *Practical Theology: International Perspectives* (Frankfurt am Main/Berlin, 1999), p. 308.

12. Johannes A. van der Ven, *Practical Theology: An Empirical Approach* (Kampen, 1993), p. 38.

13. Gerben Heitink, *Practical Theology: History, Theory, Action Domains* (Grand Rapids, 1999), p. 49.

A New Interest in Religion

Whereas the focus tended to be mostly on the meaning of the church for society in the 1970s and 1980s, it shifted more and more toward interest in religion from the 1990s onward.[14] There was a slow discarding of the idea that secularization and modernization are indissolubly linked. At first scientists had silently endorsed the so-called zero-sum theory, that is, that the sum total of modernization and religion will always be zero: the more religion, the less modernization, and, especially, vice versa — the more modernization, the less religion. Gradually this thesis of secularization is headed in a different direction; religion and modernity are seen in a more positive relationship toward each other.

Secularization is no longer exclusively viewed as a continuous process of decreased religiosity but as a change in religious consciousness. We cannot deny the process of unchurching and secularization; but the question is, how do we interpret it? The demise of institutional religion, we are told, does not necessarily point to the end of religion, though it may well point to a change in religion. Hans-Georg Ziebertz believes that our times will not see the extinction of religion, but what remains an open question is this: Which of today's religions have the best chance of survival?[15] It is the task of the church, he continues, to connect with modern forms of religion. Therefore, Wilhelm Gräb argues, practical theology must be a theory of religion rather than a theory of the church.[16] We may note in passing that the use of the word "religion" indicates that the theistic notion is more and more disappearing into the background. The focus shifts from God to the human subject, from revelation to experience, from the institutional church to the local community. Henning Luther, for example, develops a practical theology of the human subject in which the evolving subject plays an important role.[17]

14. "While in the 1970's the trend of the unchurching of Christianity (Jesus, yes; church, no) dominated the discussion, this was displaced in the 1980's by the tendency towards a de-christianizing of spirituality (religious, yes; but why be a Christian?)." Wilhelm Gräb, *Lebensgeschichten, Lebensentwürfe, Sinndeutungen. Eine Praktische Theologie gelebter Religion* (Gütersloh, 1998), p. 32.

15. Hans-Georg Ziebertz, *Religie in een Tijd zonder Religie?* (Utrecht, 1996), p. 27.

16. Gräb, *Lebensgeschichten*, p. 25.

17. Henning Luther, *Religion und Alltag. Bausteine zu einer Praktische Theologie des Subjects* (Stuttgart, 1992), p. 30.

Luther is of the opinion that the traditional forms of religion will die out, but that this does not lead to the disappearance of the importance of religion. Religious life will be less precisely delineated than in the past; it will be less guided by tradition and increasingly by one's own life experiences. This is at the root of the growing interest in the biography of the individual.

Finding Our Own Position

What is our perspective as we look at religious praxis? We may take our point of departure from the church, the work of the pastor, or the interaction between church and society in all its complexity. Each of those approaches can be justified to a degree. Yet we may well ask the question whether, in doing so, we may ignore one of the most fundamental concepts amid these various perspectives. The questions are: (a) What does the church want to achieve? (b) What purpose is served by the work of the pastor? (c) What is at stake in the interaction between church and society? For whatever difference there may be in the various perspectives, they all reflect the dimensions of the praxis of faith. It is remarkable that the very notion of *faith* has received scant attention in recent practical theological proposals. Karl Nipkow feels that the focus on ethical and political issues has put the theme of faith on a side track in practical theology.[18] I believe there are a number of reasons for this development, of which I will mention four: (1) Through the influence of dialectical theology, revelation became the central pursuit of theology, and the concept of faith was thereby moved to the sideline. (2) The more liberal traditions, with their emphasis on the concept of faith — due to their anthropological anchoring of religious life — continued to have problems with the concrete content of many aspects of faith. The result was that they replaced the concept of faith with the much broader concept of religiosity. (3) Because of the increasing influence of the social sciences in the domain of practical theology, theologians increasingly avoided doctrinal concepts. Practical theological studies made an increasing use of anthropological categories, with

---

18. Karl Ernst Nipkow, "Practical Theology and Contemporary Culture," in Schweitzer and Van der Ven, eds., *Practical Theology: International Perspectives*, p. 104.

the result that the life of faith was no longer analyzed by means of the theological criteria from the faith tradition. (4) The paradigm of action theory has also contributed to something of a discrediting of the category of faith; for it implied that in religious praxis decisions are reached in the sphere of action. The primary role of action has caused the more spiritual-intellectual dimension, which does play a role in the concept of faith, to move to the background.

In this book I will call for an analysis of religious praxis from the perspective of *believing*. The praxis we will study is to be viewed as the praxis of faith; that is to say, we will be dealing with believers. In the Christian tradition, faith is the central function of religious life. Religious practices may be expressed in many different ways and may be explained by the use of all kinds of concepts, but through it all faith remains the underlying category. Of course, the way faith is shaped by the church is important, and in that sense we may thus speak about the praxis of the church. But faith constitutes the core element. Without a living faith, the praxis of the church would be no more than an empty shell. When the concept of faith has a central place, human beings enter the picture. But this does not mean that I intend to construe a practical theology on the basis of anthropology.

Human beings do not stand alone; they live in a relationship with God and their fellow humans. Indeed, I consider faith as an active involvement, as an existential relationship between subjects. As this book unfolds, I will work this out in greater detail. This means that, as we pursue practical theological reflection, we must consider both the human and the divine subject in our analysis of the praxis of faith. The communion between God and humankind does indeed presuppose human subjectivity and an adequate functioning of our intellectual capacities. Therefore, giving central place to the concept of faith implies that we are faced with an anthropological dimension as we analyze the praxis of religion. But there is more. Since faith understands itself as a living relationship with God, it also expresses that our human existence refers to the reality of God and his salvation. And this divine reality is such that we speak about our communion with that reality in terms of encounter, relationship, dialogue, and so forth. Therefore, the connection between God and humans is understood as personal in nature, in the sense that God is seen as the subject of word and action, that is, as a person full of initiative and energy. This means that faith is more than an anthropological category in and of itself. In theological terms, faith implies the actual communion between God and humans. We are dealing with a view of reality that presents God as the subject of word and action, and in which such notions as "encounter" and "communion" are present from the very start, that is, as part of our human nature. This communion is not simply an assumption rooted in our human self-consciousness; rather, it is the other way around: humans learn to know themselves in their encounter with God. God makes himself known as the one who calls and saves us. The faith relationship is thus a receptive communion: there is always a bipolar situation — speaking and hearing.

Partners in Dialogue

The study of religious praxis from the perspective of faith provides me with a solid point of departure in the academic discourse of practical theology. While taking the results of the work done by the social sciences and the humanities into account, I believe that it remains important for practical theology to profile itself as a theological discipline. The conceptual framework for the analysis of praxis cannot be satisfactorily developed without full use of the concepts and distinctions used by the faith tradition. At the same time, we should not forget that religious praxis is embedded in daily life. It is a way of doing things — a lifestyle — and it consists of certain customs, habits, attitudes, and sentiments. And the faith concept has those two sides. On the one side, I will explore the theological connotation. We will see that, in the light of the Protestant tradition, faith is indissolubly linked with a gracious acquittal from God. That, in turn, indicates that God's role has priority in this relationship of faith. On the other side, I will explore the ways in which faith is embedded in the human mind and in everyday life. The functions of the human spirit are enlisted in the act of faith, and the psychosocial aspects of life fully resonate with it.

From this position, I believe that I am able to enter into a meaningful dialogue with practical theology that is primarily anthropologically oriented. Faith is a fully human phenomenon. I agree with the older theologians who are more anthropologically oriented, for example, Schleiermacher and Tillich; and I also agree with the younger generation (represented by Henning Luther and Wilhelm Gräb) that the human subject has a central role in the praxis of faith. I do object to the failure of this latter group to give adequate attention to the theological aspects of the concept of faith; in their propositions, the pole of the divine "Other" has disappeared. They appeal to Luther's *adagio* of the "justification of the sinner," but this receives no theological weight. The reason I refer to these German theologians is that they explicitly intend to continue the tradition of Protestantism as a cultural phenomenon *(Kulturprotestantismus)*. As we continue our explorations, we will meet other practical theologians who advocate a primarily anthropological approach to the praxis of religion; indeed, I am in dialogue with this tradition as I develop my own ideas. I also wish to enter into dialogue with Johannes A. van der Ven, a practical theologian at the University of Nijmegen. He belongs to the empirical school in practical theology and is an internationally renowned thinker. I will deal with his work in Chapters 7 and 8 of this study, where I will also state my own position with regard to practical theology. Since Schleiermacher is generally regarded as one of the founding fathers of the study of practical theology, and his vision of the life of faith has greatly influenced what I refer to as the anthropological model, I will outline his position in the section on the communication of faith. In Chapter 10, I will give ample space to the anthropological approach to the praxis of religion.

There is still one other practical theological tradition that is part of the dialogue: kerygmatic theology. This current of thought analyzes religious praxis solely on the basis of theological concepts. Divine revelation, particularly, plays a central role. Praxis, we are told, follows God's self-revelation. We cannot hope to understand human praxis when we ignore God's praxis — his words and actions. Faith, as life in communion with God, thus receives its specific content in this communion with the divine. God's words and deeds shape our faith. And this praxis of faith is thus closely linked to the salvific revelation that received its form in the history of Israel and in the life, death, and resurrection of Christ. Chapters 3 and 4 will cover the theology of praxis. But I will show that salvation is not simply revealed but must also be realized in our lives as human beings. It also includes the "indwelling" of this salvation and the renewal of humanity. I believe that it is precisely the Reformed tradition that has developed a balanced theology in this regard, a theology that is constructive and useful. The revelationary model, I feel, does not do enough justice to the actualization of salvation in human existence (see Chapter 9). I consider revelation and faith as correlates: the former accentuates the divine initiative, and the latter the anthropological appearance.

The Structure of This Book

This book has four sections, each of which forms a thematic unit. The first part, entitled "Faith and Life," deals with the way faith is embedded in actual life situations. Chapter 1 deals with some aspects of the anthropological context of our faith and with metaphysical presuppositions about God. Chapter 2 focuses on the position of the human subject in the praxis of faith and the intertwinement of faith and everyday life.

In Part II, "The Theology of Praxis," I deal with a few fundamental concepts that have arisen over time from a systematic reflection on praxis. I will restrict myself to some notions related to the concept of faith and closely linked to the life of faith. Chapters 3 and 4 describe the two sides of this relationship of faith — Chapter 3 with the divine imputation of salvation and Chapter 4 with the indwelling of salvation.

Part III, "Building a Practical Theological Theory," deals with the development of practical theological theories, pointing to interpersonal communication as an important key in the analysis of praxis. I will particularly investigate the role of interpersonal discourse in the process of shaping faith — and the resulting shape of faith. I will focus explicitly on the way we name God. In this section I seek a dialogue with the hermeneutical-communicative and the empirical paradigms.

In Part IV, "Reconstructions of Praxis," I wish to reconstruct the praxis of faith from two perspectives. In Chapter 9, I describe praxis from the point of view of revelation theology, and in Chapter 10 from an anthropocentric perspective. In illustrating this perspective on praxis, I take my point of departure in both cases in preaching and pastoral work. In Chapter 11, I analyze some fundamental aspects of the formation of practical theological theories. The building blocks for this foundational discussion do appear in other chapters, but the theoretical argumentation reaches its final unfolding in Chapter 11. Chapter 12 is a concluding chapter that describes the reciprocal connections between the faith relationship and the communication of faith.

PART I

Faith and Life

The Structure of Faith

Charting Our Course

Faith is enacted in a constant interaction with the vicissitudes of life. The social, economic, and biological parameters within which our life is lived matter. Meanwhile, faith remains an act of human beings. When we say "I believe," we thereby indicate that it is an act in which the subject, the "self," is involved. Even though people are interconnected through numerous structures and social networks, and even though the community plays an important role in Christian faith, it is nonetheless the individual human subject who believes. The sociologist Peter Berger even speaks of the "solitary believer."[1]

But what kind of activity is faith? At first glance, it seems to be an umbrella concept: it covers a large series of attitudes and activities. By referring to a person as "a believer," we intend to say that that person is religious or has a religious lifestyle. But the term "faith" may also be used concerning the sum total of a person's religious ideas and convictions; or it may have an even more pregnant meaning, one that points to one's trust in God or to the conviction that God reveals himself in his Word.

The word "faith" is also often used in a more specifically Christian sense when we refer to a life in communion with Christ: it implies that Christ has a determining significance for the believer. Through this communion with him we receive God's salvation, and our faith

---

1. Peter L. Berger, *A Far Glory: The Quest for Faith in an Age of Credulity* (New York, 1992), p. 87.

then is our bond with Christ. God comes to us in his grace and compassion and grants us a share in the salvation of Christ. This approach clearly underscores the fact that faith is a divine gift. The point of gravity is not with humans but with the God who comes to meet us with reconciliation and liberation. God is the source of our faith. This brings an important aspect of the structure of the Christian faith to expression: faith is an answer, a response to a God who speaks, a reply to God's promise. It is not a man-made product, but it results from the revelation of the living God. Faith, therefore, is something that takes shape in our lives, but its actualization is of divine origin.

This chapter will be devoted mainly to the anthropological and metaphysical structure of faith, both of which play an important role in this book. By way of introduction, I will make a few remarks regarding these aspects.

1. Since our faith is part and parcel of the way we lead our lives, we are able to trace faith as a phenomenon in the human sphere of life. We are dealing with people who believe, and since these people have a concrete existence, their faith will also assume a concrete form. Their faith is anchored in their human existence. For that reason we want to explore how the act of faith is embedded in the human subject.

2. But faith also has an "object" dimension: it consists in a relationship with God. Theology does not analyze faith as a purely human phenomenon but views it from the perspective of communion with God. This immediately raises a number of metaphysical questions. In what sense can we speak of God as a subject over against the human subject? Is God — if there is to be a mutual relationship — also a subject who speaks and acts just as we do? The very moment we talk about God (and we do this, of course, in the praxis of faith), we are faced with numerous questions regarding our knowledge of God and the way we can speak about God. We will not be able to avoid these questions, along with the metaphysical problems they entail.

This chapter will not try to explain faith on the basis of the structure of the human mind. The Christian faith finds its identity and particularity in the history of salvation. But this does not deny that, based

18

on this peculiarity, faith receives its concrete form in the lives of human beings. It is embedded in human life and receives its *gestalt* in the infrastructure of the human mind. If this were not the case, faith would remain a strange element, unconnected to human existence, neither integrated in life nor in the person. And this would not be in tune with the nature of the Christian faith. For God's salvation does not hang in the air; it is experienced and practiced in a concrete way. People become involved with God and live in expectation of God's salvation. The whole human being is drawn in.

Yet this analysis of faith in anthropological and metaphysical categories continues to raise questions. If we use these categories, don't we run too much of a risk of thinking too exclusively in general human categories and viewing faith exclusively as a human act? Doesn't this force the words and concepts that have come to us through the process of revelation into a strange straitjacket? Isn't there the risk that the concepts derived from insights of the human sciences will dominate our faith analysis? Revelation theology, in particular, poses these critical questions. Noordmans warns that, in that scenario, Word and Spirit may easily be reduced to human processes; as a result, we may leave the Word of God behind. He argues that the gospel, which consists of Word and Spirit, will "thus be reduced to a philosophy of life, the church to a sociological concept, and faith to mere experience."[2]

But, in spite of these concerns, I believe that we must choose this route in order to gain insight into the praxis of faith. Otherwise, faith would remain a phenomenon alien to the human mind, and the infrastructure of the human mind would play no role in the way faith functions in daily life. The practical theologian must make an independent judgment about theological and nontheological theorizing about the human being and human faith. It turns out that not just any metaphysical theory is compatible with a theological perspective on faith. An anthropology whose primary roots are in naturalism and behaviorism will interpret the human consciousness as a biological phenomenon: a natural "brain process" that is subject to stimuli. Does such a theory allow us to speak about a consciousness and a "self," notions that I believe are presupposed in the concept of faith? If we want to give a place to anthropological and metaphysical theories, we must be alert

---

2. O. Noordmans, *Verzamelde Werken*, vol. 2 (Kampen, 1979), p. 204.

19

to the presuppositions and consequences of those theories; and we should especially be aware of the possibility that they may result in a reductionist impact on our faith. For example, based on his naturalistic view of humans, John Searle says:

> For us, the educated members of society, the world has become demystified. Or rather, to put the point more precisely, we no longer take the mysteries we see in the world as expressions of supernatural meaning. . . . For us, if it should turn out that God exists, that would have to be a fact of nature like any other. To the four basic forces in the universe — gravity, electromagnetism, weak and strong nuclear forces — we would add a fifth, the divine force. Or more likely, we would see the other forces as forms of the divine force. But it would still be all physics, albeit divine physics. If the supernatural existed, it too would have to be natural.[3]

This is an example of how naturalistic anthropology puts its stamp on the interpretation of reality. Why would we follow such a view in all respects? It offers scant perspective if we want to make faith comprehensible. I should note, however, that Searle rejects a totally "flat" form of materialism in his anthropology. He believes that human consciousness is caused by biological processes in the brain, but that it represents a higher order in brain functions. Thus he attempts to highlight subjectivity, which is part and parcel of the human consciousness, and thereby to explain our intentional involvement with existence. In other words, the open space he creates in his anthropology disappears as soon as God enters the picture.

Whatever approach we choose, our theories will always contain presuppositions that are in tension with a theological perspective. That such tension exists is not altogether problematical; after all, we view many things in life from various positions. In the various currents of Idealism, material reality disappears into the background, and the human consciousness becomes the pivotal point of our existence. These imbalances are not stumbling blocks in themselves, for they do provide us with a certain view of reality. But we must be sure to recognize the specific perspective of these anthropological approaches, while at the

3. John R. Searle, *Mind, Language and Society: Philosophy in the Real World* (New York, 1999), p. 35.

same time we create an open space for a theological view of faith as it is lived.

Attention to Human Beings as Spiritual Beings

Insofar as faith receives its concrete shape in everyday life, the human subject is involved. But how? Faith is characterized by action, that is, it expresses itself in a concrete lifestyle, in actions and behavior. But those actions are rooted in motives, considerations, choices, and aspirations. This points to the "inside" nature of our faith, its anchoring in the infrastructure of the human mind. Thus faith takes the form of an attitude. It is a lifestyle in which living-in-trust, compassion, and humility play an important role. Faith also takes the form of emotion or state of mind, expressing itself in feelings of dependence, remorse, joy, and gratitude. Although it makes itself known in a particular way through behavior and actions, it is also an intellectual condition. Further, faith is also a matter of beliefs. These beliefs may refer to God or to humanity and the world, but they are nonetheless a function of the human mind. Of course, these beliefs may evolve through a process of education and tradition, but that does not take away from the fact that they develop in the human mind — in, for example, a noetic act. Faith, therefore, is a phenomenon that receives its form in the functions of the human mind, and this requires that the human being be a spiritual being. The same is true for the various dimensions of faith praxis, such as giving thanks, worship, confession, and so forth. These activities presuppose the functions of the human mind and human consciousness. Thus faith is not an isolated function, detached from knowledge, feelings, and the will.

Let me make a few observations about the terms I intend to use. I use terms such as "human spirit," "human mind," "inner self," and "spiritual abilities" interchangeably. I also use the term "consciousness" as synonymous with our mental abilities and not as a counterpart to the subconscious. In speaking generally about the human mind, we may see it as that aspect of our being that knows, feels, and wills. Knowing, feeling, and willing provide the rubrics for the countless functions performed by the human mind. These three categories should be regarded as an ordering of a multifaceted event: they provide useful and practical structure to an utterly complex phenomenon. But is the human mind also synonymous with the human psyche? Not entirely. A reflection on the life of the human psyche does indeed deal with a similar phenomenon, that is, our inner life; but here the emphasis is more on the relationship between inter- and intrapersonal processes. Depending on the perspective we choose, we will consider these processes from the angle of the physical-biological or the social reality of the person. When I speak of the human psyche, I mainly refer to the psychosocial dimension in which the human mind functions. But when I mention the functions of the human mind, I am pointing to the three elements of knowledge, feelings, and the will.

I will now pay further attention to the ways the human mind functions in the act of faith. Why is our consciousness essential for our human nature as such, and, consequently, why is it relevant to our understanding of faith? Perhaps I can best explain this by pointing to certain aspects of human action. It is characteristic of human action that it not only consists of concrete deeds — our actual behavior — but that it also involves a decision-making process, that it has to do with motivations and aspirations. In that sense, action — more than just behavior — always points inward, to the sphere of commitment and involvement. When we act, we ask ourselves questions such as this: What do I have in mind? What are my motives? On what expectations do I base my actions? Based on this dimension, we say that our actions are an intentional activity. Actions involve an acting person, a subject who makes conscious considerations with respect to his or her actions. This points to an "inside" world of intellectual and spiritual life that participates in our actions.

Human existence thus has a spiritual side; the inner life is a unique dimension beyond our physical existence. This does not necessarily lead to a form of dualism; but we do recognize two facets of the human person, a physical and a spiritual sphere that constantly interact. A third aspect that must be added is the function of language: we can express our inner selves through language and thereby articulate our thoughts and feelings. This is important. Without the ability to express our thoughts in language, many of our thoughts, feelings, and experiences would remain vague and diffuse — even to ourselves. It is precisely this interaction between our consciousness and language that sharpens the functions of the human mind. We clarify things for ourselves as we name and describe our thoughts; our feelings only take shape as we put them into words. And I have not even explored how language enables us to communicate our inner lives to others.

I am often conscious of something in my perceptible world: I feel a nagging pain in my left leg; I see a leafless oak in the garden; I remember a phone call I received last night; I enjoy a glass of wine; I fear I will be late. All these observations express a certain relationship I have with the world I live in. This phenomenon — that is, this ability of our selves to be involved with and relate to the world in which we find ourselves — is a unique characteristic of human beings. By means of our mental activities we become somehow involved with the "external" world.[4] This is precisely what constitutes human subjectivity. The world does not consist merely of objects that portray certain characteristics but also of subjects that exist in a conscious relationship to their environment, subjects that act intentionally. And it is because of these mental functions that we can relate in a specific way to reality (to objects, events, and other people). By and large, this happens through the three central functions — knowledge, will, and feeling — into which our mental functions are usually divided. Our *knowledge* enables us to arrive at a picture of what is happening around us. We use our *will* when we try to initiate or achieve something. Our *feelings* cause a dynamic of attraction or rejection, so that this reality does not leave us indifferent. This is how we approach life and find our way. Because we have these mental abilities, we are able to intentionally focus on the world we live in. We have all kinds of opinions about this world; we cherish numerous expectations about what life will be like a few years hence; we love some people and we dislike others; we fear for the future or hope for the best.

Berger and Luckmann have pointed out that everyday life — and especially as it presents itself to us in the here and now — is present with overpowering intensity in our consciousness.[5] We are able, in our involvement with life, to somewhat regulate this intensity, but we will always remain deeply involved in a situation that has an impact on us directly. For example, the moment the train does not depart, I am aware of the traffic congestion in the country where I live. The moment there is a problem with one of my children, my responsibility as a fa-

---

4. Cf. Searle, *Mind, Language and Society*, pp. 67-83.
5. Peter L. Berger and Thomas Luckmann, *The Social Construction of Reality: A Treatise in the Sociology of Knowledge* (New York/London, 1966), p. 22.

ther takes over, and for the time being my work becomes of relative un-importance. Not everything is always massively and forcefully present. The degree of intentionality varies, and this enables us to distinguish between the center and the periphery — and thus to prioritize. Whether these choices are made on rational or nonrational grounds is another matter.

Practical Theology and the Human Being as Acting Subject

In the preceding paragraphs I have attempted to show that the functions of the mind play an important role in the analysis of faith as it is lived. I do not think that recent practical theological studies have paid adequate attention to this. In the practical theological discussions of the last quarter of the twentieth century, the paradigm of the theory of action took center stage. The following quotation from Yorick Spiegel, which describes the turnaround in the 1970s, indicates that the human being was primarily perceived as an acting being.

> Instead of starting from the basic concept of man as a mental and speaking being, as in philosophical anthropology, man is here defined as a being in action.[6]

The theoretical framework in which religious praxis is explained in this paradigm is primarily inspired by the work of the social philosopher Jürgen Habermas. As a result, human action becomes the object of practical theology. Firet defines praxis as "communicative action in the service of the gospel," and Heitink elaborates this into a practical theological theory of action. He positions religious action within a hermeneutical, an empirical, and a strategic perspective. Van der Ven, in proposing an empirical theology, follows Habermas and gives center stage to the hermeneutical communicative praxis.

During the turbulent 1960s and 1970s, action was apparently perceived as the very core of the praxis of religion. Rolf Zerfasz, for instance, maintains that in an action-theory-oriented practical theology, praxis must be understood in terms of the actions of the church and of

6. Yorick Spiegel, "Praktische Theologie als empirische Theologie," in *Praktische Theologie Heute*, ed. Ferdinand Klostermann and Rolf Zerfasz (Munich, 1974), p. 178.

24

Christianity.[7] Simultaneously, we see the social sciences taking the lead in practical theological studies. Social and ecclesiastical reality is studied in the form in which it actually presents itself to us. Practical theology studies the *Ist-Zustand* (present reality) of society and inquires into the human need for the gospel.[8] At the same time, this paradigm often includes an ideology-critical theory with references to notions of liberation theology. Social issues are given center stage, and oppressive powers are denounced — in society in general as well as in the church. Gert Otto, in his criticism of ideologies, argues in line with the Frankfurt School — particularly with Horkheimer and Habermas — that we should not analyze human action from the angle of "mind," or "intentionality," or "inner life," but on the basis of social conditions.[9] Otto criticizes the status quo from the perspective of a critical theory, which is informed by the idea of an ideal or desired situation, such as Habermas's idea of a *Herrschaftsfreie Kommunikation* (communication without oppression). We also see this approach in Van der Ven: he borrows, without any attempt to justify it, the normative criteria for the communicative praxis from Habermas (equality, freedom, solidarity, and universality) and suggests that, when interpretations clash, we should opt for the interpretation that promises some real liberation potential.[10] In retrospect, Albrecht Grözinger says that there is here an assumption that the final concretization of life occurs on the level of action, that religion primarily consists of concrete actions.[11] I believe, however, that this fails to do justice to the role of the human mind in the faith act. Faith is not just an act; it is also a state of mind.

7. Rolf Zerfasz, "Praktische Theologie als Handlungswissenschaft," in Klostermann and Zerfasz, eds., *Praktische Theologie Heute*, p. 167.

8. Alois Müller, "Praktische Theologie zwischen Kirche und Gesellschaft," in Klostermann and Zerfasz, eds., *Praktische Theologie Heute*, p. 25.

9. Gert Otto, *Grundlegung der Praktische Theologie* (Munich, 1986), p. 76.

10. Van der Ven, *Practical Theology*, pp. 48-49.

11. Albrecht Grözinger, "Praktische Theologie als Kunst der Wahrnehmung," in *Gelebte Religion. Im Brennpunkt Praktisch-theologischen Denkens und Handelns*, ed. Albrecht Grözinger and Jürgen Lott (Rheinbach, 1997), p. 315.

The Life of the Mind

There is no doubt that our actions play an important role in religious practices. Our intention is revealed in our actions, and Christian faith expresses itself in everyday life. We might even regard the more intellectual dimensions of faith as actions of the mind. Nevertheless, I believe it is incorrect, or at the very least one-sided, to consider action as the point of departure in our practical theological reflection. We may, of course, try to stretch our concept of action somewhat in order to bring additional intellectual and linguistic dimensions into the picture. But that would be artificial, and it would still indicate an underestimation of the meaning of our inner life. Life has aspects that are not, at least not immediately, directed toward action. Life is not simply a matter of activity, but also one of being and feeling. We find ourselves in a relationship with existence in general, and with our own existence in particular. We are mentally involved with the situations we find ourselves in and with the conditions that shape our lives. This spiritual life has a value of its own. For example, we are aware of the nice weather, or of the grief we carry within us, or of the love we receive. We experience friendship and trust; we feel that life is not always easy; we look forward to a party. Further, we are conscious of ourselves. And what about our ability to know things? I know that it's raining; I think I closed the windows. We could go on and on. These are not actions. The more affective things, and the things that are associated with knowing, are indirectly related to our actions, but they are not actions as such. Thus faith undoubtedly includes an action component, but we have as much reason to say that it is a dimension of our intellectual life. Faith receives its concrete contours in the functions of the human mind.

Knowing and Trusting

Concrete faith is embedded in everyday life. We just saw how the human subject-functions are actively involved. But let us not forget, in the meantime, that we are dealing with faith in God. Faith is a relationship between subjects, a communal bond between God and humans. A life of faith is not just a matter of taking certain beliefs about God and his salvation to be true; it is also a matter of our trust in God and of God's trustworthiness. These notions are given with the structure of faith as a relationship between subjects.

Trust and trustworthiness also play an important role in interpersonal relationships. Let's take a closer look at the word "believing": we use this word in both its meaning of holding something to be true and its meaning of trusting. "I believe I have locked my bike" is a statement indicating that I consider a certain state of affairs to be true; when I say "I believe you," I am indicating that I trust you as a person (it refers to an interpersonal relationship).

In common usage we encounter the word "belief" in three different shades of meaning. In a first usage, it is a "weak" form of knowledge (i.e., "I believe something to be true"). This meaning creates considerable confusion within the context of religious belief. Should we think of our faith as a weak kind of knowledge, in the sense of having a vague opinion? Or is faith knowing something with certainty? In everyday usage, "believing" is not as strong as "knowing." We consider something to be true, but it has a lower epistemic status, so to speak. We can't be absolutely sure about it: "I *believe* I put the safety catch on when I locked the door." But because I am not entirely sure and cannot say, "I *know* I put the safety catch on," I will have to get out of bed to go check. "Belief" in these examples has the meaning of taking certain propositions to be true; it is about forms of knowledge concerning certain matters or facts. And religious faith is almost automatically associated with this weaker kind of knowledge. Religion, people say, has to do with matters about which one cannot be entirely certain.

In addition to this propositional meaning of "belief," we find two other shades of meaning of "belief" that have more to do with interpersonal interaction. One way is in the sphere of trust: when we say, "I believe you," we are dealing with a relationship between two people where one person expresses trust in the other person. We cannot immediately check the truth of what you are saying, but we trust that you are not lying. Of course, we should not underestimate the social component, and this is also true of a relationship based on the kind of knowledge we discussed in the preceding paragraph. For doesn't all knowledge begin with trust and a recognition of authority? Ideally, our knowledge is based on immediate observation and immediate insight. I see with my own eyes, or I understand because of my own insight — as an autonomous, mature, educated, intelligent person. Ever since the Enlightenment, we in the Western world have not thought highly of belief that is based on what other people say. My own observation has primacy, and even when I depend on others, I must be able to make it part of myself. Nonetheless, many thinkers have pointed out that our "knowledge-society" is a "faith-society," in which we trust the knowledge and skills of others. And today, when "high-tech" has become so all-important, we are obliged to trust the experts even more. We have no direct access ourselves to most of the truth and knowledge that has been discovered. We are at best "believing co-experts"; we accept many things because we have to trust our scientists. H. Richard Niebuhr emphasizes that even our knowledge of nature is largely a matter of trust — of "belief" in our fellow human beings.

> The contemporary age is an age of faith, that is, of trust in science, that is, in the scientists. Only a small fraction of the people have much direct knowledge of the objective order with which the natural scientists are concerned.[12]

This leads Niebuhr to conclude that faith can never be seen as an isolated act of the human subject, of the "self," but always includes the recognition of another subject. It consists of a triadic relationship of at least two subjects and an object. And, Niebuhr continues, when we take something to be true, it does not spring from an isolated situation, in which the subject confronts an object, but from a social situation, in which the "self," in the company of other people, is confronted with a common object.[13]

Third, the term "belief" is used with regard to future action. In such a usage it has to do with the trustworthiness of a person — with promise and expectation. When someone makes a promise, we may expect that the promise will be kept. Our "faith" will be quite strong when we trust that we are dealing with someone who will fulfill what he or she promises. Here again, our faith depends to a large extent on the measure of trustworthiness we attribute to the other person.

12. H. Richard Niebuhr, *Faith on Earth: An Inquiry into the Structure of Human Faith* (New Haven/London, 1989), p. 39.

13. Niebuhr, *Faith on Earth*, p. 34.

Trustworthiness and Truth

Two things emerge from this brief discussion: (1) Faith has a social dimension: trust and trustworthiness are at stake, and we are dealing with a relationship between subjects. (2) Faith has to do with cognitions regarding the reality in which we live, with the belief about whether something is true or not. It is thus a characteristic of "faith" — in the sense of trust — that it is embedded in the interaction between subjects. And Niebuhr reminds us that even our cognitions possess a social dimension. Our mental involvement with situations cannot be detached from our trust in the people who educate and teach us. We are always faced with a social setting in which the subject and co-subject are involved in particular situations; without such mutual trust, cognitions are hardly thinkable.

This insight is important in our reflection on religious belief. The act of faith *(fides)* cannot be detached from the two poles of trust *(fiducia)* and trustworthiness *(fidelitas)*. In faith we place our trust in God; we do so because we believe God to be trustworthy. The Christian faith identifies trustworthiness and goodness as fundamental characteristics of God. In his faithfulness God allies himself with his people, and the people continuously appeal to this trustworthiness. Israel placed its trust in God because God revealed himself as the one who keeps his word (covenant) and fulfills his promises. Faith, therefore, stands in a constant tension between human trust and divine trustworthiness. God's truth is that God is true, that is, trustworthy and utterly dependable. And this is where our faith finds its certainty: in who God is.

This intersubjective structure of the concept of faith points to an analogy between the religious and the everyday meanings of "belief." In our social interaction with people, we learn to trust them; as we experience the trustworthiness of other people, we can be trustworthy ourselves. But we also meet the other side in our social interactions. We also experience from time to time that people, including ourselves, can be untrustworthy. Human beings can also be deeply suspicious. People make promises, and others believe those promises; but those promises may be broken, and that trust may be betrayed. As human beings, we are shaped by this contradictory social interaction as our psyche sustains its impact. When we look at life from a psychological angle, we may say that this basic sense of trust is already developed in the earliest stages of the child's development, when the care of (in most cases) the mother is crucial. But there may also be early signals of untrustworthiness that give rise to mistrust and suspicion. It seems logical to surmise that these interpersonal relations also play a role in religious faith. From a theological perspective this is quite obvious, for the Bible portrays God and man in a covenant relationship in which trust and mistrust are significant factors. And thus we may imagine that our experiences in our own social interactions — for example, between parents and children — influence, both positively and negatively, the way we experience faith in God. If our trust has been betrayed, can we still trust God? And can a renewed trust in God, in turn, possibly help to mend and renew our social interactions? It is hardly surprising to find a reciprocity in these trust interactions.

Even though faith in God is, because of its intersubjective structure, doubtless characterized by human trust in the divine trustworthiness, this does not in any way take away from the fact that all kinds of cognitions are also involved. It is not a blind trust but a trust that is linked to what we know and understand, including the knowledge of who God is and what God does. For there can be little abiding trust if we cannot answer the question, Whom do you trust? Who is God and what do you expect from God? In other words, while faith certainly has to do with a relationship of trust, we cannot exclude the propositional dimension. There is no trustworthiness without truth. It is thus wrong to pose the notion of trust over and against the aspect of knowledge. Trust is nurtured through knowledge: what we know about someone determines whether or not we find that person trustworthy.

Existential Involvement

So far we have seen that religious faith is embedded in the subject-functions of the human mind and that both knowledge and trust are at issue. A primarily intellectual function of the human mind finds its mode of expression in our knowing, while, because of the interpersonal relationship, trust is clearly linked to the social component. Faith is both a cognitive and a social activity. But we still do not have a full picture of the concept of faith. For it is also characteristic of faith that it inspires and motivates. Faith is a dynamic force: it motivates our actions, it generates trust, and it intensifies our emotional life. Believing is more than having religious opinions, as we have already seen in the discussion of the notion of trust. A definite measure of existential involvement is also typical of a living faith. Knowing and trusting are not merely rational matters, but they resonate in our affections and ambitions. Our inner drives, our emotions, and our goals play their part. Faith is able to lead people to do things. Our affections are stimulated, and our inner drives and ambitions are involved.

Our faith is a dynamic part of life and of our personality. It is directed toward our daily life, but also toward God and God's salvation. What is the link that causes this engagement? Where is the connection that causes the human subject not only to be carried along but to enthusiastically agree, and that ensures the involvement of our total life?

> [Acts] of notitional assent and of Inference do not affect our conduct, [while] acts of Belief, that is of Real Assent, do (not necessarily, but do) affect it.[14]

In this statement, J. H. Newman wishes to indicate that "real assent" includes something we directly encounter and experience. But how does this work? Does this have something to do with the nature of the assent — with the fact that our total being is involved from the very beginning? And does it also have something to do with the nature of the involvement with the object — with the fact that the object touches us with immediacy? Throughout the Christian faith tradition, the unique nature of faith has often been explained as being in a degree of opposition to our intellect. At times the emphasis was placed on man as a moral being, but there is also a rich tradition that anchors the receptivity for the holy in the affective part of our being. The underlying idea is that the uniqueness of religion is not expressed in concepts and ideas but is experienced through our affections. Religion is a matter of actual involvement in life, and of receptivity to the workings of the divine. Rudolf Otto says:

> It is one thing merely to believe in a reality beyond the senses and another to have experience of it also; it is one thing to have ideas of

14. J. H. Newman, *Grammar of Assent* (Garden City, NY, 1955), p. 87, cited by Niebuhr, *Faith on Earth*, p. 8.

"the holy" and another to become consciously aware of it as an operative reality, intervening actively in the phenomenal world.[15]

If faith is a concrete interaction between God and man, this must have an impact in some way. Otto refers to this as an energetic moment: it expresses something of the "vitality and passion of an affective being," a kind of "will, force, movement, excitement, activity, impetus."[16] And this is what activates the human heart.

Does this create too much tension with, for example, the intellectual aspect of faith? Should we perhaps be suspicious of this aspect of knowledge when we speak of faith? According to Newman's statement above, we should distinguish religious faith from knowledge based on logical reasoning. Religious faith has its own unique dynamic; it is part of and inspires everyday life, and it is rooted in revelation. Schleiermacher says that it will take hold of a person.[17] Apparently, for theologians such as Schleiermacher, Otto, and Newman, engagement — being absorbed — is an experience that is essential to faith. And the ability to "know" is then mostly associated with intellectual abstraction.

This anti-intellectual reaction is understandable, but it should not tempt us to place knowledge in total opposition to affections. I agree that faith has to do with receptivity to the dynamic divine influence; but that does not eliminate our cognitive faculties. The theologians above are merely referring to a concern that a cognitive approach might only deal with objective and abstract matters, which could lead to an intellectual reductionism. This danger is found in Cartesian thought, in particular, where the subject becomes so central that everything else and everyone else becomes an object.[18] The object of the inquiry becomes detached from its context and is mostly described and analyzed from a purely theoretical perspective. But where, then, is the

---

15. Rudolf Otto, *The Idea of the Holy* (London/Oxford, 1972), p. 143.

16. Otto, *The Idea of the Holy*, p. 23.

17. Friedrich Schleiermacher, *On Religion: Speeches to Its Cultured Despisers,* trans. Richard Crouter (Cambridge, 1988).

18. John Hick points to a change in the epistemology of the Western tradition with Descartes: "Instead of being in acquaintance with the fully (as distinguished from the imperfectly) real, knowledge has become awareness of the truth of either self-evident or necessarily (as distinguished from contingently) true propositions and their implications." *Faith and Knowledge,* 2nd ed. (London/Ithaca, NY, 1970), p. 201.

point of contact? Where is the reciprocal relationship and impact? Indeed, when we express what we know in propositions, it can easily lead to an abstraction from the time and space in which we find ourselves. I can imagine why this isolation of the human ratio has given rise to many questions in the religious debate. And why, as a reaction, do the "irrational" elements of faith and the role of our affections come to the forefront so vigorously in some antirationalist streams of the Enlightenment. The core of this reaction was: My faith has to do with an actual relationship! But it would be incorrect — and this is what I want to emphasize — to understand this relationship at the expense of the role of knowledge. Faith is not only a matter of experience but also of truth. But knowing should not be reduced to the ability to discern the objective and the abstract.

I bring to mind two classical theologians, Thomas Aquinas and John Calvin, who assign an important role to knowledge but do not detach knowledge from experience and contact. In this respect they stand in a long tradition, which we already see in Plato: cognitions are caused by a relationship or commonality between the human mind and what is observed. The human mind comes in contact with the reality of things, and in the knowledge that results we find echoes of such notions as proximity, intimacy, and communion. Cornford uses the phrase "having intercourse with" for this contact of the human mind with the realm of Ideas.[19] Knowing the Good is an activity of the human mind that implies community.

Subject-Side and Object-Side

I have described faith as a relationship between God and humans, and I would like to focus on the structure of this divine-human interaction. Just as on the human level, the interaction between God and humans is not a static situation but a living and dynamic process. I have already noted that subjectivity (i.e., the life of the "self") plays an active role in this interaction. Now I would like to emphasize that we are relating to the Other as a reality outside of our own "selves." We recognize the Other as subject, or as co-subject; but does the Other also become ob-

19. Dewey J. Hoitenga, *Faith and Reason from Plato to Plantinga* (Albany, 1991), p. 7.

ject, for example, the object of my knowing? Theology makes the distinction between the *fides quae* (the faith content) and the *fides qua* (the faith relationship). We have certain opinions about God, humans, and the world. We believe, for example, that humans have a responsibility, that God is gracious, and that it is meaningful to live with God's promises and commandments. In this sense we may speak of an object of faith — the propositional content. We tend to express this content in "that" sentences (also sometimes referred to as "is" statements): "I believe that . . ." and so forth. This refers to a degree of objectivity and abstractness. But this object of faith is not identical with the concrete "others" with whom we have relationships. In our daily lives we meet concrete human beings, and in these encounters we meet the other; we experience the other as subject; and we experience some things about the other. The other represents a reality outside of our "selves" — in that sense an "objective reality" — whom we recognize as subject in the encounter.

Of course, we have all kinds of ideas and opinions about the other. But we may hope that in that existential encounter we will actually meet the other, and not just our own opinions about the other. Looking at the object-side of our mental functions, we face two different aspects: (1) the object of our faith, that is, the propositional content, and (2) the encounter with the other as existentially over and "against" me. These dimensions, naturally, are not detached from each other. For example, I have certain opinions about my colleagues; if someone asks me about a particular colleague, I can relate what I think of that person. In preparing for a meeting where an important decision must be made, my knowledge about this colleague will be helpful in giving me some idea of how he or she thinks, or might vote, on a given issue.

We can form pictures in our minds of other people and of certain situations. But we are often surprised by what happens when we meet people face to face. When the other meets me as subject, I may have to correct my mental picture because the reality may differ from my projection. I interact with a certain image (a sum total of cognitions), but I will have to correct this image during the actual encounter with a real person. Does the same apply when we meet God? We have opinions about God, we form a mental picture of God, but do we also encounter God as subject?

This leads us to a controversial theme in our thinking about faith. The German language has a word that points to the otherness that is outside us and, in a sense, the opposite of what we are: *Gegenständlichkeit* (there is no adequate translation in English). When used with respect to God, it points to the object-side of the faith, or, to put it differently, to God as subject. It ascribes freedom, independence, and *aseitas* to God. When we discuss faith as it is lived, our reflection automatically turns to the side of the human subject. Doesn't that present a danger? Is it still possible to do justice to the other pole of the relationship? Is the recognition that something precedes faith — as a human activity — not of fundamental importance? At this point the Protestant tradition will lead us to such notions as revelation and Scripture, while the Catholic tradition will turn our attention to the mediation of the church in our understanding of revelation and Scripture. But, in the final analysis, shouldn't the object-side have priority? Barth, for example, strongly emphasizes that faith is *nachher* (something that follows): it is neither more nor less than our response to God's revelation. God is always the *unaufhebbar* (unremovable) Other. I might also refer to the core concept of the Protestant view of faith: the justification of the sinner. Because, when all is said and done, so we are told, it is not human faith that matters but the gracious acquittal we receive from God. Our faith recognizes that God's activity has an impact on us. This underscores the idea that God must indeed be seen as the acting subject who enters our lives. And this, again, results in the fact that faith will not seek its certainty at the subject-side, but rather *extra nos* — in God's promises and saving activity, that is, at the object-side.

Metaphysical Models

Are we allowed to speak about God in this way? This problem is not just theological but also metaphysical in nature. What is at stake is how we understand the relationship between the world outside of us, on the one hand, and the world of the human spirit (and human language) on the other. When we act, think, or speak, we assume that our acts, thoughts, and words somehow relate to the world around us. But how does this world around us influence our thoughts and the words we speak? How do we access that world? And this applies even more when we speak about God. Would it not be better to stay completely on the subject-side and remain content with mere mental images of God? For images of God are purely subjective, embedded in the social and cultural environment and thus apt to change. Or can we say that our words and concepts do indeed point to God and that our faith also contains an element of knowledge about God? When we address God as the compassionate one in our prayers, do we then indeed trust that God is compassionate? Or is our prayer based on the mental picture we have of God?

Since this problem will play an important role in my later discussion of our God-language, I will take the opportunity here to briefly sketch the contours of the different metaphysical models that the students of Western theology will constantly encounter. In Chapters 8 through 11, I will return to these models when I analyze the ways we speak about God. The main point is whether we can, in fact, speak about the object-side of faith. Can we say something about God? How adequate are our human concepts? Can we indeed say that we know God? Or is there a gulf between our world and God's world that cannot be bridged?

These kinds of questions are usually embedded in the conceptual frameworks of particular cultural or philosophical traditions. We find it difficult to move outside of these frameworks because they have shaped the way we experience reality. In our Western tradition, theology has had to deal with the heritage of the Enlightenment. This tradition attributes major importance to the role of the human mind and the subject's role concerning the way he or she perceives reality. It argues that the human mind brings structure to reality. Of course, external reality exists: there is a world of rivers, chairs, and tables, cars and computers, and, don't forget, other humans. But their conceptual order and the conditions for our knowledge about them is based on the powers of the human mind. For that reason, we will not be able to say anything about this objective order without recourse to human perception. We cannot speak about truth and falsehood without enlisting our noetic capacities. Our concepts are not directed toward the structure of external reality; it's the other way around: realty is shaped after our mental images.[20] We will never know whether this reality actually has a

20. For a short description, see Alvin Plantinga, *The Twin Pillars of Christian Scholar-*

structure, but we do know that we have ideas and concepts in our head. The phenomena of the world around us do have their impact on us, but the conceptual construction is a human activity. We cannot understand German Idealism and the more liberal Western theologies if we fail to take this foundational pattern into account. This has led Nicholas Wolterstorff to write an article with this critical title: "Is It Possible and Desirable for Theologians to Recover from Kant?"[21]

The position of postmodernism is more recent. This term serves as an umbrella for a number of currents of thought that have one thing in common: they are critical of Idealism and the Enlightenment. Postmodernism denies the possibility of one uniform conceptual ordering through the human mind, because the human mind and the "self" cannot be regarded as "objective" entities. Human subjectivity is not the origin but the outcome of speaking and writing, the result of human discourse. The adherents of Social Constructionism maintain that interactions rather than the individual are the basis of intellectual and social life. Intellectual abilities are *entia per alio,* byproducts of the discourse. And this discourse is fully contextual: it is a social artifact, that is, a human convention.[22] Following this route, both our conceptualizing of the external reality and our knowledge of that reality become a matter of mere perspective; it just depends on the point where we happen to be, on the group to which we happen to belong, on the prejudices we happen to have, the political party we subscribe to, and the economic goals we strive for. All forms of objectivity have disappeared.

Analytical philosophy in particular has many influential currents of thought that not only reject the conceptual subjectivism of the Enlightenment but also the postmodern perspectivism, and advocate a form of external realism. One example is the aforementioned John

ship (Grand Rapids, 1990), pp. 9-20. Plantinga himself is a "realist" and belongs within that category of "theists." For a fundamental analysis, see his *The Nature of Necessity* (Oxford, 1974).

21. Nicholas Wolterstorff, "Is It Possible and Desirable for Theologians to Recover from Kant?" *Modern Theology* 14:1 (January 1998): 1-18.

22. See Kenneth Gergen, *An Invitation to Social Construction* (London/Thousand Oaks, 1999). For my analysis, see "Human Discourse and Preaching," in *Social Constructionism and Theology,* ed. C. A. M. Hermans, G. Immink, et al. (Leiden/Boston, 2002), pp. 147-70.

Searle, who defends a form of naturalistic metaphysics: (a) there is a real world that is independent of us and our interests; (b) things in this world exist in an objective way; and (c) we can access this real world in an epistemic way.[23] But numerous other philosophers (Alston, Chisholm, Plantinga, Wolterstorff) defend a form of realism, in some cases in combination with a theistic view of reality. Usually they reject the idea that concepts are mental presentations or images. Objects as well as co-subjects have properties that we understand with our mind. The whole point is that the mind is, in fact, able to understand reality. These properties are external to the human mind and to language, but we can understand them with our minds and express them via language. We do not shape the structure of reality ourselves, but we do understand it.

Realism concludes that there is a world independent of the human mind — and that we have access to that world. But we should keep in mind that realism is a broad term. Plato, for example, was a realist because he believed in a world of ideas behind the visible reality. The Scholastics borrowed heavily from this in their doctrines of God and of the sacraments. But modern analytical philosophers see properties as abstract entities.[24] However, my point is that properties are not manufactured in the human mind: a cognition or statement is true when what has been thought or said is indeed the case. Truth and falsehood have to do with the actual state of things and not with our perception of it.

No Theoretical Vacuum

Theology does not occur in a theoretical vacuum. Wherever we turn, we will meet conceptual frameworks that provide terms with which to reconstruct our faith. This should not be a problem in itself. But it is essential that we tune our theological motives as well as we can to the theoretical framework. I have already drawn some base lines regarding the

23. Searle, *Mind, Language and Society*, p. 15.
24. For a detailed study of this problem, see my book *Divine Simplicity* (Kampen, 1987); see also my article "Theism and Christian Worship," in *Christian Faith and Philosophical Theology*, ed. Gijsbert van den Brink et al. (Kampen, 1992), pp. 116-36; see also my article "Human Discourse and Preaching," pp. 147-70.

anthropological structure. We have seen that the functions of the subject — such as knowledge, feelings, and the will — are in their very nature intentional; that is, they are directed toward the object-side. Religious faith also has, as we have seen, an object-side: God and his salvation. So the question is, can we speak of God as an "opposite"? Shouldn't we be more reticent in speaking of God? Do we actually have more than our own "images" of God? I will in several places in this study defend a form of external realism, not only concerning the world around us but also concerning our speaking of God. I believe that there are good grounds to do so. On the other hand, we must also take the subject-side into account as we reconstruct faith as it is lived. For faith is a reciprocal relationship between God and humans.

What does this mean with regard to the object-side of faith? First, it means that the propositional content of our faith, the sum total of our cognitions (the *fides quae*), is closely linked to the referential object: God as the "opposite" person, the subject of acts and words. Beliefs about God and his salvation refer to God himself. Second, it is precisely this referential aspect that underscores that God is more than an object of our knowledge. God is subject, co-subject, a person who acts intentionally, who makes himself known, and allows us to experience his presence. Only in this way can we speak about faith as involvement, as a living relationship.

Communion with God

After this excursus on the subject-side and the object-side, I want to return to actual communion with God through faith. How do people relate to God? As I have said above, our attention to the human subject does not mean that we should neglect the object-side. When we discuss our faith, the object-side will play an important role. God is an acting subject, involved with people and their world; God is a person with passion, power, and will. In our faith we recognize that the Other is a subject, for faith is defined in the Christian tradition as "a firm and certain knowledge of God's benevolence towards us."

Calvin

That last definition comes from Calvin. It suggests that, in the act of faith, we come to know the Other in his love for us; we see the Other in his heart. This approach to the Other does not exclude our own subject-side; in fact, it embraces it. Christ, Calvin says, is of no profit to us as long as he remains outside of us. "Therefore, to share with us what He has received from the Father, he had to become ours and to dwell within us."[25] On the subject-side, notions such as assurance and doubt play a significant role. Calvin says that faith "consists in assurance rather than in comprehension."[26] Faith understands that God's promises are not just true outside of us, because we accept them internally and appropriate them to ourselves. But "we cannot imagine any certainty that is not tinged with doubt, or any assurance that is not assailed by some anxiety."[27] On the contrary, believers face a continuous struggle against their own unbelief. The certainty they do achieve does not result from a rational proof but from "a persuasion of divine truth." And because of this subject-object relationship, faith remains in a constant bipolar tension.

> The godly heart feels in itself a division because it is partly imbued with sweetness from its recognition of the divine goodness, partly grieves in bitterness from an awareness of its calamity, partly rests upon the promise of the gospel, partly trembles at the evidence of its own iniquity, partly rejoices at the expectation of life, partly shudders at death.[28]

The degree of assurance, we might say, depends on the degree to which one is able to rely on God and becomes conscious of God's compassion. The certainty is inherent in the object of our faith, in this instance the trustworthiness of God. But in addition to this focus on the object there is also introspection: the recognition of my own misery. Calvin expresses this tension between the two poles by his distinction between spirit and flesh.

25. Calvin, *Institutes of the Christian Religion* (Philadelphia, 1960), III.1.1.
26. Calvin, *Institutes* III.2.14.
27. Calvin, *Institutes* III.2.17.
28. Calvin, *Institutes* III.2.18.

Tillich

It is interesting to find this tension between the poles of subject and object in the work of a theologian such as Tillich as well. He also speaks of the bipolar relationship between assurance and doubt. But Tillich brings a completely different structure to his theology: it is in the way he introduces the object-side of the faith relationship. God is no longer a reality that can be named, but has become the totally Other. For Tillich, faith is, on the one hand, a central act of the human mind; but on the other hand, faith is also the expression of ultimate concern. "Faith is the state of being ultimately concerned: the dynamics of faith are the dynamics of man's ultimate concern."[29] In this reconstruction of the life of faith, the polarity in the structure of faith is determined by the pole of this finite being, which — and that is the second pole — interacts with the infinite.

> Faith is certain in so far as it is an experience of the holy. But faith is uncertain in so far as the infinite to which it is related is received by a finite being. This element of uncertainty in faith cannot be removed, it must be accepted. And the element in faith which accepts this is courage.[30]

In this approach, doubt is inherent in faith itself, as it is implicit in religion as such, since it is a relationship with the infinite. Existential doubt and faith are poles of the same reality. In Tillich's understanding of faith, humans are being touched; but because of the intrinsic indefiniteness of the object-side, faith is primarily an attitude of the subject rather than a relationship toward another (divine) subject. I believe that Tillich is the classical example of a theologian who feels that we can never refer to God with our language and concepts. In this he joins Schleiermacher. God does resonate somehow in our lives and in our inner being; we are being touched, but the object remains indefinite. Indeed, God becomes the wholly Other, and no description can be adequate. God is the ground of being.

> Without the manifestation of God in man the question of God and faith in God are not possible. There is no faith without participa-

29. Tillich, *Dynamics of Faith* (New York, 1957), p. 1.
30. Tillich, *Dynamics of Faith*, p. 16.

tion! But faith would cease to be faith without separation — the opposite element. He who has faith is separated from the object of his faith. Otherwise he would possess it. It would be a matter of immediate certainty and not of faith.[31]

We meet this indefiniteness regarding the object-side with other theologians who tend toward postmodernism. David Tracy believes that God is bipolar: on the one hand, God is totally abstract and absolute; on the other hand, God is fully socially determined and relational. But in our religious praxis we deal with the God who makes himself available, the God who is, just as we are, determined by an "ever-changing and ever-affecting actuality."[32]

I would like to summarize this chapter by mentioning two themes that are going to play an important role in this book. (1) Our life of faith is embedded in the functions of our intellectual makeup. Through our knowledge, feelings, and will, we relate to God and experience his workings in our lives. Faith is thus an intersubjective event in which God and humans are the subject of consciousness, language, and action. (2) Faith as a human activity has an object-side. Faith is not restricted to human action, for there is also an object of faith: God and his salvation. This leads us to the question of how we can name God in the praxis of faith.

31. Tillich, *Dynamics of Faith*, p. 100.
32. David Tracy, *Blessed Rage for Order: The New Pluralism in Theology* (Chicago/London, 1996), p. 183.

CHAPTER 2

How Faith and Life Interconnect

The Dynamic of Faith

Faith and life are intertwined. The one is not detached from the other. As we go through life we have all kinds of experiences, and we face situations that call for decisions. Faith is a part of all of this. Faith is something dynamic rather than static: its connection with life keeps faith alive.

Human life does not develop like a clock that will tick imperturbably; it is characterized by care, commitment, and passion. We are actively involved in responsibility and freedom. Amid ever-changing situations we must find our orientation and determine what needs to be done. I have shown in Chapter 1 how our mental abilities are part of human nature. We do not merely react to stimuli and impulses and blindly follow our instincts and compulsions; we weigh the options, we consider, we think of causes and consequences. In addition, our emotions come into play as we react to people or situations: we miss a loved one, we experience sorrow, we are pessimistic about a friendship that appears to have soured, we fear surgery, we long for kindness. This kind of involvement can be very intense. Sometimes we are overwhelmed by grief, but we will do everything possible to see things in the proper proportion. We will focus on things that we find interesting, or try to think of something else and concentrate on something different. Apparently, we have that ability to distinguish and to weigh our options.

Faith receives its shape in this life. It is involved in everyday existence, with its joys and cares, its challenges and conflicts, and with the miseries and passions that are often part of it. Faith is lived: it accompanies us in our daily lives and is part of our journey through life. Since our mental makeup is characteristic of our human existence — for we live with intentionality — we may assume that our faith is part and parcel of that intentionality, of the functions of the mind. This is where it is entrenched, and thus it touches all aspects of life. Faith presupposes the proper function of the human mind. I don't intend to say that faith is a self-evident correlate of our mental makeup, for we know that many people go through life without religious faith. What I mean is that faith, if it does take shape in our life, is embedded in the functions of the mind. It becomes part of our personality and manifests itself in the ways we relate to the world we live in. Or, to put it more strongly, faith is a dynamistic factor that intensifies our relationship to our world. It is not a drug that allows us to escape from the world; rather, it is a stimulating factor that motivates and inspires us in the praxis of life. Faith is like the salt that flavors our food, like the leaven that makes the bread rise.

Faith puts life in a particular perspective. It points to a life that is lived in the light of God's involvement with us and with the world. Faith allows us to stretch beyond our natural confines and beyond human nature. For faith directs itself toward God and salvation. We know God as the one who is life and who gives life. Our encounter with God makes us appreciate life.

In this chapter I will investigate in some detail two aspects of this interconnectedness of faith and life. First, I will focus on the shift toward the subject that took place in practical theology during the latter part of the twentieth century, which resulted in the subjectivizing of faith. I will clarify this by referring to the views of Wilhelm Gräb. (This theme will return once again in Chapters 10 and 11, where I deal with the anthropological model.) Second, I will look at the intertwining of faith and life by asking how faith interacts with everyday life. Does faith offer a *basic trust* in the midst of all the vicissitudes of life? Or does faith rather instill in us a critical attitude toward what happens in daily life? That discussion will also deal with the social and personal dimension of faith.

Human Beings as Subject

Toward the end of the twentieth century, anthropology and the human sciences came to dominate practical theology. Initially, it was the sociopolitical significance of faith that took the front seat in this so-called anthropological shift. Gert Otto describes it this way:

> Due to the reality with which practical theology is concerned, the dogmatic-ecclesiological current in practical theology must give way to the complex relationship between religion and society (of which the church is a part) as the point of departure.[1]

This rejection of a dogmatic-ecclesiological approach to the praxis of faith has remained.[2] But the predominantly institutional approach to religion and faith is, via the detour of the sociopolitical interest, being replaced by an increasing attention to the individual or, to put it more correctly, to the human subject in the context of everyday life. In Germany the term *gelebte Religion* (religion as it is lived) has become quite popular.[3] It expresses the notion that the subject herself actually shapes her religion and is not so much bothered by customs and traditions. As a result, two aspects receive considerably more attention: the experience of faith and the person's own faith history or biography. Henning Luther is a practical theologian who has been a trendsetter in this area.[4] Dietrich Rössler is also significant in this discussion: he explains the prominence of the individual as a result of the demise of the public manifestation of Christianity. Religion, Rössler says, is not confined within the walls of the church. Besides the institutional forms of faith (liturgy, pastorate, diaconate, etc.), we must also recognize a public form. By this we mean that our society is heavily influenced by all kinds of religious convictions and customs. But in Europe, in particular, this public form of religion is rapidly disintegrating. In addition to these institutional and public forms, Rössler tells us, a third form has emerged: individual or private faith. While the church withdraws

---

1. Gert Otto, *Grundlegung der Praktische Theologie* (Munich, 1986), p. 69.
2. See Gräb, *Lebensgeschichten*.
3. See Albrecht Grözinger and Jürgen Lott, eds., *Gelebte Religion. Im Brennpunkt Praktisch-theologischen Denkens uns Handelns* (Rheinbach, 1997).
4. Henning Luther, *Religion und Alltag*.

within its walls and public religion gradually disappears, the individual must not be left to his own devices in the sphere of religion. For that reason, Rössler pleads with us to once again place subjective religion on the agenda.[5]

Subject versus Institution

It is remarkable how theologians who make everyday life and the subject a theme in practical theology create a contrast between, on the one hand, a subjective faith that is being lived and, on the other hand, a faith that is present within church structures and is attached to doctrinal content. The impulse behind this is the view that subjective faith is real to life and is purified by daily experiences, while doctrinal-institutional faith would be more detached and abstract. In this view, being intertwined with real experiences in daily life makes subjective faith concrete and authentic. And, according to Gräb, this authentic faith is under threat when it is placed under the canopy of a truth that has already been defined by the Bible or the church. Here Gräb refers to Troeltsch: "Religion is not some communal or ecclesiastical or official activity; it cannot in any case take on some communal form. It is rather the *Privatsache des Einzelnen* (private business of the individual)."[6] And thus the point of departure is found in humans themselves.

Gräb believes that the search for meaning has not disappeared from our postmodern society. He maintains that all human beings are looking for meaning and that religion provides us with the symbolical resources that enable us to express such meaning and direction for our lives. But it begins with the existential questions people ask; for these are, by definition, real to life and plausible since they originate in people's own experiences and self-understanding.[7] If the church were to add to this from the outside, it would only cause alienation. What the church does is provide a system of symbols through which these private experiences can be worded. In other words, the church helps us sort out our private experiences, and in this respect the church does

---

5. Dietrich Rössler, *Grundrisz der Praktischen Theologie* (Berlin/New York, 1986).
6. Quoted by Gräb, *Lebensgeschichten*, p. 83.
7. Gräb, *Lebensgeschichten*, p. 91.

have a role. Gräb is looking for a church that follows, that explores the ways in which people search for meaning, and that fully respects the ways in which people do this. This would be a church that does not in any way prescribe anything and does not offer anything — at least not to begin with. It would simply provide a supportive environment, a language tradition that would help people express their experiences, and the company of other people who would have some understanding of religion.[8] What's at stake are the real-life experiences of the subject as the starting point in the search for meaning and the absence of restrictions on the freedom of the subject. The church would not act paternalistically in any way. And if the church desires to retain any significance, it would have to relate to the life experiences of the people.

Religion of the Subject: Appreciation and Criticism

What should we make of this form of subjectivizing? Gräb rightly points to the fact that we should not, in our reflection on our faith, exclude the aspect of human subjectivity. And the faith that is lived may indeed stand in a certain tension with the tradition of the church. Church teachings will remain at a distance if they no longer touch us and if we can no longer make them part of our internal lives. The institutional church restricts our life when it kills new initiatives and seeks to limit our freedom. Following in the footsteps of the Reformers, we must always remain critical about the mediation by the church. The Word itself makes salvation accessible; the Holy Spirit is given to the believers individually and is not primarily present in the institution. Particularly those currents that have emphasized subjectivity have pointed to the need for an unmediated encounter with God. We have seen this, for example, in several pietistic movements. And this motif also emerges in the cultural Protestantism that Gräb defends. It is important that people be independent in the exercise of their faith and not be restricted by any external authority.[9]

But Gräb's views do give rise to an objection. Tjeu van Knippen-

8. Gräb, *Lebensgeschichten*, p. 94.
9. Friedrich Schweitzer, "Gelehrte, gelernte, gelebte Religion," in Grözinger and Lott, eds., *Gelebte Religion*, p. 145.

berg has appropriately commented that we should not evaluate the Christian faith only in terms of a philosophy of life. The question "Can the Christian faith have any function for contemporary people in search of meaning?" puts undue pressure on faith to be relevant and useful. "If this is the way we look at faith," says Van Knippenberg, "we run the risk of only finding what we ourselves have, either from above or below, put into it. The role of the Christian religion is not to provide labels of meaning to the residuary problems of our society."[10]

The search for meaning and faith, of course, are related. Faith gives a certain content to life. The nature of faith is such, Van Knippenberg says, that it plays an important role in our journey through life. Here he is referring especially to the defining moments in the human life cycle and in the Christian calendar. But Van Knippenberg believes that we should not play off the objective church-related meaning against the subjective search for meaning. The ecclesial praxis has its own unique role.

Gräb, however, approaches spiritual life primarily on the basis of subjective experience. Institutional life and the liturgy of the church are, in this respect, secondary to the experience of the subject; even interaction with the community plays a secondary role. Interpersonal subjectivity and the conviction that people shape their own lives come first. Thus subjective relevance becomes the determining factor. Where does this absolutizing of the human subject originate? To understand this, we must keep in mind that Gräb wants to continue with the tradition of cultural Protestantism, one of whose goals is to express the Christian faith in such a way that it can be appreciated by modern people. Gräb is convinced that we do not have to leave the Christian faith behind us as a religion dating from premodern times. On the contrary, faith is utterly relevant for modern people. But human freedom and dignity must be safeguarded in the way faith is experienced. Following Hegel, Gräb regards the right of the subject to full freedom as the particular turning point toward modernity.[11] Humans must be free to define their own history and thereby to find the meaning of life.

Gräb then asks whether humans are able to accomplish this. We

10. Tjeu van Knippenberg, *Tussen Naam en Identiteit. Ontwerp van een model voor Geestelijke Begeleiding* (Kampen, 1998), pp. 142-43.

11. Gräb, *Lebensgeschichten,* p. 27.

may have high ideals that we try to realize, but we also fall victim to fear and doubt, and we discover many shortcomings. We are often quite ambivalent and do not have full control of ourselves. Precisely at that point, Gräb declares, religion enters the picture. Apart from the things we do ourselves, we recognize a foundation that supports us, a sense of affinity. There is a kind of knowing that reaches beyond what we can say about ourselves and others. This is the religious component in our search for meaning, a *Gefühl unseres absoluten Gegründetseins* (the feeling of having some ultimate foundation).[12] This undefined religious sense, which, according to Gräb, we should not too hastily label with our ecclesiastical vocabulary about God, constitutes the core of this subjective religion. It is a form of basic trust, and it is prior to any religious description. The church then provides a vocabulary to describe this basic trust in concrete representations; but at its very core this basic trust has a religious linkage with a transcendent source that we cannot further describe. Religion deals with a sense of the infinite, a place where our quest for meaning will eventually come to rest. The true source of support in our life is this basic trust — "out of which we live long before we speak about it or use it to develop our vision for our life."[13] The fact that people long for this foundation in finding direction for their lives is not, according to Gräb, a sign that they lack maturity, nor is it a threat of autonomy or rationality. Rather, religion makes a positive contribution to our humanness.

Remarkably enough, Gräb points to the notion of the "justification of the sinner" as the theological foundation for his ideas.[14] He feels that this doctrine from the Lutheran tradition gives expression to our feeling of being unconditionally accepted by God. It cuts through every form of human self-justification. Gräb takes the subjective interpretation of Pietism and of the Enlightenment even further with regard to this principle of justification. But he refers to it as a *weltimmanente* (immanent to the world) experience. And we get some idea of what that means when we experience unconditional love from others in our own lives.

12. Gräb, *Lebensgeschichten,* p. 67.
13. Gräb, *Lebensgeschichten,* p. 69.
14. Gräb, *Lebensgeschichten,* p. 197.

Evaluation

In this approach to religious life, the intentional object of our faith — that is, the one to whom the believer relates — disappears from view. The object of faith lies beyond the boundary of what can be named or known, with the result that it becomes absolute or infinite. It falls outside every conceptual framework, and thus faith is described as a basic feeling. Faith is a postulate of our human freedom and dignity and offers us a basic trust. Piety and religion remain integrally connected with life, but merely as dimensions of anthropology. Man's trusting takes precedence over trust in God.

Gräb's approach fails to do justice to some fundamental aspects of the praxis of faith. I will remark on four of these points. First, the notion of the justification of the sinner presupposes the external character of divine judgment: *iustificatio* reaches us from the outside. It is an imputation and form of address in which God is the acting and speaking subject. In Gräb's model, humans themselves find meaning; but in the doctrine of justification, by definition, God initiates the relationship between God and humankind. Jüngel warns us in his study of justification that we should not confuse the Christian faith with the human quest for meaning. We are indeed delivered from the meaninglessness of our existence through this justification, but there is a tension between the human quest for meaning and justification. In Christian practice the human subject is not the one who provides meaning. Faith points to the revelation of truth and the discovery of salvation.[15] It has to do with deliverance from captivity, with trust that sets free. Faith brings us in touch with a liberating movement that issues from God; it does not originate with us but comes to us as "Word."

Second, Gräb's model hardly does justice to the historical dimension of the Christian faith. God has revealed himself to Abraham and has made himself known in the history of Israel and the life and person of Jesus. This revelation history not only provides us with a system of symbols that may help us describe our life experiences, but it also con-

---

15. Eberhard Jüngel, *Das Evangelium von der Rechtfertigung des Gottlosen als Zentrum des christlichen Glaubens. Eine theologische Studie in ökumenischer Absicht* (Tübingen, 1999), p. 224.

tains identifying stories about the communion between God and humans. If we wish to discover who God is, we have to hear an external word, which is transmitted and proclaimed to us. The concept of salvation history points to the fact that "God has brought to fulfillment and will yet fulfill in Christ, in a final and decisive way, his salvific work that embraces man, world and history."[16] Scripture is not a resource in our *Selbstauslegung* (interpreting ourselves) but a testimony to God's salvation.

Third, I agree with Gräb that the life of faith definitely does involve the human subject. God's liberating word is understood and experienced, and this results in movement and change in life. But the question is how we see the subject. We are not dealing with a solitary "self" but with a "self" that has an essential connection with God, the other, and the world. In religious life, J. H. van den Berg believes, humans cannot revert to a complacent subjectivity, nor can they be made into mere objects.

> Man is originally and essentially the "second person." Man is addressed by the Other; he has been created by the Word and owes his reality and sustenance to the Word. He is the one who is seen, and the Eye which sees him brings him to completeness and freedom. He can only be truly himself as "second person." Only then does he know his true duty, does he know his goal and does he realize the significance of his freedom.[17]

Viewing this from a theological angle, we must affirm that humans are God's image. Humans are being addressed and are known. Humans are, so to speak, designed to be responsive — "respondable beings."[18]

Fourth, this also implies an inherent openness to the other. From the very beginning, we are not without the other. The other is given to us, and without him or her, we are not human beings. "Inasmuch as I meet the concrete other," Henning Luther says, "the concrete individuality of the other will always break through the equalizing influence of

---

16. Herman Ridderbos, *Paulus. Ontwerp van zijn Theologie* (Kampen, 1971), p. 47.

17. J. H. van den Berg, "Psychologie en theologische anthropologie," in *Van gisteren tot heden. Godsdienstpsychologie in Nederland,* ed. J. A. van Belzen, vol. 1 (Kampen, 1999), p. 115.

18. Berkhof, *Christian Faith,* p. 186.

colorless reciprocity."[19] Becoming a subject is not primarily a matter of self-development and autonomy. Notions such as receptivity and accessibility are at least as important; they bring openness and compassion into our lives. The quality of life is found not only in our self-development but just as much in the fact that we are able to receive and share love, friendship, and care.

Daily Life

Faith receives its form in the concrete lives of human beings, but it also finds different ways of expressing itself. We may distinguish three aspects. We saw in the preceding section that it involves the human subject: the life of faith is one of personal involvement where the human heart, the inner self, plays an important role. The mental functions, such as knowledge, feelings, and the will, which are characteristic of human life, also have their impact on our faith. But there is more than that.

Various explicitly religious activities — which may have a personal or communal character — are also part of our life of faith, such as prayer, singing, Bible reading, and meditation. In our faith communities we celebrate Sundays and the Christian feast days, expressing the liturgical dimension of our faith. Josuttis says, "Religious praxis is operational in the individual as well as in the community as the cultic act."[20] The social aspects are inherent in the nature of pastoral and communal care. But even when we add this second dimension, we have not fully defined the life of faith. Faith also finds expression in everyday life. Besides the liturgical-ceremonial and the devotional praxis, we must distinguish the praxis of actual life as such, in which faith plays a significant role. Our daily life, with all its joys and cares, is an important dimension of human existence, and it would be strange if faith were not a part of this.

These three aspects together form the praxis of faith. It would be incorrect to emphasize the institutional church praxis at the expense of our personal spiritual life or the praxis of everyday life. And we would

19. H. Luther, *Religion und Alltag,* p. 81.
20. Josuttis, *Die Einfürung in das Leben,* p. 85.

also shortchange the breadth and cohesion of our faith praxis if we were to turn our spiritual life and our everyday and professional lives into opposites. We live our faith through sacred activities — prayer, attending worship services, Bible reading, and so forth; but these special activities that help us maintain our contact with God do not take place outside of everyday life. There is, of course, a distinction between those "sacred actions" that mark the religious life and our professional and social lives; but it is a mistake to separate them. Liturgical expression has its own value, but it should not be detached from daily life. Because we have become aware that rites and symbols refer to the questions of life, we do not detach Christian rituals from the fundamental questions that are raised in people's daily lives. Liturgical acts — like the weekly pattern of Sundays in general — interrupt the weekday activities of everyday life, but they are also connected to them. The day of rest surely implies a critical idea — that the labor and hassle of daily life should be interrupted.

This places our everyday life in a different perspective: we become aware of definite boundaries. Prayer, for example, is a specifically religious act; but in our prayers we introduce our experiences in the outside world into our dialogue with God. Liturgical or "sacred" activities do not remove us from life; they emerge from our life and return us to life in a new way. Life is interrupted for the sake of life itself. Singing a song may differ from caring for someone who has asked for help, but the two things are connected. The hymn may motivate us, and it can provide vision or give words to distress; thus it may lead us toward the other. As we go through the liturgical year, we become more aware of the path God reveals in Jesus Christ: we travel from Advent to Christmas, through the Passion to Easter, and via Pentecost to the end of the world. But this does not remove us from real life. We learn how to place death and life, disappointment and expectation — the things we encounter daily — in a different perspective, namely, in the light of God's involvement with us humans.

Theological and Historical Backgrounds

So we have found how three factors play a role in the praxis of faith: the institutional church, the spiritual life of the individual, and daily human life. The Reformed tradition places the emphasis on the latter two. Because of its deep reservations about the sacral, ritualistic, and institutional elements, that tradition has made the believer's practical life of faith its most prominent feature. True religion is found in the life of the Christian. Religion does not find its point of gravity, Noordmans argues, in the cult but in everyday life: "It has been Rome's mistake to overemphasize the cultic element in the sacrifice. Paul underlines the full breadth and depth of the life of faith."[21] Noordmans says that the Reformers removed the sacrifice from the mass and returned it to the life of the believer. Here he appeals to Romans 12:1: "I urge you, brothers, in view of God's mercy, to offer your bodies as living sacrifices, holy and pleasing to God — this is your spiritual act of worship." Sacrifice is found within the context of life, Noordmans argues. Ehrensperger, too, points out that the Reformers brought the worldly and everyday character of religion back to the forefront.[22] We find the same idea in Martin Luther. The life of the Christian, he says, is played out between the two poles of faith in God and help for one's neighbor. That is what the gospel teaches, and that is what parents should say to their children — at home and everywhere.[23] There is a deep conviction that God himself touches people and renews their existence through Word and Spirit. The kind of worship we find in the Reformed churches also reflects the fact that the service on Sunday is intimately connected with everyday life.

The office of the deacon is not primarily liturgical in nature: she or he serves at the table but then turns to "the ministry of compassion towards the church and to the world" and strives for "a society that is characterized by justice and gives space to every human being to live and work." And the elders, together with the pastors, supervise the church "with respect to confession and walk of life." Don't forget the role of the Ten Commandments in the church. They are read in the main worship service to remind the church and the society of the rule for our lives; and they are dealt with in detail in catechetical instruction, as "the rule of thanksgiving," that is, as the

21. O. Noordmans, *Liturgie* (Amsterdam, 1939), p. 119.
22. Alfred Ehrensperger, *Gottesdienst. Visionen, Erfahrungen, Schmerzstellen* (Zurich, 1972), p. 20.
23. Quoted in Ulrich Nembach, *Predigt des Evangeliums* (Neukirchen, 1972), p. 70.

directive for the sanctification of the daily lives of the saints, as a response by believers to the Word they have heard.[24] The church service is thus characterized by instruction, not primarily concerning doctrine but instruction for everyday life. True religion is in the Christian's life, and that life springs from the renewing influence of the Spirit. The Holy Spirit provides the bridge between Scripture and the human mind. And we should not place too much church ritual in between, for that will only distract. Noordmans says:

> We stand with our faith in the midst of life and in the midst of the world. Everything is part of the business of life, in the most direct sense of these words. The soul lays itself bare to the impact of the world. And the world is the immediate object of the activity of faith.[25]

We find this emphasis on the Christian life in the various currents of Reformed Protestantism. The basic idea is that faith receives its concrete form in the everyday life of the person — spiritually and ethically. I will mention three currents of Protestantism that emphasize this aspect: the Second Reformation (Dutch eighteenth-century Pietism), Puritanism, and the school of ethical theology. Gijsbertus Voetius refers to practical theology — sometimes also called *ascetia* — as the "practice of godliness": by this he means the application of the doctrine of salvation. He believes that the entire theological discipline deals with "the method and skill needed to apply theology to daily life, and to use it for the development of our spiritual life, the steering of the will and the passions, and to a proper walk of life."[26] He distinguishes between practical theology and the *credenda* (systematic theology); it comprises not only the *agenda* (theology of ethics) but also spiritual exercises.

The second movement I have mentioned, English Puritanism, with its clearly identifiable influences on Dutch and North American Protestantism, strongly emphasizes the sanctification of life. Salvation does not come through participation in the sacramental life of the

24. J. Schweitzer, *Zur Ordnung des Gottesdienstes* (Zurich, 1944), p. 49.

25. O. Noordmans, *Verzamelde werken*, vol. 3 (Kampen, 1981), p. 394.

26. Gijsbertus Voetius, *De praktijk der godzaligheid*, trans. C. A. de Niet (Utrecht, 1996), p. 24.

church but results from personal commitment, which will be expressed by the way we lead our daily lives. Spiritual goals and everyday existence are closely linked to each other. Salvation remains the work of God, but it is affected directly through the Spirit in humans.

Charles Taylor, in his study *Sources of the Self*, emphasizes that "the affirmation of ordinary life" constitutes an important consequence of the Reformation heritage: "The rejection of the sacred and of mediation together led to an enhanced status for (what had formerly been described as) profane life."[27] The affirmation of ordinary life and the particular impetus it receives in the modern era comes first of all from the Reformation. As a result of the rejection of the mediation of salvation by the church, the emphasis has shifted to (1) the personal commitment of the believer and (2) the concrete practice of ordinary daily life, which is to be hallowed. Taylor believes that, as a result, the emphasis in religious praxis is to be found in "the activities of this life, in one's calling and in marriage and the family. The entire modern development of the affirmation of ordinary life was, I believe, foreshadowed and initiated, in all its facets, in the spirituality of the Reformers."[28]

We find this same connection between spiritual commitment and our daily walk through life with the theologians of the "ethical school." We must understand Noordmans's warning that the Word can be dissolved in the human consciousness against the background of this ethical theology, which emphasizes the life of the Holy Spirit in the believers. The Spirit dwells in believers, and human consciousness thus receives an important role in the motivation for our life of faith and our lifestyle. In reflecting on the seriousness of the Reformed-ethical approach to the life of faith, Noordmans says:

> We certainly met and felt the seriousness in the church, in the official proclamation, the administering of the two sacraments, during the sobering liturgical moments. But the true deep seriousness which we know is, in particular, connected with the personal sphere, where we came close to God. Close to God the Holy Spirit. Where we were to some extent able to discern and experience the influence of the Holy Spirit in and on the human heart. At that

27. Charles Taylor, *Sources of the Self: The Making of the Modern Identity* (Cambridge, 1989), p. 216.
28. Taylor, *Sources of the Self*, pp. 211-33.

56

moment we felt an enormous distance from anything liturgical and hierarchical, from the church in the more institutional and formal sense of the word. We felt the presence of the invisible church. There was a direct relationship to God, without any detour. Three words say it all: God, Spirit, faith. From there a straight road leads from our heart to the heart of eternity.

To stand before God, without any apparatus, any organization, any solemn form of mediation, this is what gives Reformed life its characteristic seriousness. God is near, for it is the work of the Spirit that takes center stage.[29]

We clearly see the emphasis on God's *immanence*. The fundamental religious attitude is spiritual in nature: being touched by the Holy Spirit, the human mind can focus on a higher order, the kingdom of God. The human mind does not latch onto the status quo of empirical reality, but it seeks its goal in divine love and righteousness. And this makes a world of difference in daily life. Our faith tells us of another reality, the coming of the reign of God. This direction motivates our life and actions: faith becomes the source of inspiration and motivation.

"Basic Trust" and "Differenz"

But how do we go through everyday life? Joy and sorrow are at times very close, and they seem unevenly distributed. Some people seem to have opportunities for development: they meet life partners, they find pleasant jobs, and so on. All conditions for a happy life seem to be there, and it would appear that they will successfully take advantage of them. There are some negative experiences and situations that are in the way, of course; but somehow they will be overcome. Life, by and large, is good and blessed.

But things could go quite differently. Not all people have the chance to get a good education, at least not in the same measure as others. Some suffer from physical, economic, and social disadvantages that force them to begin with a serious handicap: a physical or mental malfunctioning, limited social skills, a poor environment, a sickness

29. Noordmans, *Verzamelde werken*, vol. 3, pp. 391, 392.

that throws a wrench in the works, the inability to develop relationships, professional disappointments or the loss of a job, troubled relationships, chronic illnesses, the early loss of loved ones, and so on. Life can bring many worries and sorrows.

Anyone who is alive has certain expectations of life — for herself and for others. We are created for life, and we should affirm life and live with joy. But is that possible when our personal experience of life is far from perfect, and we have to conclude with disappointment that life is different from what we hoped it would be? Surely we cannot and should not deny life's potential for brokenness. For even if people are successful, do they not remain connected as social beings with the world and the people around them? And do they not thereby also share in the misery of life?

Our daily life manifests these two sides of human existence: the expectation of life, with its accompanying joys, and the difficulties and trials, the misery and death, with their accompanying sorrow. There are enormous differences between the lives of different people. But it is important to see both sides, not allowing our joy to be constantly tempered by sadness, and even less to make light of our sorrow by constantly pointing to the good things we are left with. Life can be very paradoxical. We long for wholeness and love, and in the meantime we destroy and demolish so much. What basic approach to life may we then expect? Will we be left with the circumstances we happen to find ourselves in, and will these determine our attitudes and our feelings? Is the climate of our spiritual life conditioned by our daily life? We have already seen how, according to Berger, the "here and now" is present in our consciousness with an overwhelming intensity. We are always involved in situations that directly affect us, and that is the situation of our daily sphere of life.

How does faith play a role in this? Is it something that affects us directly and determines our fundamental approach to life? We may see faith as a basic sense of trust, that is, one day things will be all right! Thus it will provide support in crises, and it will keep us up as our lives are about to fall apart. It will protect us when what we do in life disintegrates, and it will provide light on the horizon when everything turns dark. Our life receives cohesiveness, and faith has a stabilizing and integrating function in this process. Our faith holds together the bricks that combine to form our life shelter, and religion is the mortar of society. This is how, from a sociological perspective, we may give faith its place. Gräb calls it a form of *Kontingenzbewältigung* (provision for contingencies).[30]

Faith offers cohesiveness in a world that appears to be haphazard in so many ways. Kuitert believes that this fundamental trust forms the basis of all religion. It is given to humans, as part of their nature, to provide meaning for their lives. It is a basic trust that we are given at birth and that is developed in the first years of our life. This core of faith provides us with assurance and is, Kuitert believes, also a faith that brings salvation, for it is faith in a good ending.[31] In this way faith acquires a somewhat homely character. Faith, as a trust in the ground-of-our-existence, tends to put the last bit of support in and under our life, most often as a form of consolidation.

Henning Luther, who also places great emphasis on faith and *Alltag* (daily life), approaches the meaning of faith from the perspective of *Differenz* (difference). Religion breaks life open, and religious language helps us break through the self-evident. It is not always necessary to calm the unrest in our lives, for it can also provide us with an opportunity to look at things in a different way. Luther gives priority to the protest against the status quo. From a theological standpoint, he emphasizes the eschatological perspective, but as a perspective on our daily life. The parables of Jesus, says Luther, concern daily life, but they are told in such a way that the result is alienation and surprise: "God's reign is found where the self-evident and the routine is done away with, is interrupted. We always discern the light of this perspective of God's kingdom where our daily routine is placed in a surprising and liberating new perspective."[32] There is no attempt to simply protect what is already there, but there is a perspective of renewal. Faith directs our attention to the other and to the new.

Living with Trust and Expectation

We should not emphasize either of the two elements just discussed, the basic trust and the *Differenz*, at the expense of the other. As we go

30. Gräb, *Lebensgeschichten*, pp. 48-61.
31. Kuitert, *Wat heel geloven?* pp. 74-85.
32. H. Luther, *Religion und Alltag*, p. 216.

through life, we meet good and evil, love and hate, faithfulness and betrayal, and so on. And in this we are ourselves intensely involved, both actively and passively. We cannot pull away, either with respect to our actions and our behavior, or spiritually, with respect to our inner selves. Yet we are caught in neither a natural course of events nor an eternal contest between good and evil. Our life is not a random natural process that leaves us with no option but to accept our fate and to acknowledge the facts. We live our lives as subjects; that is, we are involved in it through our intellectual capacities. We do not exist as robots in a causal network of relationships, but we live through spiritual relationships. We live consciously and through the possibilities of the human mind: knowing, feeling, and willing — that is, making judgments and distinctions.

This does not mean that we deny the factuality of the *condition humaine*. We are faced with the hard facts of life every day, but we live with a full package of convictions, values, and expectations. That is a characteristic of human existence. This capacity for making judgments, in particular, determines how we go through life. And our religious faith is, without a doubt, an important factor in making judgments. Of course, there is more: the way we are educated, the culture we live in, and so forth. But our faith reinforces the awareness that we are spiritual beings. Faith leads us to conclude that life is more than a series of natural processes. We are God's creation: when we view life as creation, we know about the "Other," about relationship, interaction, and communion. Faith clearly presupposes the subjectivity and intersubjectivity of life: we live before God in fellowship with our fellow humans.

What does this imply about the way we go through life? It implies a strong affirmation of life and a basic posture in which trust and commitment play an important role. When communion and reciprocal involvement become fundamental in our life, the lie cannot indefinitely reign and mistrust cannot be the rule. For truth and sincerity are essential for intersubjective relationships; otherwise, the social fabric disintegrates and we are merely motivated by self-interest. That is why a good creation presupposes a good God. We consider the creation to be good because we trust in the goodness of the Creator, who has the best of intentions for us. God gives us the pleasure to exist, and we may therefore affirm life. But does that mean that we affirm anything that might happen to us? Absolutely not. We know life in its brokenness, even in its terror — hatred, war, and death. At times life is without any perspective and seems useless. But that doesn't mean that life in itself would be worthless and can no longer be called good. When we believe in God, we look at life in the awareness of God's involvement in our lives. In his history with us God reveals his salvation and rescues our life from extinction. To believe in God means to know the distinction between good and evil, creation and sin. Good and evil are not in a constant equilibrium, but evil and sin are being challenged. God himself fights for the disappearance of evil. Evil and sin are parasites that threaten shalom — strange, inexplicable, and disastrous perversions of the good. As Cornelius Plantinga observes, sin is deviant and perverse — an *in*justice or *in*iquity or *in*gratitude.[33] On the other hand, we mention God's salvation in the same breath with words such as redemption, renewal, judgment, deliverance, and rescue — terms that are central to the Christian view of life. And that is why we focus radically on the person of Jesus Christ, in whom — so we believe — truth and life have been revealed. And salvation in Jesus Christ offers the final and deepest trust in the goodness of life.

So is there a basic trust? Yes, because of our faith in God. And what about the *Differenz*? Yes, because we know that life has become different, that it has already changed in the revelation of Jesus Christ, and that it has been broken open into a new future. Faith in God is not the same as the shelter and safety of the old and the comfortable. This was not true for Abraham, nor for the New Testament church. The notion of basic trust may carry a deceitful element. Living through faith will call for courage to change and renew. But we must also pursue the *Differenz* when speaking of God; if we fail to do so, it will merely remain an anthropological reference.

I have asked the question, How do we go through life? I have argued that we are intentionally involved in the things of daily life. And I concluded that this intentionality has an important place in our faith. Faith allows us to view life from the angle of our communion with God, of God's salvific and revealing manifestation in our lives. With this as their point of departure — that is, beginning with God's partici-

---

33. Cornelius Plantinga, Jr., *Not the Way It's Supposed to Be: A Breviary of Sin* (Grand Rapids, 1995), p. 88.

patory and saving love — humans accept life and shape life. This implies, then, that we can also speak *theo*-logically about life, from the perspective of God's salvation.

Henning Luther has demonstrated that the human subject is not detached from the *Alltag* (the everyday). Besides religion's social function of binding together — the angle from which sociology views religion — Luther rightly demands attention to the subject and his biographical identity. Boundary situations and transitional phases of life become important: birth and death, puberty, the start of a relationship, finding a life's work, retirement, and so forth. Often these are enervating and shocking experiences that can cause a good deal of turmoil, and we should not be too eager to immediately smother this. Of course, in such moments religion can have a calming and stabilizing role. Of course, critics of religion such as Feuerbach and Marx have shown how religion may also have a dangerously anesthetizing effect. Therefore, Henning Luther chooses a different kind of critical approach: religion as protest. He joins the Frankfurter Schule in claiming that religion "can mobilize dissatisfaction with the here and now."[34]

This is precisely the core experience that is at the root of our Christian hope. It is particularly during crisis situations and during times of transition in the course of our lives when the obvious elements of the "self" become problematic. "When our life takes a different turn from what we expected *(Differenz)*, the subject moves into a mode of sadness, or into the mode of expectation." In both cases the subject feels "dissatisfied with the here and now."[35] Sorrow and expectation are related: they both carry the awareness that we are not totally at home on this earth. In other words, in our sorrows and longings we become aware of our finiteness. This brings a sense of dependence and a need for salvation, and these are again notions with theological content.

> A theology without the tears of grief and without a sigh of hope, a theology that has lost sight of man in his distress and in his expectations, has also lost its real theme: God.[36]

34. H. Luther, *Religion und Alltag,* p. 248.
35. H. Luther, *Religion und Alltag,* p. 249.
36. H. Luther, *Religion und Alltag,* p. 252.

So that is where it ends: the link between the experiences of sorrow and longing and the name of God. But in his further explorations, Henning Luther remains too much on the side of the subject. He does refer to the longing for salvation, but he does not elaborate. He has forcefully focused our attention on the entrenchment of our faith in everyday life, and then he goes on to tell us that God, being the actual theme of theology, is not detached from our sorrow and longings. Unfortunately, he speaks of God no further, at least not as a speaking and acting subject. And thus he gives no further particulars of a soteriology. But life does, in fact, take on a new perspective when viewed from a soteriological angle.

Social Relationships

We live within a social framework, and it fills a major part of our lives. We grow up in a family, within a network of relatives and acquaintances, as part of a neighborhood and a school. And thereby we acquire many values and skills. We refer to this as the process of socialization, a "process whereby the knowledge and control of relationships, norms, values, skills and social techniques are transferred."[37] (I am not concerned here with all the sociological and psychological theories by which we can analyze this process of socialization, but merely with the social interactions in which we are involved.) Through schooling and other kinds of training we are educated toward being able to participate in social life, and through this participation we get to know life in all its facets. The functions of the human mind are developed through this interaction with parents and educators.

This also applies to our faith: religious education belongs to our social development. And even though the learning subject nowadays plays an important role in the process of faith development, this does not take away from the fact that religious education remains a transmission of faith in the form of a process of socialization.[38] For it is in

37. I. J. van der Molen, *Opvoedingstheorie en Opvoedingspraktijk* (Groningen, 1994), p. 156.
38. Friedrich Schweitzer, "Gelehrte, gelernte, gelebte Religion," in Grözinger and Lott, eds., *Gelebte Religion,* pp. 142-56.

this process of social interaction that we learn about the different dimensions of life and faith. We meet pain and sadness, and we have to face disappointments and discover that we will not always succeed in what we undertake. But we also experience joy concerning the good and pleasant aspects of life; satisfaction about the progress we make in knowledge and skills; amazement in love and friendship; happiness in our work; delight in beauty; and zest for life. Life brings with it dimensions of both burden and joy, and for this reason, social interaction is not purely a private matter. Even though I feel no pain myself, I perceive the pain of the other and cannot ignore it. Sharing in joy and sorrow is part of life. Living in a social framework means that we enter into relationships and assume responsibilities.

The social dimension of everyday life constitutes an explicit theme in the praxis of faith. Labor and care have long been important foci in diaconal work. People find fulfillment in meaningful work, and we should always be concerned when a person, for whatever reason, has lost employment. Alternative jobs and tailored work situations are essential to keep as many people as possible in the labor process. Good work relationships are important for people's spiritual well-being. Employment should not merely be viewed from an economic perspective, because it is also a matter of social justice and has much to do with optimizing our joy in life and work. In addition, the church has been involved in caregiving, with the realization that illnesses, handicaps, and the deterioration of old age can place terrible restrictions on life. The motivation for the humanitarian work that the church undertakes springs from the appreciation we have for our life as given by the Spirit. God gets personally involved in our lives and descends into our earthly existence to bring salvation. The diaconal work has its basis in the communion of the church around the Lord's table. Where the bread and wine are distributed as symbols of our communion with Christ, we are sent into the world to share in compassion with others.

Gerard Dekker points out that social life does not merely consist of interaction between people. He distinguishes between *social* communion and *ideal* communion, using the latter term to refer to "having a commonality" or "participating in something." The social communion mainly applies to the frequent and regular mutual contacts, while the ideal communion applies to a sharing in fundamental values and norms.[39] For the faith community, this is realized in the relationship with Jesus Christ. The social is, so to speak, anchored in the ideal; communion with Christ motivates our social life. This dimension of the ideal is continuously used as a resource and is actualized in the activities of the church, for example, in the ministry of Word and sacrament. Interaction within the faith community is thus both a social and a theological event: communion with God is not only embedded in interpersonal communication but, further, has an impact on interpersonal relationships.

As we direct our attention to the social dimension of life, we should also take the institutional aspect into account. Our social life is not merely a product of human interaction; it also takes on concrete form in social institutions, which in turn influence life. The church itself is such an institution, but it also serves as the context for other institutions, such as worship services, the sacraments, and ecclesiastical offices. We continue to be institutionally incorporated into the church through baptism. The diaconate and the pastorate also have institutional aspects since they are linked to the offices of deacon and elder and are closely connected to the communion service. Praxis demands institutions. "Religious institutions," Berger says, "function precisely to make a tradition *available* in this manner."[40] A certain event from an era long past is brought to the present through the institution of the church; thus is faith handed down from one generation to the next.

De-institutionalization is one of the major problems that today's church has to confront. The church's diaconate will find it difficult to survive without some institutional form, for only in institutional form can the church take on concrete shape in society. And we should also remind ourselves, as part of this discussion, that it is precisely the institutional form that directs us to the dimension of the "ideal": God's involvement in our lives as the source of our efforts of labor and care.

39. Gerard Dekker, *Zodat de wereld verandert. Over de toekomst van de Kerk* (Baarn, 2000), pp. 183-97.
40. Berger, *A Far Glory,* p. 172.

Personal Life

What significance do we attach to the personal dimension of everyday life? We have just seen that the social aspect constitutes the binding element, but don't we also develop our own individuality? Don't education and development also result in individualization? Nowadays personal choice and self-development are receiving much attention. No longer are we easily led by traditional values and the social codes of our group. People see themselves as the authors of their own biographies. We have already seen how freedom of choice is deeply rooted in our modern approach to life: the fragmenting and the individualizing of human existence have generally been praised as achievements of modern culture. Education is not merely adaptation to a cultural pattern that has been handed down, but is now primarily a matter of individual development.

It would be incorrect to speak of these differences as though they were absolute opposites. What has been handed down as the tradition or belongs to the social code of our community must also be internalized if it is to become a part of our personal life. On the other hand, self-development is not an automatic process — a simple development of potent seeds that germinate and already carry everything in them. Human life takes place through interaction, including our psycho-social life; and human identity takes shape in and through this social interaction.[41] We should note, however, that the human subject experiences his own unique development in that process. This does not automatically imply that the subject is the author of this process, but it does mean that our walk through life has a personal dimension. In that sense we can agree with Henning Luther that humans are always in search of their own identities.[42]

But doesn't this go too far in the direction of self-realization? Isn't there a real danger that this will produce an egoistic, self-satisfied, and arrogant personality? Not necessarily so. We are not talking about unrestricted growth at the expense of others. For as we go through life we also encounter the brokenness of human existence — if we don't

41. Siebren Miedema, ed., *Pedagogiek in meervoud. Wegen in het denken van opvoeding en onderwijs* (Houten, 1997), p. 327.
42. H. Luther, *Religion und Alltag*, p. 162.

shut ourselves off from it, that is. If we care for the other, we learn to share and to give. At times the other will take precedence, and we will need to come in second place. The Christian tradition calls this "self-denial." In the midst of difficulties and setbacks we discover how life acquires depth when we are ready to face misery. It takes courage to face life realistically. Sooner or later we have to confront things that we have not chosen but have crossed our path nonetheless. We encounter our limits and at times find ourselves in a blind alley.

Of course, some people are able to achieve much in their lives, both socially and personally, and it would not be right to call that meaningless. But it would be just as wrong to constantly idealize life. For our lives — or the lives of the others in any case — are too fragile and brittle for that. It may happen that we gain our strength at the expense of others. Life is both a matter of growth and disintegration, and human aspirations falter at the walls of illness and death. Henning Luther correctly emphasizes that thinking in terms of development will only bring us to a halt or send us in the wrong direction if we fail to consider the crises and situations of loss that characterize human life. "Every phase of life also has its cracks, its losses, and not only its growth and profit. In that sense we are always the ruins of the past. We experience this factual situation in a dramatic way when we meet a crisis. But in every phase of life we are also a ruin of the future, a building plot of which we do not yet know what will be built there and by whom; we only know that the building process is incomplete."[43]

What is the role, then, of the Christian faith in this personal dimension of life? We would be wrong to think that we can or should develop a theory of the identity of the self based on the Christian faith. But our faith does offer insights about that identity. Apart from the linkage between our personal and social life — as rooted in the divine image and the communion of faith — we should consider two things when we deal with the personal sphere of life.

    1. The development of our personalities is not an uninterrupted process of growth. A believer knows this and recognizes that life also has its failure and sin. Remorse follows our awareness of sin.

43. H. Luther, *Religion und Alltag,* p. 170.

Repentance and remorse, therefore, are fitting exercises of our spiritual life because they contribute to our self-knowledge. Unlimited autonomy leads to hubris and unholy ambition. Do we need, then, to be restrained? Should our passions be constrained? Not all the time and in every respect, but in such a way that we do what is good and refrain from evil. We cannot ignore the bitter reality of sin in the formation and development of the human "self." For pride and an inflated ego — wanting to be like God — constitute a threat to our life on earth.

2. Discipleship and cross are a part of the identity of the Christian life. Jesus says, "If anyone would come after me, he must deny himself and take up his cross and follow me" (Matt. 16:24). Discipleship implies a willingness to follow the path of Jesus: self-denial, solidarity with the other, and unselfish love. This will ensure that life takes on the dimension of serving others, which is not without cost. Discipleship has to do with conversion and change, and in some cases this demands a new solidarity. Consider Abraham and Paul. Discipleship is a highly significant notion and suggests that the human subject dares to go his own way in spite of the environment in which he finds himself. The development of the human subject is stimulated by discipleship.

The Pauline idea of the justification of the sinner plays an important role in the Protestant concept of faith. Our life is defined by the fact that we died with Christ and are raised with him: "Now, if we died with Christ, we believe that we shall also live with him" (Rom. 6:8). This is symbolically expressed in our baptism. The communion with Christ, therefore, is such that the cross and the resurrection define the identity of the believer. Both aspects, the death of the old life and the resurrection to a new life, are operative in our lives: *simul iustus et peccator*. This clearly contradicts the idea of a constant kind of life — and even of growth and development. For we find that we fall short and fail all the time. In each succeeding phase of our lives the wreckage and failures of the past catch up with us. Life presents us with much unwanted repetition. But this does not necessarily lead to a sense of helplessness or meaninglessness. Our name is linked to the name of Christ, and the path of Christ is our path. Human identity is becoming who we are in Christ. What is at stake is that we become, genuinely and actually, the new persons we already are in the judgment of God.[44] This implies a continuous appeal for change and renewal. Our attitude of faith is that of a future-directed life, rooted in God's revelatory action in the resurrection of Jesus Christ. *Simul iustus et peccator* as our faith identity provides space for repentance and remorse, but also inspires us toward struggle, renewal, and victory.

---

44. Godwin Lämmermann, *Einleitung in die Praktische Theologie. Handlungstheorien und Handlungsfelder* (Stuttgart, 2001), p. 87.

PART II

The Theology of Praxis

CHAPTER 3

The Imputation of Salvation

Salvation as a Gift from God

Believing in God does not mean that one has a distaste for life; rather, it implies the joyful acceptance of life in the expectation of salvation. The believer trusts that life is not to be relinquished, since God himself is the source of life and redeems it. Thus faith carries with it a distinctive appreciation for life; it does not leave us indifferent to what happens. Those who know God as the God of life — of justice and love — find themselves in a new tension: a life full of expectations in the midst of the difficulties and the needs of their everyday existence. Like anyone else, a believer shares in the grandeur and the misery of life; but he or she does not experience this merely as a natural process, and does not submit to the fateful concept of an eternal or fortuitous interconnectedness of good and evil. The name of God carries a unique dynamism: it means compassionate and loving care for our tattered lives and a cheerful and courageous attitude toward the renewal of our existence.

In the next two chapters I turn our attention to the praxis of faith in the context of a few fundamental theological categories. I will focus on concepts that are related to the expectation and experience of salvation. To believe in God is to believe in God's salvation: the basic feature of salvation, at least in the Christian tradition, is that it is the work of God and a gift from God. God moves toward humans and takes the initiative. But how does this relate to humanity as subject? What role is left for us?

In the Protestant tradition this subject is crucial to our understanding of faith. Faith is a gift of grace. The Reformation underscores this in the expression "the justification of the sinner" — the *iustificatio*. This declares that the experience of salvation is intimately connected with the imputation of grace. The sinner is declared righteous by God, despite all the sin and guilt found in him or her. On the other hand, we find that something occurs in and with the person: the word of grace has the effect that it brings change and leads to conversion and renewal of life. It is correct to say that the Reformation emphasizes the work of God *in* us and *in* our lives: the point is that God's word of grace finds access into the human heart. Word and Spirit are closely connected as the Holy Spirit lives in and with us. This makes the movement of God toward human beings effective; the heart is touched and this results in faith and trust, assurance and commitment. The testimony of the Holy Spirit gives birth to faith, hope, and love. Calvin refers to the Holy Spirit as the "internal teacher," the one who convinces us from within of the salvation we have received in Christ, so that we begin to live accordingly.

This tension between the imputation of salvation and the indwelling of salvation is the central theme of this section on the theology of praxis. This is also an interesting subject from the perspective of historical theology. As a reaction against the anthropologizing of theology at the end of the nineteenth and the beginning of the twentieth century, dialectical theology returned explicitly to the *iustificatio* as the divine judgment over our lives. The terrors of World War I evoked a critical reaction in theology. In its earlier phase, dialectical theology was first of all a critical theology that emphasized the distance between God and humanity. We should not bring God down to the human level, so the thinking went, for if we do, there is a great danger that we will use God for our own interests — thus making God dance to our tunes and become identified with our political goals. Thus, between World War I and World War II, Barth and Thurneysen, in particular, rendered the *iustificatio* operational for religious praxis.

We have seen in the Introduction how practical theology made an anthropological turn at the end of the twentieth century. Theological reflection began to pay more attention to human reality. The category of experience, particularly, received more emphasis, while the notion of revelation became less self-evident. Whether we should regard this shift as a reaction against the one-sided revelation theology, or whether we are dealing with an ongoing school of thought that had temporarily lost some of its authority because of the popularity of dialectical theology and is now back again in all its force — this is hard to determine. In any case, in these two chapters I want to focus on the relationship between the *iustificatio* and the indwelling of salvation. And I will defend the view that the notion of imputation does *not* weaken the notion of the indwelling. For faith receives its concrete shape in the arena of human life.

The External Source of Salvation

The fact that we have expectations for our lives is closely linked to our faith in God. Life and salvation become manifest in God's words and actions, and through his presence life receives a different dimension. His involvement with us means the revelation of true love and justice, which gives life a new value. The salvation we expect, therefore, originates with God; without God's presence there is no wholesome existence. Practical theology studies the praxis of faith from the perspective of the praxis of God — from the perspective of God's coming to people in their world. This movement of God toward his creation, toward humans, is essential for our understanding of the Christian praxis of faith. Salvation does not develop from within the human world but comes to us from without. Van Ruler rightly says: "This matter has a measure that can only be caught in a theological concept. Salvation must be proclaimed. Through the proclamation it will come into our existence, where it is absorbed. It reaches out in order to be absorbed. But it never originates there. However common and familiar it may become, it will never completely lose its otherness. Christ is and remains an other to the Christian. . . ."[1]

We can express this movement of God toward humanity in various ways, all of which often come together under the term "revelation," though that word sometimes has a certain ambiguity. Revelation implies, among other things, *disclosure,* the revealing of a secret.[2] That is, what was hidden comes to light, which in turn has implications about

---

1. A. A. van Ruler, *Theologisch werk,* vol. 4 (Nijkerk, 1972), p. 89.
2. Gabriel Fackre, *The Doctrine of Revelation: A Narrative Interpretation* (Edinburgh/Grand Rapids, 1997), p. 26.

knowledge: we learn something new. Revelation breaks through our human boundaries and reveals a new world to us. There is a moment of "unveiling." Daniel Migliore says that "[t]here is a gift-like quality to many of our experiences of knowing. Every knower must be receptive as well as active if true knowledge is to be attained. We must let the object that is to be known 'speak' to us rather than forcing it to conform to our preconceptions."[3] In the Bible this new knowledge is presented as having a life-transforming effect: revelation is salvific, imparting new life. It is a power for life. Revelation takes hold of us and opens our eyes for a future of salvation. In his revelation God shows who he is and what his presence means for our life: "In him was life, and that life was the light of men" (John 1:4).

But there are other words and concepts that express this coming of God, and especially the fact that God takes the initiative. He is a calling, promising, and electing God, which tells us that he acts in freedom and sovereignty.[4] All of these different terms emphasize that we are dealing with a movement of God toward humans. It creates communion, an actual contact, and even reciprocity. But God is its source; the initiative and the implementation originate with God. Like the biblical notion of the covenant, we find that the origin and the concrete actualization of the communal relationship between God and humans spring from the free choice and love of God.

Faith and Revelation

Thus the expectation of salvation is intimately linked with God's coming, with God's movement toward people, with God's revelation in our life. While faith is primarily an anthropological category, revelation is in the first instance a divine action. When we say that salvation comes from God, we mean that its origin, progression, and completion are God's work. It is, of course, operative in our lives, and we are fully involved; nonetheless, it remains a divine work. In our analysis of faith praxis — with a view to developing theological theory — we must go

3. Daniel L. Migliore, *Faith Seeking Understanding: An Introduction to Christian Theology* (Grand Rapids, 1991), pp. 19, 20.
4. W. Zimmerli, *Grundriss der alttestamentlichen Theologie* (Stuttgart, 1972), p. 15.

further than a mere conceptualizing of our faith. We must approach this relationship between God and humans, which is a relationship between subjects, from the basis of a correlation between faith and revelation. In our theologizing we should take the concept of revelation into account, particularly as we approach the praxis of religion as a praxis of faith. For if we fail to do so, we run the risk of subjectivizing religion.

In looking at faith as an activity of the human mind, we might gradually reduce revelation to an awareness of the human mind, and that would simply turn revelation into a dimension of our human experience. Thus might revelation easily become divination, that is, an experience of the human mind that leads us to conclude that God speaks to us. G. J. Heering has convincingly shown how liberal Protestantism of the late nineteenth and early twentieth century fell into that trap: "God" became the label for a consciousness of God. Insofar as the concept of revelation continued to play a role at all, it was simply understood as human awareness, an activity of our own mental makeup — reduced to a dimension of the mind.[5] Admittedly, this allows us to do justice to the receptive character of faith; but the element of divine action disappears completely behind the horizon. Revelation no longer stands for something that is revealed, with the result that the attention shifts from the salvific facts to the inner work of the Spirit. The *extra nos* of God's revelation in the historic person of Jesus Christ is replaced by the revelation of Christ *in nobis*.

If we wish to get a clear picture of the concept of revelation in its relationship to the praxis of faith, we must always remember the following distinction: revelation as (1) God's action in Jesus Christ's coming into this world, as opposed to (2) our understanding of this coming through faith. The first aspect precedes the second, just as the Cross and the Resurrection precede the birth and growth of the church. We may speak of both phenomena in terms of revelation, in the sense that God is the subject of proclamation and action that create a new reality. Seen from the perspective of the believing subject, the first is external and the second internal. The first happened in the history of Israel and in Jesus of Nazareth; the second happens in the human heart. The first is Christological and the second pneumatological. But we may see both aspects as divine revelation, and both dimensions play a role in the

5. G. J. Heering, *Geloof en Openbaring,* vol. 1 (Arnhem, 1935), p. 222.

praxis of faith. Faith is a spiritual event in which the subject arrives at insight and trust; but this insight and trust is related to one object: God's coming in Jesus Christ and the salvation revealed in him.

Revelation and Life

The result of God's coming toward humans is not merely that humans start to believe. God comes to people in order to reveal true life, and this revelation is an event in which the communion with God develops. The Christian tradition refers to this as "salvation." God not only wants us to have existence and life; he also wants to give us his salvation. And this salvation is a very special divine gift. Therefore, we also refer to this as "redemptive revelation." In this process of revelation we come into contact with the salvation that originates with God. The church confesses that in the coming of Jesus Christ the fundamental revelation of salvation has occurred.

This understanding of the revelation as God's coming toward humans has a connotation of something breaking through. The unapproachable, inaccessible, and self-directed sinful existence is broken open. That is to say, God's coming brings change: it implies criticism and renewal — both sides — and without this coming there would be no change. It is indeed a revelation of salvation, or, in other words, a change for the good. Thus Jesus calls himself the light of the world and the bread of life, because he brings salvation and redemption. The eschatological redemption becomes concrete in the coming of the Messiah, who is the resurrection and the life. God's coming in his proclamation and action provides humans with a new reality, which has to do with what "no eye has seen, no ear has heard" and "no mind has conceived" (1 Cor. 2:9).

The notion of God's coming to humans also means that we should not consider salvation as an ideal that we must strive for. For in so doing we would approach salvation too much from the basis of human longing. The Bible speaks about it as a bursting forth of the reign of God, which certainly evokes expectations. But God's redemptive activity always encompasses more than fits human spiritual understanding and can be realized through human efforts. It has an abundance and richness with a divine rather than with a human measure. "For

God was pleased to have all his fullness dwell in him, and through him to reconcile to himself all things, whether things on earth, or things in heaven, by making peace through his blood, shed on the cross" (Col. 1:18, 20). The cosmic and eschatological dimension of salvation comes from the fact that God reveals his salvation, and that is more than a human being can fathom.

Thus, we would sidetrack the revelation of God's salvation were we only to approach it from the angle of the human subject. The encounter precedes the experience, and we recognize the presence of the Other in the encounter. God's revelation first creates the possibility of faith and then brings it about. However, that does not exclude the subjective acceptance and experience. On the contrary, revelation and faith travel together. The concept of revelation points to the *a priori* of God's proclamation and action, while the concept of faith points to the acceptance and realization within our human existence. We will need to deal with both aspects in our practical theological discussion. The Holy Spirit must be given priority in the divine-human relationship, even if we opt for a more pneumatological approach. Besides, the Holy Spirit takes the revelation of Jesus Christ as its point of departure. Jesus says, according to the Gospel of John, "[He] will take from what is mine and make it known to you" (John 16:15). The Spirit always refers categorically to something else. The Spirit opens our eyes, not for its own presence in us but for that of Christ outside us.

Iustificatio: Imputation of External Righteousness

I mentioned in the introduction to this chapter that dialectical theology, in particular, once again put the forensic doctrine of justification on the theological agenda. It did so from the perspective of criticism regarding the civil and religious annexation of God. As children of the Enlightenment, both liberal theology and Pietism have so strongly emphasized the work of God *in* man that it has become, in fact, the work *of* man. By placing so much emphasis on the indwelling of the Spirit, this theology eventually has the Spirit acquire our human traits and become incorporated in our interests and our aspirations. In opposition to this approach, Karl Barth underscored the total otherness of God by using the concept of revelation, which to him was one of critical importance.

For our knowledge of God, Barth argues, we are and remain fully dependent on God himself. And even with regard to faith, we cannot draw any dotted lines toward the affections or the experiences of the knowing subject. The position of the knowing person in relation to this object (i.e., God's revelation) is the position of a fundamentally and irrevocably determined subsequence *(nachher);* it is the position of grace.[6] Eventually love, trust, and obedience will be lost if we remove the objectivity of the revelation and fail to see our faith as a radical attachment to this self-revealing God. Love, trust, and obedience are fundamentally anchored in God's claim on us; in other words, the focus on the object is essential for our faith. The human subject remains totally dependent on the divine acquittal and will never have faith simply at her disposal. Faith stands or falls with God's judgment, the judgment of grace. According to Barth, the human subject is precisely the new person who has been declared righteous, the new person seen from the perspective of God's judgment. Faith brings us to the state of being declared righteous by God. We are not only what we are, but through faith we are what we are not.[7] This minimizes the act of faith in the concrete person. Brunner puts it this way: "A judgment is called over our life, from the other side, a transcendent voice, fully independent from our subjectivity, directed *de excelsis* downward, a 'judgment of justification,' an *actus forensis.*"[8]

Imputatio: Declaration and Imputation

We will first take a closer look at *iustificatio* (the justification of the sinner) in order to arrive at a correct understanding of the human subject's role, viewed from the angle of indwelling. Justification has always belonged to the core of the life of faith in the Protestant tradition, especially the Lutheran tradition. Experiencing justification is not a secondary matter. And this has everything to do with my argument that we should see God as a speaking and acting subject. For justification

6. Karl Barth, *Church Dogmatics* (Edinburgh, 1956-75), II/1, p. 21.
7. Karl Barth, *Der Römerbrief,* 2nd ed. (Munich, 1933), p. 255.
8. Quoted in G. C. Berkouwer, *Dogmatische Studiën. Geloof en Rechtvaardiging* (Kampen, 1949), p. 7.

means that God himself imputes the righteousness of Christ to humans. The background is found in St. Paul's statements about the revelation of this righteousness in Christ. In the Epistle to the Romans (5:1 — "being justified by faith"), Paul depicts justification as an imputation from God, a verdict in the divine judgment. God declares the sinner righteous because of the righteousness of Christ. It is a picture of the accused as acquitted and declared righteous; it is a matter of attributing a righteousness that does not belong to the person himself, just as Abraham was declared righteous (Rom. 4:3).

Speaking dogmatically, we are here dealing with *imputation,* the attributing of extrinsic righteousness, understood as God's righteousness of grace as revealed in Jesus Christ. It is not found in the sinner. The idea behind this forensic doctrine of justification is that "the sinner is accepted as righteous by God only on the basis of a totally external divine righteousness, as has been revealed in Jesus Christ."[9] The human subject does not make any contribution whatsoever, nor does it become our own property that we can dispose of at will. It comes completely from God.

This line of thinking clearly believes that we are completely dependent on divine judgment: humans are only justified because God declares them righteous through the imputation of this external righteousness. It is a word that comes to us from outside: something *extra nos* is imputed to us, namely, the righteousness of Christ. The notion of Jesus' vicarious role is crucial: Jesus stands before the tribunal and takes the place of others so that they may be acquitted. We come to understand that "one died for all" (2 Cor. 5:14), and that through Christ we shall also all be made alive (1 Cor. 15:22). In him alone are all included, and thus are sinners accepted as justified and holy. In this view of forensic justification we find a strong emphasis on the subject's being completely dependent on an external event with regard to his faith. The subject is outwardly directed. We are not dealing with something that humans themselves have acquired or earned, with something they could discover in themselves, with a process in which they can actively participate, let alone contribute to. But this would make it seem as

9. Eberhard Jüngel, *Das Evangelium von der Rechtfertigung des Gottlosen als Zentrum des christlichen Glaubens. Eine theologische Studie in ökumenischer Absicht* (Tübingen, 1999), p. 175.

though people themselves have no role in justification and that there is no indwelling of Christ in believers.

Iustificatio as Actual Change

This last conclusion, however, would set us off on an entirely wrong track. For *iustificatio* as a divine judgment places our life on the cutting edge. Salvation and damnation are presented as opposites, not with the intention of expressing the ambivalence of life but to point to the last support in our temptations — God's judgment. Even when we find ourselves caught in the snares of mischief and evil, it does not mean that the last word has been spoken about our lives. For God has the final word, and God judges life from the perspective of his coming into the world. What is at stake is that our faith is focused on a reality that transcends our own selves. Not the reality where we find ourselves, nor the horizon of our own experiences, nor our own feelings have the final word. God's word of promise is the final word. Helmut Tacke suggests that we must view the kerygmatic pastorate from this angle. The *extra nos* is brought into the equation in order to free people from all burdens that oppress them.[10] And Thurneysen adds that thus justification needs to be proclaimed, even in the setting of a pastoral conversation. For this proclamation is connected with *iustificatio* as a matter of course. (I will return to this in Chapter 9, where I discuss the revelationary model).

The notion of *iustificatio* makes it possible to call sin and evil by their right names, for God breaks through the world of evil, sin, and death. God pulls humans away from the present evil world (Gal. 1:4), where wicked powers hold them in their grip: "What a wretched man I am. Who will rescue me from this body of death?" (Rom. 7:24). And believers confess, "Salvation is found in no one else, for there is no other name under heaven given to men by which we must be saved" (Acts 4:12). In him appeared salvation and true life, in him "who was delivered over to death for our sins and was raised to life for our justification" (Rom. 4:25). Even when the human condition is one of hostility

10. Helmut Tacke, *Mit dem Müden zur rechten Zeit zu reden. Beiträge zu einer bibel-orientierten Seelsorge* (Neukirchen-Vluyn, 1989), pp. 68-77.

and not of longing for God, even then — or precisely then — are we dependent on the Word that comes from the outside.

The forensic character of salvation does not point to a movement of withdrawal, which would leave our lives untouched. The fact that salvation has an external origin brings an enormous dynamism to our lives, which are broken open and exposed to a new daylight. The justifying judgment of God is a powerful word that effects this breakthrough. It calls forth a new life, just as Jesus is not destroyed by death but rises renewed on Easter morning. It has validity when the sinner is declared righteous. "The imputation of this external righteousness is only correctly described," says Jüngel, "when this *declaration* of divine righteousness is understood in the sense that it actually changes man's *being*."[11] God's judgment is a word that re-creates; humans are set free from bondage to the powers of sin and death. The justified person enters life with a new motivation and inspiration — living out of this reconciliation and with renewed expectation.

To believe is to affirm the truth of God's judgment and to live on that basis. So there are concrete consequences in humankind, in the subject. Affirming the truth means viewing life from the perspective of God's judgment, of the life and death of Christ, of God's reign. Martin Luther said this was living on the basis of a "happy exchange." If we want to enter life in this way, we don't need to first acquire all kinds of guarantees or assemble proofs in what we see around us. Even though the present reality is full of injustice, violence, and lovelessness, it does not have to paralyze us. In faith we know of another reality, of the revelation of God's kingdom in Jesus Christ. Paul says that the righteousness of God has been revealed . . . through Jesus Christ to all who believe in him (Rom. 3:21, 22).

Believing thus means living our lives on the basis of the saving and liberating Word, having the courage to let the reality of that Word rule in our own existence. God's declaration of grace does not leave us untouched. God's imputation calls for the affirmation of the human subject. We accept it as a valid judgment, and that acceptance has a major impact on our lives.

---

11. Jüngel, *Das Evangelium*, p. 180.

The Realization of Salvation

The Reformed tradition in particular has always paid attention to God's work in humans. Calvin refers to the Holy Spirit as the internal teacher and to our communion with Christ as Christ's "indwelling" in us. Furthermore, in the theological reflection on the life of faith, we meet not only the concept of *iustificatio* but also that of the *applicatio salutis*. Humans make salvation their own. Acquittal in judgment is accepted and receives concrete shape in our hearts and lives. Dutch Calvinism, in particular, has pursued this line of thought. The basic idea is that humans truly receive a new life through the imputation of Christ's righteousness. This word awakens new life, not as a torrent of rain that washes the seed from the field but as a refreshing shower that makes seeds germinate and grow. Humans are brought to life.

This divine work in us does not in any way detract from the *iustificatio*. The focus is on the *communicatio cum Christo*, but as a concrete event in us. Surely this faith is aroused by the Holy Spirit, and in that sense it is again a matter of God's coming to man — but in this case as *pneuma*. Therefore, if faith is to be real, the human subject will somehow have to be involved. When a human being accepts God's love, that very fact is an act of the human spirit. Even if we approach faith, as Martin Luther does, on the basis of *iustificatio,* and if we strip away from faith any human contribution, the point remains that the human being approves of divine judgment. We are resigned to God's promise in Jesus Christ. If we were to remove this last remnant of human input, this assent, we would eliminate faith as such and would be left with only the revelation of Christ — with humanity being of no importance. To me, that conclusion would be absurd.

J. H. Gunning, Jr.

Before we move on to the next chapter, I want to briefly describe the position of two influential Dutch theologians: J. H. Gunning, Jr. (1829-1905) and A. A. van Ruler (1908-1970). Both paid attention to the relationship between the Holy Spirit and the human subject, and both attributed an important role to the concept of indwelling.

Still fully in tune with the spirit of optimism of the nineteenth century, Gunning considered the inner life as the place where the Spirit of God dwells. In his writing he differentiates between a mechanical external dwelling *through* us and an internal essential dwelling *in* us. In this second instance we find that "He who knows is in turn known by the one he knows; and this knowledge is from the Image of the First that arises in him, through which the second, the one who is known, becomes aware of the living indwelling of the First. This indwelling knowledge may be referred to as a marvelous mystery, a joy for the heart, both to the One who knows and to the one who is known, when the eyes of each of them meet. Thus God is reflected in his image in man." As long as there is only a dwelling-*through,* man remains under the law. "But when God dwells in the human person, then he knows as he is known, and he lives in the freedom of salvation, and, as Thomas à Kempis says, God and the soul meet in the holy kiss of love. Here we see the intimate bond between divine life and that of the creature."[12]

Two matters take center stage. (1) There is reciprocity in the relationship: God knows humans, but humans also have a genuine knowledge of God. But there is more. An important link in this reciprocity is (2) the image of God that emerges in humans. As a result, there is a degree of intimacy with God. The human subject is able to know affectionately and deeply because of the image of God that rises up in him. It is because of God's presence, the divine indwelling in the human heart, that the knowing subject develops a trusting relationship with God. To me, this means not only that we know God as the object of our knowledge (object-directed faith) but that there is also a subjective connotation: humans have become familiar with God and experience God in their own world.

This is not the place to investigate Gunning's theology in detail, nor to deal with ethical theology as the outcome of nineteenth-century modernism. But a few remarks are in order. Gunning does not agree with Spinoza's monism and attaches great value to humans as persons — and to faith as a relationship between persons. God is personal; therefore, God is not revealed in a mechanical manner, as, for example, water flows into a vessel.

---

12. J. H. Gunning, Jr., *Blikken in de Openbaring* (Rotterdam, 1929), vol. 3, pp. 86-87.

In this way the divine revelation would not really come to man, but would remain more or less outside of him without uniting with his inner being, just as water, though surrounded by the staves of a barrel, does not become part of the barrel. It would also conflict with the human personality. Man is a person, because he is what he is through his own action; because, and to the extent that, he made himself into what he is. An impression, a divine voice, will only genuinely come to him if he is receptive. For otherwise the voice will reach no further than his ear and will not reach his heart, his inner self.[13]

For Gunning, this receptivity has everything to do with the image of God. He does not deny that the image has been thoroughly destroyed as a result of sin; but it is immediately revived through God's work on the heart. Gunning points to an impact that comes from God and enters man. The human spirit is the point of contact where progress and development play an important role, not just on the individual level but also on the level of the history of the world. The genesis of a spiritual communion is at stake. The first Adam became a living soul, the last Adam a life-giving being. "Had sin not intervened, the natural would have gradually developed, here as anywhere else, through constant communion with God, into the spiritual."[14]

Gunning clearly starts from the personal relationship between God and humans, while he wants to do justice both to the revealing work of God and its impact and to the development of the life of faith in the human subject. Regarding the latter, Gunning makes the image of God, as God's gift in the human spirit, the central principle. That we become aware of God through our self-consciousness is no problem for him, as long as we remain dependent on revelation and the miraculous. "Since human receptivity has been aroused by God, it can only find its satisfaction in the Miracle and the divine Revelation."[15] And Jesus Christ is the ultimate revelation, for in "him *dwells* the fullness of the godhead bodily."

13. Gunning, *Blikken in de Openbaring,* vol. 1, p. 52.
14. Gunning, *Blikken in de Openbaring,* vol. 3, p. 41.
15. Gunning, *Blikken in de Openbaring,* vol. 1, p. 53.

A. A. van Ruler

Just as Gunning assigns a crucial role to the human subject, Van Ruler likewise emphasizes that the human self forms an important link in the salvation process. "The work of the Holy Spirit," he says, "is characterized by the fact that it puts us to work." If we think pneumatologically, we "realize that there is also a crucial point in the salvific process within man: there is a decision in the human heart just as much as there was one on Calvary."[16] The decisions that were made in Christ are not just proclaimed over us, but new decisions are required — and they are made in us. Van Ruler refers to the work of Christ as one of vicariousness, while he refers to the work of the Spirit as indwelling, and he believes that we should always speak of God's salvation from these two vantage points. Salvation is realized in Jesus Christ, in the once-and-for-all atoning sacrifice. The reign of God was realized in Christ and not in us. But, Van Ruler continues, we cannot comprehend the terms "presence" and "realization" in a purely Christological sense. This unique sacrifice of atonement is realized in us as the sacrifice of sanctification and glorification; in that sense, Christ manifests himself in us. Thus Van Ruler's notion of indwelling takes on the sense of actualization: salvation, God's reign, actualizes itself in everyday human existence. "The divine salvation, which appeared as a historical reality in Christ, has a salvific orientation toward createdness. And therefore it seeks to be actualized in, that is, to be turned over into, the reality of our daily life."[17] This applies to the full scope of human life: the church, our thinking, our inner selves, our social relationships, our culture, and the nation we live in. Paul Fries summarizes this in his study of Van Ruler in the following words: "The central category for pneumatology is not representation, but *indwelling*. In our real existence, in our particularity, God the Spirit dwells within us, witnessing not only *to* us but also *with* our spirits. This 'with' means that we are not simply acted upon, but that we act along with the Holy Spirit. There is a full reciprocity between God and man."[18]

16. A. A. van Ruler, *Theologisch werk,* vol. 1 (Nijkerk, 1969), p. 182.
17. Van Ruler, *Theologisch werk,* vol. 4, p. 90.
18. Paul Roy Fries, *Religion and the Hope for a Truly Human Existence: An Inquiry into the Theology of F. D. E. Schleiermacher and A. A. Van Ruler with Questions for America* (1979), p. 102.

Van Ruler insists that God himself dwells in us as the Holy Spirit. It is an intimate relationship that should not, however, be confused with a deification of the creature. "The creature must remain creature. This is of supreme importance. Everything falls apart if man becomes God. We must differentiate between the self-ness of God and the self-ness of man. Both remain unscathed only if we stay with the formula that God dwells in and with man."[19] More than does Gunning, Van Ruler points to struggle as a characteristic of the indwelling: we are not merely touched and enlightened; there also is a battle between Spirit and flesh. "This battle is a fight, and the fight is a tournament, and the tournament is a love play, and the love play is a dialogue. It has all these facets. And many more. And all of them — fight, play, and dialogue — continue forever. They last for as long as we live. And there is no decision until the Spirit penetrates our world and touches us with the magic wand of his almighty power."[20] And this, Van Ruler maintains, is the real pneumatological mystery; this leads to the term that qualifies the reciprocity between God and humanity. "What is referred to as vicariousness in christology, is called reciprocity in pneumatology. Theonomous reciprocity: the Spirit does and gives everything. For instance, he liberates our will so that we receive a free will."[21] Van Ruler uses the term "theonomous reciprocity" to indicate that God's motion toward us has priority. When God touches us, we will reach the point where we accept God. "The touch is enlightenment, is conviction, is liberation. All this penetrates man: it touches his mind, his will, his heart, the self, man's being." This touch as the almighty work of the Spirit can only be described in terms of a turning around. "The new birth marks a turning point in man's existence. Why, then, should we not also use categories such as in-pouring or infusion?"[22]

Both Gunning and Van Ruler want to do full justice to God's work in us, and in such a way that the human subject receives a constitutive and active role in the communion with God. Gunning still leaves us with a taste of the unbroken idealism and optimism of the late nineteenth century. God brings life to development through the miracle of

19. Van Ruler, *Theologisch werk,* vol. 1, p. 185.
20. Van Ruler, *Theologisch werk,* vol. 1, p. 186.
21. Van Ruler, *Theologisch werk,* vol. 1, p. 181.
22. Van Ruler, *Theologisch werk,* vol. 1, p. 186.

creation, the crown of creation being humans as God's image. God embodies true life in his Son, and through the Spirit the miracle of communion with God is completed. Everything is full of progress and drive. Life develops because of the miracle of divine revelation and finds its perfection in the communion with God. Even though Gunning gives a prime role to God's motion toward humanity, that is, to revelation, that approach is not critical. God's coming is edifying, renewing, perfecting, but not judging and directing. Life must indeed be set free from sin and evil, but this is not, to all appearances, a cancerous evil that must be fought tooth and nail. The never-ceasing temptation of sin and the fragmentation of our existence never come to the forefront. Notions such as struggle and temptation, therefore, do not become central issues in anthropology. God comes close to us, and life develops as God finds a place in the human heart. In Gunning's theology, the receptivity of a person's self is accompanied by a kind of coziness: God lives with the people. Van Ruler is more critical. Because of the unruliness of life, he puts more emphasis on the element of struggle, and he also attributes to life a more fragmentary and pluriform character.

CHAPTER 4

The Indwelling of Salvation

Salvation has been revealed in Jesus Christ. It is imputed to us by God in justification, through which we get involved. I have already hinted at this activity by using the term "indwelling": God dwells among us. But how does that happen? How does salvation take shape in our lives? I will deal with that question in this chapter. When God's salvation has an impact on us, it leaves a trail in our lives. But does this also imply a genuine change in us? Is a new person born? Here we will investigate, in particular, the way of salvation in human existence. What does participation in God's salvation mean for our journey through life?

Exploring Some Theological Concepts

Reformed theology distinguishes between justification and sanctification. Berkhof prefers the word "renewal" to "sanctification." Other terms that we often encounter are "conversion" and "new birth." Calvin speaks of "a reformation into the newness of life."[1] Lutheran and Reformed theology both also use the term *ordo salutis* to describe the salvific process in our life. It would be incorrect to think that the difference between justification and sanctification is that in the first case God is the acting subject, while in the second the human being is the actor. Sanctification is just as much a matter of faith. In other words, we remain fully dependent on God's grace and live on the basis of God's compassion; it is not a matter of cooperation in the sense that it

1. Calvin, *Institutes* III.11.11.

is now our turn to do something. Sanctification also centers on the ongoing implementation of God's work, but the difference is that it is now God's work *on,* and specifically *in,* the human heart. For God also works in the inner parts of people. Jeremiah hears God say about the new covenant that will be established: "I will put the law in their minds and write it on their hearts" (Jer. 31:33). And we read in Ezekiel: "I will put my Spirit in you and move you to follow my decrees and be careful to keep my laws" (Ezek. 36:27). Moreover, sanctification is not something detached from the human being, for communion with Christ is precisely the core of sanctification. Berkhof believes that conformity to Christ is, in fact, the purpose of renewal.[2]

Thus it is important that we have a theological understanding of the salvific process in our lives. Van Ruler points out that we must focus on a pneumatological rather than a Christological analysis: "Speaking about ourselves, the church, the Christian or Christendom, we must do so, if we take our relationship with God seriously, not christologically but pneumatologically. All we have in and through ourselves, and are, with respect to salvation — it is all fully a divine reality, but in the modus of the Holy Spirit and not in the modus of Christ."[3] Van Ruler is of the opinion that there are major structural differences between a Christological and a pneumatological analysis. Pneumatology emphasizes that we humans, as individuals, are ourselves and remain ourselves while the Spirit dwells in us. We are, Van Ruler says, destined to be dwelling places of God in the Spirit. In the realization of salvation, the human subject remains the one who is over against God.

The human subject, therefore, has a constitutive role in the communion with God. We have an important place. But what does this mean for the subject role of humans if God is also an acting person? I have observed in Chapter 1 that Calvin emphasizes the subject-side by saying that Christ, in order to transmit to us what he has received from the Father, must become ours and must dwell in us. This takes place, Calvin says, through the work of the Holy Spirit, for he is "the bond by which Christ effectually unites us to himself."[4] The elevated Christ

2. Berkhof, *Christian Faith,* p. 430.
3. Van Ruler, *Theologisch werk,* vol. 1, p. 176.
4. Calvin, *Institutes* III.1.1.

himself works through his life-bestowing Spirit; we are dealing with a spiritual unity. The Spirit is "an inner teacher by whose effort the promise of salvation penetrates into our minds, a promise that would otherwise only strike the air or beat upon our ears."[5]

Through the work of the Holy Spirit humans receive understanding and insight, in such a way that an actual relationship ensues. The Spirit brings enlightenment and change in the subject, says Calvin: "For light would be given the sightless in vain had that Spirit of discernment not opened the eyes of the mind. . . ." We see in Calvin's thought a constant movement back and forth between God and humanity. God manifests himself in his Word, and through faith we know his will toward us. God draws us to himself and enables us to embrace him. But it is always a human activity — aroused by the Spirit, but nonetheless a human act. In that light, we are not surprised to hear Calvin speak of the Spirit as the internal teacher. The human mind and heart are fully involved. When we believe, it is God who is active with and in us. Van Ruler observes that we should remember, precisely at this point, that God is a subject. Otherwise, our understanding of his work in us becomes too object-directed, too physical, too materialistic. It is an intersubjective event. There are no "things" placed in existence, but "God Himself is, as God the Holy Spirit, present in existence through the *gratia interna*. And this means that He — in the manner and power of the Holy Spirit — is working in and with human existence toward its salvation."[6]

A Change in Humanity's Essential Being?

The Reformed tradition often speaks of an actual transformation or change of the inner person. This seems to suggest that a new germ is placed in us that gives us a new and sanctified potential. The Canons of Dordrecht refer to a powerful work of renewal through the Spirit.

> He opens the closed and softens the hardened heart, and circumcises that which was uncircumcised; infuses new qualities into the

5. Calvin, *Institutes* III.1.4.

6. A. A. van Ruler, *De vervulling van de wet. Een dogmatische studie over de verhouding van openbaring en existentie,* 2nd ed. (Nijkerk, 1974), p. 216.

will, which, though heretofore dead, He quickens; from being evil, disobedient, and refractory, He renders it good, obedient, and pliable; actuates and strengthens it, that like a good tree, it may bring forth the fruits of good actions. . . .

Whereupon the will thus renewed is not only actuated and influenced by God, but in consequence of this influence becomes itself active. Wherefore also man himself is rightly said to believe and repent by virtue of that grace received.[7]

This points out how the subject herself, through the work of the Holy Spirit, is renewed and how she, as a renewed subject, is able to come to discernment and action. This leads to a question: How independent does the human being become in this respect? Are we perhaps infused with new attributes? Abraham Kuyper uses the terminology of the human being as an "opposite" of God, with an "essence" and certain "habits." "God's love is infused into our heart through the Holy Spirit." It is not something that rebounds but something that is infused: a divine seed is inserted into our souls, and thereby the state of our souls is changed. For our human habits can be either unholy or holy. Kuyper insists that we are transformed through the new birth.

> Just as He has the power to transform in the new birth the *root* of your life, God also has the possibility to transform the manifestation of your affections from their previous state of unholiness into holiness.[8]

Bavinck, though a bit more reticent, also speaks of the renewal of our nature. God not only imputes to us the righteousness of Christ, but he also allows us to participate in this "in our inner being through the process of rebirth and the work of renewal through the Holy Spirit, until we fully reflect the image of his Son. . . . This sanctification is ethical, it continues throughout life, and it ensures that, through the renewing impact of the Holy Spirit, the righteousness of Christ becomes our ethical possession."[9]

7. *Canons, Ratified in the National Synod of the Reformed Church, Held at Dordrecht, in the Years 1618 and 1619* (Third and Fourth Heads of Doctrine), pp. 11, 12.

8. A. Kuyper, *Het Werk van de Heiligen Geest*, vol. 3 (Amsterdam, 1889), p. 67.

9. H. Bavinck, *Gereformeerde dogmatiek*, vol. 4 (Kampen, 1930), p. 233.

In this way the human subject does indeed acquire a constitutive role, not only in the sense that humans accept and agree with the judgment of justification; but there is also something that happens inside of them: a transformation of the inner self that results in a new *habitus*. It results from God's action, but at the same time it is more than merely an external judgment that is accepted "subjectively": the subject himself actually changes. Or there is something in him that is transformed. Nonetheless, Bavinck hastens to add that a reborn person is not changed into an essentially different being from what he was before his new birth.[10]

What is at stake here? We are dealing with the role of the human subject in our life with God. We have noted that, with respect to faith, the Reformation gave great weight to God's justifying judgment. We are faced with the imputation of an alien (that is, external) righteousness. And we note that God as subject has the primacy in the communion between God and humanity. Yet we must continue to ask further questions about the concrete human being who is addressed and involved. Does he or she actually hear the word of grace and liberation? Does this result in any change in his or her life? How does this word have an impact on the person, and how far-reaching is it? For this is what we need to know: What does it actually mean in a person's daily life? And another, closely related, question is: In what way does this involve a person's intellectual powers? By this I mean a person's inner being, where the knowing, feeling, and willing takes place. For if divine justification is to have any impact on our lives, it must somehow involve the inner self, where our thinking, our emotions, and our intentions are shaped. And if we speak about the renewal of life, we must assume that this will not be a fully external event — something outside of the person. The salvation that God imputes receives its concrete form in our lives. That is the classical theme of the *ordo salutis*.

I hope it is clear that I do not argue that humans come to God through their own power and thus, as it were, begin to cooperate with God. And I do not ignore the fact that humans can be totally enmeshed in evil and may only harden themselves. There are many instances in the Bible where we read about the stubborn heart that is broken, or the

---

10. Bavinck, *Gereformeerde dogmatiek*, vol. 4, p. 418.

heart once closed that has been opened. Think of the example of Lydia: "The Lord opened the heart of Lydia to respond to Paul's message" (Acts 16:14).

A Theological Controversy

Let us now examine a theological controversy. We find especially — but not exclusively — in the Reformed tradition a tension between understanding our faith from the perspective of justification and understanding it from the perspective of new birth and conversion. We encounter this latter line of thought mostly in Pietism, Methodism, and Evangelicalism. The first approach is particularly found in "confessional" traditions, both Reformed and Lutheran, with the followers of Kohlbrugge and, let's not forget, the Barthians. We are dealing with differences in emphasis, but they do make a real difference in the praxis of our faith. A major objection to taking new birth as our point of departure in the understanding of our faith is the resulting categorization into "converted" versus "unconverted." This may lead to lines of demarcation that are too easy and too visible between the church and the world, or even, within the church, between those who are presumably converted and those who are not. A further objection is that the difference between a believer and an unbeliever is further extended when conversion or new birth is understood as giving someone a new "quality" through which that person, in essence, becomes a new being. Furthermore, if this new life is seen as ethically superior, then we will soon find ourselves in a self-satisfied and rather exclusive Christianity: a group of true believers that differs from other humans. Thus the drive toward holiness can easily become detached from remorse and from the fundamental equality of all people, which is so forcefully expressed in the justification of the sinner. And this opens the possibility of the pious person or the worshiper or the ethically correct person or the socially active person climbing onto his throne and assuming the right to judge others.

Theologians such as Kohlbrugge and Barth voice their objections to this self-sufficiency of grace *in* us. They do not deny that there is change in the life of the converted person, but this will never become that person's own possession. Grace becomes active in us, but its subject is and will always be Jesus Christ and not the converted individual. Therefore, it is hardly possible to speak about humans outside of Christology. Our life is with Christ hidden in God; what we are, we are in Christ, once and for all. Faith thus points away from itself: the obedient person is Jesus Christ. If we want to know what human obedience and integrity truly are, we can only point to him. "Faith is not," says Barth, "a standing, but a being suspended and hanging, without ground under our feet."[11] What is behind this, I believe, is the deeply entrenched fear that we, at the very moment that we take matters into our own hands, will reduce and change the richness of God's grace, and particularly the scope and fullness of this grace. As soon as we make it our own, we will absorb it and will relegate it to the sphere of civility and decency. Barth wants to prevent the domestication of grace.[12] But there is also in the background a deep mistrust of human piety. For we are enemies of grace, and will we not cunningly place ourselves on the throne and revel in our own honor and hubris under the guise of piety?

The Externality and Intimacy of Salvation

We must take this warning to heart, that is, we must always critically look at our renewal and sanctification, realizing that there is no complete overhaul of the inner self. Otherwise, we would simply ignore the stubbornness of the "old life" and the constant struggle against it. Moreover, we should remain clear that renewal is brought about by the Spirit of Christ. Faith is an abiding relationship, not an infused substance that develops autonomously. Having said that, however, I must also say that the theological approach that we have just considered remains too much caught in criticism. Can something positive be said about the human acceptance of salvation and grace? In other words, does faith make a difference? If faith matters, then the human being also matters. This does not deny the external origin of salvation; but it does leave room for its intimacy. And this intimacy refers to the indwelling, both in our inner being and in our daily lives. Reformed theology, with its attention to the work of the Holy Spirit, has an abun-

11. Barth, *Church Dogmatics* II/1, p. 159.
12. Barth, *Church Dogmatics* II/1, p. 141.

dance of terms at its disposal for speaking about salvation: besides the *iustificatio* is the *applicatio;* besides tradition (as the mediation channel for salvation) is the reception of salvation; besides the Word is faith; besides the promise is obedience; besides the sacraments is the experiential dimension. Externality and intimacy do not exclude one another; in fact, they go together.

I will now examine three of these aspects in greater detail. (1) If there is a movement from God toward us, how does it enter a person? In what way is that person touched so that she is able to make it her own? On this subject Van Ruler uses a beautiful image, though he gets carried with the metaphor: "Then the Spirit jumps over the wall of the human heart and incites man so strongly to open the gates of his heart that — another jump! — man takes the initiative to open these gates."[13] I want to explore in more detail what role our intellectual capacities play in this transaction. (2) *Iustificatio* as the imputation of the righteousness of Christ implies a relationship between the believer and the historical revelation in Christ. For this reason the journey of faith is not only typified by justification but also by conversion and renewal. This is clearly manifested in our baptism: we have died with Christ and are raised with him. This communion is actualized in the concrete praxis of life. (3) In this journey through life, our faith receives a preliminary and fragmentary shape. How is it expressed — in remorse and repentance or in actual renewal?

The Impact on Our Inner Self

Let us now direct our attention toward the intellectual capacities of the human subject in the life of faith. The function of knowledge plays an important role in the Reformed tradition: we learn to *know* God's goodness. Calvin refers to the Holy Spirit as the internal teacher with good reason. The first book of the *Institutes* begins with the thesis that faith pertains to both the knowledge of God and the knowledge of ourselves. We have already discovered (in Chapter 1) that this knowledge must not be associated with conceptual objectivizing and intellectual abstraction. This knowledge implies an eager affirmation and leads to

13. Van Ruler, *Theologisch werk,* vol. 2, p. 92.

communion. When we know Christ, we know the goodness of his deed. It is interesting to note what Calvin has to say about this: faith is, he says, "a firm and certain knowledge of God's benevolence toward us, founded upon the truth of the freely given promise in Christ, both revealed to our minds and sealed upon our hearts by the Holy Spirit."[14]

The knowledge of God's mercy is revealed to our minds by the Spirit and is sealed in our hearts. Our inner beings are involved from the very beginning. "And it will not be enough," says Calvin, "for the mind to be illumined by the Spirit of God unless the heart is also strengthened and supported by his power."[15] The cognitive and the affective are closely related, and we get the impression that the passion to accept God's promises as true and genuine does, in fact, arise from the stirring of our affections. For through the work of the Spirit the enlightened soul receives, as it were, a new acuteness, and the human mind now gets a true taste. The images and metaphors Calvin uses have a strong affective connotation. The Spirit directs the feelings and the mind toward God's promises, and as a result we see how God's loving compassion lights up in them. "For truly, the abundant sweetness which God has stored up for those who fear him cannot be known without at the same time powerfully moving us. And once anyone has been moved by it, it utterly ravishes him and draws him to itself."[16]

It is this converging of mind and emotion that stirs the human subject to action. "How can the mind," Calvin asks rhetorically, "be aroused to taste the divine goodness without at the same time being wholly kindled to love God in return?" So the human subject arises and turns toward God. It is abundantly clear that the intense affections originate when heart and head are directed toward the love of God in Christ. God's love has an infectious quality. It is remarkable to note, however, that Calvin does not mention the human will. Not because he does not attach great importance to this dimension — on the contrary. But Calvin deals with that aspect when he discusses conversion and renewal and not when he treats of faith and justification. When his focus is on faith, he keeps the cognitive and the affective aspects together.

14. Calvin, *Institutes* III.2.7.
15. Calvin, *Institutes* III.2.33.
16. Calvin, *Institutes* III.2.41.

Jonathan Edwards

I want to compare Calvin's approach with a strain of theology that takes a slightly different route, American Puritanism, particularly the theology of Jonathan Edwards (1703-1758). Strongly influenced by the English empiricists Hume and Locke, Edwards put great emphasis on the way the human mind functions. Edwards emphatically maintains that he belongs to the Calvinistic tradition, but he differs from Calvin when he does not point primarily to the role of knowledge but to a combination of the affections and the will. The communion with God, we might say, is not primarily a matter of our heads but rather of our hearts, in the sense that our emotions — or the impulses of the human self — direct our will. Edwards sees the will as a rather neutral function; however, it does have the inclination to either attract or reject. The affections make the will go in one particular direction. Edwards argues that the Creator not only endowed us with affections but also made them the source of our actions. "And as true religion is of a practical nature, and God hath so constituted the human nature that the affections are very much the spring of men's actions, this also shows that true religion must consist very much in the affections."[17]

Edwards distinguishes between two functions of the human mind: (1) the cognitive function of observation and speculation; and (2) the function that makes it possible for us to have a certain drive or inclination with regard to the things we observe and know. We do not remain indifferent; we are either attracted to or repulsed by them. This second aspect is the ability of the human mind to regard the things we observe, not as unaffected observers, but in a state of attraction or rejection, pleasure or displeasure, love or loathing. We refer to these inclinations, according to Edwards, as the *heart;* and when we express these inclinations in action, we speak of the *will,* meaning that there is a close connection between the heart and the will. Edwards also uses the word "passion" for the inclinations and feelings, to describe the intense emotions that may stir the human mind. These may be positive emotions, such as love, hope, joy, and gratitude, but may also be negative ones, such as hatred, anxiety, sorrow, and anger. All of this means that we must make a clear distinction between the *habitus* of the heart on the

17. Jonathan Edwards, *The Religious Affections* (1746; Edinburgh, 1997), p. 29.

one hand and conceptual abilities and rational arguments on the other. Affections have an intense emotional component that we experience as something coming over us: we are being moved.

Here religious life finds its source. "I am bold to assert," says Edwards, "that there never was any considerable change wrought in the mind or conversation of any person, by anything of a religious nature that ever he read, heard or saw, that had not his affections moved. . . . And in a word, there never was anything considerable brought to pass in the heart or life of any man living, by the things of religion, that had not his heart deeply affected by those things."[18] No one becomes a believer if his inner being has not first been touched by emotion. This aspect of being-touched-by-love plays an important role: love is the fountain of all emotions. Spiritual life consists of an intense feeling of the spiritual beauty and glory of God; a new world opens itself to us as soon as we make this discovery. We are not dealing with rational arguments but with emotions that arise in the heart and express a direct contact. The Spirit of God opens our eyes for this beauty, with the result that we experience a change from within. The primary thing is not that we receive new knowledge through the Spirit but that our own spirit receives a new status — a taste for the beauty and glory of God's love.[19]

> I have shown that spiritual knowledge primarily consists in a taste or relish of the amiableness and beauty of that which is truly good and holy. This holy relish is a thing that discerns and distinguishes between good and evil, between holy and unholy, without being at trouble of a train of reasoning.[20]

By giving such central place in their inner lives to the affections, believers acquire direct and evidential insight. Arguments, reflection, deductions from other principles — they are not the issue. "He who has a correct musical ear knows whether the sound he hears be true harmony; he does not need first to be at the trouble of the reasonings of a mathematician about the portion of the notes."[21] Likewise, she who is led by

18. Edwards, *The Religious Affections,* pp. 30, 31.
19. Edwards, *The Religious Affections,* p. 203.
20. Edwards, *The Religious Affections,* p. 207.
21. Edwards, *The Religious Affections,* p. 207.

the Spirit knows instantaneously what she must do, and she spontaneously arrives at a sound judgment, without any deduction, on the basis of the beauty and goodness she has tasted.

Our Inner Life

It is clear that, in both Calvin's and Edwards's approaches, our intellectual capacities are spoken to and activated by the working of the Spirit. Or, to recall Van Ruler's metaphor, the Spirit jumps over the wall of the heart and so stimulates the person to open the gates of his heart that he will decide to open them. In a theological reconstruction of this event, we encounter such categories as intellectual capacities and the dimensions of knowing, feeling, and willing — admittedly in diverse ways. Calvin emphasizes the combination of knowledge and affections, while Edwards makes a close link between emotion and will. But it is remarkable how both assign an important role to our inner life — with respect to this lively involvement that is so characteristic of the faith concept. Apparently, faith is not anchored in the center of one's personality and does not become a motivating power in daily life if one's feelings are not involved. There must be an existential involvement of the subject in the faith process if there is to be a genuine communion.

Neither Calvin nor Edwards denies the cognitive aspect of our faith. Calvin emphatically refers to the knowledge of God's benevolence toward us. But it is a knowledge that touches our feelings and moves us; it has a concrete impact on us, both with regard to our emotions and to the intentionality of our actions. And this results from the fact that the subject has encountered the reality and the activity of God and has thereby discovered communion with God, which shows how the subject-side and object-side are both presupposed in our faith. Both dimensions are needed if faith is to be a genuine encounter. Does this mean we can say that the Spirit transforms people from within, so that a new mentality or a new *habitus* originates in our heart? That depends on how we formulate this. It cannot mean that a button has been pushed in our minds that allows us to live with a new frame of mind from now on. For this would imply that we have detached it from our faith relationship.

The human subject must continue to depend on external input. In that sense, our inner selves completely depend on keeping the loving and gracious benevolence of God in view. And we need to hear that time after time. That is the impact of the *imputatio*. Unfortunately, those who are fearful of human subjectivity often forget that the subject does play a pivotal role, in the sense that faith needs to be interiorized in our minds — in our knowledge, our affections, and our will. And, I hasten to add, it leaves a vivid impression. The work of the Spirit is not like a glancing blow that bounces off; it touches a sensitive nerve in our inner being, and it sounds like music in our ears. Human subjectivity also implies a certain continuity. Think, for example, of the functions of memory and conscience. Our faith and the work of the Spirit are more than cursory hunches or sudden fireworks displays without any lasting consequences. There is a continuity in our consciousness: remembrance, memory, conscience, reflection, and internal dialogue. In that sense we could speak of a new approach to life and a new *habitus*. If the impact is powerful and profound, there will be a long-sounding echo. And then the human mind will truly be a dwelling place of the Holy Spirit.

Tied to the Revelation in Christ

Concepts such as conversion, new birth, and renewal indicate that salvation enters human existence. These words refer to the effect of God's salvation on human lives. God has saved us, we read in Titus, through the baptism of the new birth and of renewal through the Holy Spirit. Paul also refers to this when he prays that God may "strengthen you with power through his Spirit in your inner being, so that Christ may dwell in your hearts through faith" (Eph. 3:16, 17).

We arrive at important decisions in our hearts and our inner beings, where our approaches to life are shaped and our motivations are made operational. We have seen in previous chapters that our inner self is not an isolated monad. As human beings we are essentially communal beings: we are the image of God and are also dependent on fellow humans. This is also true of the new life. You have put the "old man" with his practices away, says Paul, and have put on the new person, "which is being renewed in knowledge in the image of its Creator." Paul immediately mentions Christ in this context (Col. 3:10, 11); he speaks further about "putting on" Christ (Rom. 13:14) and about becoming like the Son (Rom. 8:29). These are all figures of speech telling us that this renewal of the person takes place in his inner being but is directed toward the Other — toward Christ or toward the Creator.

The nature of this renewal is closely related to our bond with Christ. It has to do with the internal acceptance of God's eschatological revelation in the history of salvation, and with its effects in the lives of individual human beings. Here we may ask whether we are not dealing with two unequal concepts: on the one hand, the historical-eschatological revelation in Christ, and, on the other, the salvific effect in our own lives. Should we not distinguish between the *ordo salutis* and salvation history? Of course, faith, new birth, and renewal are rooted in the revelation in Christ, but it surely is of a different order when seen as a process in human life. Indeed, we must affirm that God's work in Christ differs from God's work in us. The revelation Paul received on the Damascus road is of a different order from the voice heard at Jesus' baptism in the Jordan River. But we should not forget that the order of salvation is always connected with the eschatological revelation of Christ in salvation history. The issue is always how we participate in this revelation process.

We find a specific expression of this in the sacraments of baptism and the Lord's Supper. Our speaking about the renewal of the person is certainly not detached from God's revelation in Christ. On the contrary, the focus is on our reception and our acceptance of this revelation in our own lives. This linkage brings a new polarity to our existence: the separation between old and new. "In the same way, count yourself dead to sin but alive to God in Christ Jesus" (Rom. 6:11). It has to do with salvation in the midst of an evil world, of truth in the midst of deceit, of life in the midst of threats of death. This is implied in such core concepts of the Christian faith as liberation, forgiveness, and resurrection.

This linkage to the historical-eschatological revelation of salvation implies that faith cannot be reduced to a mere longing or an ideal we cherish. The Christian faith is expressed in much stronger terms: "Faith is being sure of what we hope for and certain of what we do not see" (Heb. 11:1). Faith has a basis, and we do already have proof of what we do not see. The coming salvation has already broken through in the groaning of creation. God's reign has arrived among us in the ministry of Jesus, which has shown us how human life is freed from sin and death. He is the foundation of our hope; he is God's revelation in time. This invariably is the core of the gospel proclamation: "that Christ died for our sins according to the Scriptures, that he was buried, that he was raised on the third day according to the Scriptures" (1 Cor. 15:3, 4). This short summary leaves no doubt about the crucial importance of that revelation of salvation.

Salvation History and Eschatology

The Bible presents the salvation that appeared in Christ as the breaking through of the new age, the realization of eschatological expectation. Living in faith, therefore, means to be connected to that reality and letting the present be determined by it. The believer expects a different world, or at the very least the believer is convinced that injustice, lovelessness, and violence do not have the final word. To believe is to have the courage to view life in this world from the perspective of God's promises. A believer does not remain a prisoner of the here and now. In the gospel we are confronted with what "no eye has seen, no ear has heard, no mind has conceived" (1 Cor. 2:9). We are constantly drawn outward, carried along in the history that God has already revealed in Israel and in Jesus Christ, and carried forward to the glory that will be revealed to us in the future. In the midst of this tension is our faith: between the revelation in Christ and the expectation of glory.

We find these two dimensions time after time in the Pauline writings. In the salvation-historical interpretation of these writings the emphasis is on the significance of the historical revelation in Jesus Christ. The primary answer to the question of what happens in the life of a human being is that we are incorporated in Christ. Sharing in the way of Christ takes first place: that amounts to sharing in the pilgrimage of suffering and in the path of the resurrection, putting away the "old man" and putting on the "new man." The primary issue is contemporaneity with Christ. The categories of "old and new man," of dying with Christ and rising with him, refer to a new corporate connection. They refer to being included in and participating in a new era that has begun in Christ.[22] The church participates in the death and resurrection of Christ; we are incorporated in this salvation-historical process through the sacrament of baptism. In other words, not only are we involved, but the true significance is that we have been included in what happened to Christ. We are part of a living connection. Paul says, "We were therefore buried with him through baptism into death in order that, just as Christ was raised from the dead through the glory of the Father, we too may live a new life" (Rom. 6:4).

The strength of this salvation-historical approach is that we are thrown back on the revelation that has already taken place, the revelation into which we have been incorporated. This offers a tremendous freedom. We have already been reconciled and saved in Christ; but this should not diminish the eschatological thrust. The believer also anticipates the future glory, the breakthrough of a new age. This breakthrough is portrayed in the Bible as having eschatological dimensions. This is what J. Christiaan Beker emphasizes in his study of Paul: he suggests that the apocalyptic and the eschatological go together. Beker disagrees with the existentialist approach of Bultmann, who dissolves the tension between the present and future anthropologically. Beker calls for a historical-ontological interpretation that will do justice to the eschatological-apocalyptic expectation: "Resurrection language properly belongs to the domain of the new age to come and is an inherent part of the transformation and the re-creation of all reality in the apocalyptic age."[23] The resurrection is not a matter of a new way of looking at things, an intrapsychic event, but of an ontological-cosmological revelation that opens up a new age. We must position the tension between old and new in this eschatological context. This hoped-for reality is more than an open future; it centers on the glory that will be revealed to us, the redemption of the body, the appearing of Christ, and peace.

This leads me to conclude that the renewal of the believer is indissolubly linked to the historical-eschatological revelation of salvation. To believe is to accept this intimate tie to revelation in Christ and to expect the revelation of his glory. As we travel our path of faith, we are constantly pulled outward to the revelation that took place in Christ in

22. Ridderbos, *Paulus,* pp. 61, 226.
23. J. Christiaan Beker, *Paul the Apostle: The Triumph of God in Life and Thought* (Edinburgh, 1980), p. 152.

the past and toward the future glory. There is more than our personal existence and more than this moment in time. Thus every effort to "anthropologize" faith limits the fullness and scope of salvation; sooner or later it will lead to a reduction. For God's grace reaches further than our human consciousness can. Nonetheless, we are, through this bond and through this expectation, fully involved. We should never allow our focus on existence in the present moment to dissipate in salvation history, nor in eschatology. If we did, we would totally ignore God's work in us and in the flow of history. With respect to salvation, we are addressed in our spiritual as well as in our physical existence. The inner self experiences a daily renewal (2 Cor. 4:16), and this refers to a constant communion with Christ. God "writes" in our hearts through the Spirit (2 Cor. 3:3). When the risen Christ appeared to his disciples, he opened their hearts (Luke 24:45). The key issue is that we are transformed through a renewal of our thinking (Rom. 12:20) in such a way that we allow ourselves to be shaped by the revelation in Christ and the expectation of glory. All these expressions indicate that we are touched in our inner beings — in our hearts, in our minds, in our wills — and that this has an impact on our way of life. It has to do with mind as well as with body: "Glorify God in your body" (1 Cor. 6:20).

The *Ordo salutis*

The linkage with salvation history should not lead us to view the unique life of every human being as of little importance. Human existence is important, and the particularity of each life should be recognized and known: "O Lord, you have searched me and you know me. You know when I sit and when I rise; you perceive my thoughts from afar. You discern my going out and my lying down; you are familiar with all my ways" (Ps. 139:1-3). The reality of human life is like a palette of colors: the conditions of life, education, socialization, character, and development — all these elements contribute to the particularity of human existence. Our linkage to salvation history is never detached from our own social and individual conditions of life. And it is precisely this concrete *condition humaine* that makes our faith existential: our relationship with Christ has an impact on our private lives.

Again we must speak of reciprocity and interconnectedness. From the experiences of daily life, we travel to the revelation in Christ; we make the return trip to the cares and joys of daily life filled with the compassion and love of God. The kerygma offers comfort when we cross the fault lines of life, even though the problems of life may lead us to doubt the kerygma at the same time. We know of the unique significance of Jesus Christ, but in the meantime we journey along our own one-time and unique path. The joy of salvation doesn't automatically destroy all melancholy. The resurrection hope does destroy the sting of death, but that does not prevent intense grief when we face a loss. There is interaction in that the insights of faith compete with our life experiences for first place in our inner beings.

Our life experiences are shaped by communion with Christ, and new experiences lead us back to the meaning of revelation. In that sense faith is never complete: it must be conquered and internalized all the time, in each new, concrete situation. In our affirmation of the merciful judgment of God in Christ *(iustificatio)*, we believers cling to the objective salvation provided in Christ, but in our subjective experience we continue along the road of temptation, penance, struggle, progress, and endurance. When Paul speaks about justification, he also gives us an earful about the other side of the coin: "And we rejoice in the hope of the glory of God. Not only so, but we also rejoice in our sufferings, because we know that suffering produces perseverance; and perseverance, character; and character, hope. And hope does not disappoint us, because God has poured out his love into our hearts by the Holy Spirit, whom he has given us" (Rom. 5:2-5). This speaks of the journey through life, of maturing and struggling, but also of progress. We may speak of growth, but not in the sense of a continuous upward movement. Rather, it is the art of living, whatever the situation, out of this bond with Christ and the expectation of glory. We grow toward him, who is the head (Eph. 4:15).

This theme comes into play in the notion of the *ordo salutis* in traditional Protestant theology, both in the Lutheran and Reformed branches. The term is primarily used to describe the journey God travels with us concerning our living a life of salvation. Usually texts such as Romans 8:30 are quoted: "And those he predestined he also called; those he called, he also justified; those he justified, he also glorified." Heppe, for instance, moves on immediately — as soon as he has dealt with the work of Christ — to election, justification, sanctification, and endurance.[24] Bavinck takes the same route in his dogmatics. The focus is on the efficacy and the appropriation of salvation in Christ. Heppe does not believe that salvation only becomes a reality in this appropriation; but he does emphasize that the objective salvation that Christ has brought is "subjectively realized in the *applicatio salutis,* in the sense that the latter rests in the first."[25] This kind of remark indicates a constant attention to human subjectivity, but a definite refusal to end up with *only* human subjectivity. We know that Bavinck became increasingly interested in the psychology of religion and religious experience. When discussing the *ordo salutis,* he enlarges on this theme, but he maintains that the Christian faith has its own metaphysical basis, that is, a basis in the revelation of God as found in Scripture.[26]

I will not go further into a systematic treatment of the way of salvation and the various phases that have been specified. Recently, Josuttis has once again argued in favor of the significance of the *ordo salutis* in practical theology, because of the structure it provides in our spiritual life and the possibilities it offers to chart the development of the life of faith. He recognizes four stages: election, enlightenment by the Spirit, conversion, and sanctification.[27]

Repentance or Progress? A Reformed Perspective

What, then, is the way we participate in salvation? Can we truly speak of a renewal? Calvin establishes a close link between renewal and repentance and the forgiveness of sins. Renewal is the work of Christ in the believer, and Calvin sees a connection between this renewal and both the dying to sin and being made alive in the spirit.[28] As soon as we accept the grace of the gospel, we see our own errors and sins and come to loathe them. Repentance is part of our faith: as we experience the

24. H. Heppe and E. Bizer, eds., *Die Dogmatik der evangelisch-reformierten Kirche* (Neukirchen, 1958).

25. Heppe and Bizer, eds., *Die Dogmatik der evangelisch-reformierten Kirche,* p. 404.

26. Bavinck, *Gereformeerde dogmatiek,* vol. 3 (Kampen, 1929), pp. 567-604.

27. Manfred Josuttis, *Segenskräfte. Potentiale einer energetischen Seelsorge* (Gütersloh, 2000), pp. 115-24.

28. Calvin, *Institutes* III.3.

light of grace, we discover our true condition. Repentance is a turning inward, and that turning to our inner self is an important link in this renewal, since the subject changes through this experience. Repentance, remorse, conversion, new birth — all these concepts are very close to each other and point to the process that affects us as the Spirit works on us. In Calvin's thinking, being crushed and being made alive belong together. This "crushing," which may be caused by the law or by the gospel, never stands in isolation but goes in the direction of a turning to God and to a new life. Thus repentance is not just a state of mind but also implies activity. "[I]n my judgment," Calvin says, "repentance can thus be well defined: it is the true turning of our life to God, a turning that arises from a pure and earnest fear of him; and it consists in the mortification of our flesh and of the old man, and in the vivification of the Spirit."[29] The goal of our remorse and repentance is to bring us back onto the narrow road. Calvin believes that phrases such as "repent and return to God" and "do penance" have the same meaning and may be used interchangeably.

Seen from this perspective, renewal is not a jump forward but rather has the dimension of remorse, return, and the restoration of good relationships. It also expresses the awareness that much has gone wrong and continues to go wrong in our lives, and that we must constantly be guided back to the right path. Renewal goes together with a new self-appraisal, with the recognition that there are wrong thoughts and inclinations in our inner being, and that time after time we are misled and swept along by them. We need that recognition and that insight if we want to fight against them. It is the Spirit of Christ who leads us to this new self-appraisal. We discover that in him the old person has been crucified and the new person has risen. Our remorse thus emerges from our knowledge of Christ; nonetheless, it remains something that happens in the human subject. That is the value and the correct interpretation of the approach via the *ordo salutis*.

Repentance, remorse, return, turning around — it all sounds rather depressing. Can't we say something positive about our journey of faith? It would be a misunderstanding to think that penance and remorse refer merely to a state of the mind that recognizes shortcomings and guilt. That is just one aspect of the attitude of faith, only one link

29. Calvin, *Institutes* III.3.5.

in a much broader chain of faith insights and experiences. Remarkably, Calvin uses the word "penitence" as a kind of general term that includes (1) a "turning of life to God," (2) "an earnest fear of God," and (3) "the mortification of the flesh and the vivification of the Spirit."[30] And this includes the turning around, the conversion toward a new life and the manifestations thereof:

> Therefore, in a word, I interpret repentance as regeneration, whose sole end is to restore in us the image of God that had been disfigured and all but obliterated through Adam's transgression.[31]

This is renewal, but it is not something that happens in a single moment, a day, or even a year. Rather, it is a matter of continuous and often slow progress. It is characterized by struggle and by a discipline that we must gain in order to better know our own weaknesses. There can be no attitude of triumphalism, but rather of a realistic awareness that we must be called back constantly from our crooked ways and obstinate thoughts. Renewal has more similarity with the confinement of evil and the containment of our lusts, so that life will not degenerate unchecked, than with a triumphant entry of the new person who arranges for a complete house-cleaning. The person is kept small, not put up on a throne. But not everything remains as before, certainly not in the person's inner being. For, as Calvin says, when God fills our souls with new thoughts and inclinations, we may indeed be regarded as new.

Regarding renewal, we must note some differences between the classical Reformed approach and the Puritan-Methodist view. As I have already observed, the Reformed tradition teaches that in this life we will never be totally free from sin. All of our lives are a process in the discipline of repentance, and this struggle only ends in death. Sin, Calvin says, no longer reigns over us but continues to live in us. We are liberated from the guilt of sin, but not from the presence of sin: "We accordingly teach that in the saints, until they are divested of mortal bodies, there is always sin; for in their flesh there resides that depravity of inordinate desiring which contends against righteousness." There remains a constant warfare, which helps us get stronger and learn more about our own weaknesses. Even in the reborn person, Calvin adds,

---

30. Calvin, *Institutes* III.3.6-8.
31. Calvin, *Institutes* III.3.9.

there remains "a smoldering cinder of evil, from which desires continually leap forth to allure and spur him to commit sin."[32]

What does this mean when we look at it from the perspective of renewal? Certainly not perfectionism, but instead a sobering realism. The believing person, who is sanctified in Christ, will remain tainted with sin in this life. There is a process of change and renewal, both in our attitudes and in our behaviors, but we do not leave the "old man" totally behind us. We are constantly involved in that struggle that is against evil and toward what is good and pleasing to God; the battlefield runs right through the believer himself. There is no demarcation line, with all the believers on the good side and all the unbelievers on the wrong side.

Is this a pessimistic view? It is in the sense that it acknowledges that there is not just a sunny side of our existence, but also a shadowy side, and even one hidden in recesses of our soul. The "old man" must be crucified constantly; otherwise, before you know it, he is fully alive again and able to destroy all that is good and beautiful. For that reason there is this emphasis on repentance, self-examination, humility *(humilitas),* and so forth. And this is not for the purpose of belittling people, but of maintaining the awareness that we must continuously strive to be free of evil inclinations, both outward and inward.

It stands to reason that concepts such as restraint and discipline receive more attention than do concepts such as development and growth. Nonetheless, the approach is positive and focused on making our daily existence livable. Calvin argues that a degree of asceticism is a necessary condition for a good life. Discipline and restraint do not serve as means of escape from real life and from the world, but as tools to give what is good and pleasing to God a chance. The goal is the renewal of life, a renewal that will become more and more responsive to God's justice and love, even though it will only receive a partial and preliminary shape in this life.

Comparison with the Puritan-Methodist Tradition

We note a number of differences when we compare this view to the Puritan-Methodist faith tradition, which has recently become influen-

32. Calvin, *Institutes* III.3.10.

tial among Evangelicals. In this tradition we find that the new birth does, in fact, signify the genesis of a new person. The separation between the "old man" and the "new man" becomes more radical and more final. New birth is experienced as a decisive event in time, when the believer leaves the old life totally behind him. New birth is based on the divine act of the imputation of God's grace and pardon, but at the same time this act implies a real change in us. In justification and in new birth, God realizes something *in* us. The act of pardon also implies an act of purification, and we are fully and actively involved in that act. In one of his sermons John Wesley says:

> And now he may be properly said to live: God having quickened him by his Spirit, he is alive to God through Jesus Christ. He lives a life which the world knoweth not of, a life "which is hid with Christ in God." God is continually breathing, as it were, upon the soul; and his soul is breathing unto God. Grace is descending into his heart; and prayer and praise ascending to heaven: And by this intercourse between God and man, this fellowship with the Father and the Son, as by a kind of spiritual respiration, the life of God in the soul is sustained; and the child of God grows up, till he comes to the "full measure of the stature of Christ."[33]

The new birth marks a genuine transformation in human beings: sinners become saints and walk on the road toward perfection. The soul is quickened, raised from death, and renewed according to the image of Christ. The sinful heart is changed in accordance with the image of the spirit of Christ. "Immediately after regeneration," the Canon summarizes, "a harmonious moral and spiritual unity exists between the human and the divine, an interaction of spirit in which Christ is said to dwell in man and man to dwell in Christ."[34] This has an impact on our lives and characters. In the first place, the newly born person avoids sin and gains control over sin; to put it another way, grace becomes a real force in the person's life. In the second place, it becomes a source of new life; God's love is "shed abroad in the heart."

This tradition places full emphasis on complete sanctification and deems it possible for a person to live truly and fully as a new per-

33. John Wesley, Sermon 45 (1872), II.4.
34. *Canons, Ratified in the National Synod of the Reformed Church,* p. 131.

son. Sin is no longer associated with the reborn person, with her heart and deepest intentions, for she is justified and in principle also sanctified. "But sin is now, in particular, associated with the outside world."[35] The separation between old and new no longer is a lasting breach in the believer's life, for the believer is seen as a new person in the midst of an impure world. The sense of a remaining brokenness fades into the background. This also speaks to the way the human self is experienced in conversion: the new birth replaces the old, divided, and sinful self with a new self that is no longer internally divided. The new spiritual center is a unity that is sanctified by the Spirit, which controls daily life and is no longer pushed around by the powers of evil. There is thus a complete inner renewal. Moreover, the reborn person experiences this renewing presence in a very direct way.

We have already seen how Jonathan Edwards, the famous American revivalist and theologian, localized faith to a large extent in the affections. If we are touched in such an intense way as to experience the immediate presence of Christ, this empowerment by divine power will leave an indelible impression that will give birth to the new self. In human existence, enlightenment and revelation in the present take center stage, and the history of salvation is understood from its effects in the present. The emphasis is not on contemporaneity with the historical Christ in the sacrament of baptism, but on new birth through the risen Christ in the existential present. The tradition of the church and the mediation of salvation do not take priority; rather, it is the personal testimony about what Christ has done in the human heart that takes priority.

In assessing the significance of faith in our daily lives, we cannot ignore the differences between the classical Reformed view and the more evangelically inclined position. The differences come to the forefront especially in the *applicatio salutis,* the way salvation penetrates existence and brings actual change in the lives of believers. I will mention three points:

1. Contrition plays an abiding role in the Reformed tradition: believers remain caught in their daily sins and must never lose sight of that fact. Confession of sin remains an ongoing process (also

---

35. Anton van Harskamp, *Het nieuw-religieuze verlangen* (Kampen, 2000), p. 145.

in the liturgy); it does not just refer to the moment of conversion or earlier.

2. The believing subject remains caught up in the brokenness of life. In that sense, we may speak of an ongoing solidarity with the "fallen world" and with our unbelieving or other-believing fellow humans. The realization of the justification of the sinner does indeed remove the burden of guilt; in that sense, it sets people free, but they are not yet delivered from the power of sin.

3. The Evangelical movement places strong emphasis on human subjectivity. The work of the Spirit in the sphere of our solitary inner self is decisive. There the radical renewal takes place, and there the presence of Christ is experienced in its fullness. In other words, the focus is on the revelation of Christ in the present life. This view does not deny salvation-historical revelation; but it tends to fully absorb it into the salvific present. As a result, there is less room for the role of the church and for the sacramental mediation of salvation.

Summary and Conclusion

Belief in God, as I observed at the beginning of Chapter 3, does not imply a distaste for life but an acceptance of life in the expectation of salvation. Salvation comes from God and is revealed in our world. That revelation of salvation and the entrance of salvation into our world is, as we have seen, a divine action; salvation is imputed to us as righteousness that was not ours. Because of this, it is made present in our existence in a powerful way, and it thereby changes life. But what is the nature of that change? And, if we speak of the renewal of life, how new will our life become?

This has led us to the question of the *ordo salutis*. I have explored how the human subject becomes completely involved in the way of salvation, establishing a real bond with Christ, which calls the person to live in a spirit of repentance and life renewal. This is the polarity in which believers find themselves: a joyful life, filled with expectancy, in an ongoing process of remorse and renewal.

Our journey through life is thus characterized by struggle and temptation. Experiencing the brokenness of our existence, the constant pull of evil, and the threat of death may at times depress us. But at that point *iustificatio* restores the balance: we sense and celebrate the joy of God's revelation of salvation. Our sin has been atoned for, evil will stop, and justice and love will eventually find full expression in our lives. That faith and that expectation motivate us in the present. Faith is not a form of escapism, but it stimulates the imagination and motivates us toward action. Our faith, in fact, enforces our imaginative ability and increases our dedication toward change. When we are convinced that our lives and the world will really be changed, we will also, in that light, be prepared to work for concrete change in the present. This is where Christian hope and the expectation of the divine kingdom fit in. They strengthen the will to work for change and renewal of life. Perhaps we should communicate this attitude more clearly to those around us: belief in God is not a form of escapism; rather, as an expectation of salvation, it is a source of renewal for our lives.

PART III

Building a Practical Theological Theory

CHAPTER 5

Communication: A Key Concept

Faith takes shape in the daily lives of people. It is part of the ideas and values we cherish; it shapes our attitudes toward people and the world around us; it finds expression in our affections; and it becomes concrete in our actions and behavior. We have seen that faith, because of its impact on the daily life of the subject, is a dynamic event.

Interhuman communication is an important factor in the praxis of our faith (I will pay special attention to this in Chapters 5 through 8), because the faith community owes its existence to the communication of faith. Through communication we maintain our life of faith and share it with others. There is no communal praxis of faith without interhuman discourse. The relationship between interhuman discourse and the mediation of faith plays a pivotal role in practical theological reflection. That is the theme of this chapter, and it will eventually lead to the question of how God is named and presented in interhuman discourse.

The Complexity of Communication

Faith demands continuous practice. Words like "exercise" and "practice" refer to our efforts to establish a praxis. We speak of "exercising" virtues and "exercising" religion. These and related terms also have the connotation of training, for example, training for an athletic or artistic activity. Sports and music require regular practice, continuous training, and a constant maintaining of skills to be in the best possible form for the moment when we are asked to perform. In a similar way, faith must be constantly exercised and practiced. Bohren speaks about a

119

sportliche Spiritualität (a sportive spirituality) as an indication that exercise and training are a definitive part of the life of faith.[1]

Within the Christian praxis of faith, the exercise of faith finds expression in many different activities. We may think of activities in the private sphere, such as prayer, meditation, and Bible study; or of family activities, such as prayer, Bible reading at meal times, and discussions; or of church activities, such as catechesis, worship services, pastoral work, small groups, diaconate, and so forth. All these activities play a role in the exercise of our faith. They constitute the personal and interpersonal activities that actualize and maintain our faith. However, they do have a double aspect: on the one hand, they produce the life of faith, that is, they help develop and maintain the faith and serve the life of faith; on the other hand, they are also expressions and products of faith by giving concrete expression and shape to the faith. They are faith-under-construction. In all these activities we discern the nurture and instruction of the faith, but we also see its expression, experience, and celebration. Berkhof refers to these activities as having a "directive" character that helps to realize the encounter between God and his people: "Seen from the vantage point of origin, those activities aim to extend through time and space that which has once taken place in history, in Israel, and in Christ. Seen from the standpoint of goal, those activities aim at the renewal of people by means of that history, by bringing them into a relationship with God and Christ and so into a new relationship with each other, with life, and with the world."[2]

In the preceding chapters we have seen how faith is embedded in the subject functions of the human mind and in everyday life. But this does not adequately portray the praxis of faith; for faith is, by definition, also an interhuman praxis. Practical theology focuses — as the theory of praxis — particularly on these interhuman activities. This leads us into extremely complex terrain. Language plays a crucial role, just as it does in the interaction between individuals. "Faith needs its language," says Tillich, "as does every act of the personality; without language it would be blind, not directed toward a content, not conscious of itself."[3]

---

1. Rudolf Bohren, *In der Tiefe der Zisterne. Ehrfahrungen met der Schwermut* (Munich, 1990), pp. 58-74.

2. Berkhof, *Christian Faith,* p. 350.

3. Tillich, *The Dynamics of Faith,* p. 24.

By putting something into language, we not only articulate our thoughts and feelings but also open up the possibility of communicating with other people. We express our faith in language, and in so doing we are able to share it with other people, meaning that the praxis of faith is to a large extent a matter of *communicating* our faith. And when we deal with the interaction between people, we should not be thinking only of language; we should also include symbolic and social interaction. But language plays an important role even in these areas. Communication takes place in numerous and diverse activities — in discussions, in learning models, in social actions, and in various parts of the liturgy. When we speak of the exercise of faith, or of the "directive" activities of faith-under-construction, we are always dealing with forms of linguistic, symbolic, or social interaction.

Some Fundamental Dimensions

Faith communication is a complex phenomenon. If we do not establish some clear demarcations, practical theological analysis will become diffuse. We must distinguish the following dimensions: first, we are dealing with interhuman discourse; second, with the exchange or sharing of faith — or, in any case, with activating the life of faith; and third, with the fact that this exchange also activates the divine-human relationship.

I will start with a remark made by Anne van der Meiden. Following Kraemer, he argues that communication is the most fundamental human fact, also the most fundamental religious fact, and even the most fundamental divine fact.[4] The first aspect of communication as the most fundamental human fact refers to the idea that communication is an essential part of human life. It is impossible for us not to communicate. And because it is a fundamental aspect of human life, we must also note that interpersonal communication adds to the quality of life. It isn't simply that we possess the technique of speaking and hearing; communication also includes a range of human values. Communication is more than technique.[5] It creates encounter and commu-

---

4. Anne van der Meiden, *De Markt van geloven. Ontsokkeling, vernieuwing en verandering in geloofsgemeenschappen* (Baarn, 1999), p. 32.

5. D. B. van der Waals, *Het Heilig Communiceren* (Kampen, 1990), pp. 38-57.

nity, and it has to do with the ability to respond and to be accountable. Communication implies the desire for community and the intention to unite what is divided. Interpersonal discourse also has an ethical dimension: we may refer to it in terms of good and bad. This qualitative judgment of interpersonal communication may even acquire a religious dimension, leading us to speak about it in terms of salvation and mischief. And by this we mean that God's salvation is actualized in interpersonal communication, particularly in social interaction. Central concepts from faith praxis, such as love, justice, compassion, and peace, do in fact have everything to do with intersubjective relationships. And it is for that reason, says Kraemer, that communication is the most fundamental religious fact. Faith focuses on true communion, on the renewal of life and the restoration of relationships. This is very closely related to the interpersonal and the divine-human interaction. Kraemer maintains that Christ creates true communication and genuine interpersonal relationships: "This re-creation, the re-establishment of the right relationship with God, can be the only basis for a real communication between people, which does not end in emptiness."[6] Here we see how interpersonal communication is viewed theologically, on the basis of the renewed impulse of communion with Christ.

Within this same context it can be said that communication is the most fundamental divine fact: by this I mean that God is in essence the God of communion. God makes himself known in his creation and in his revelation as the one who brings us in communion with him. Since biblical revelation implies that God makes himself known to us, in our inability to know God as he truly is, communication belongs to the very essence of revelation.[7] Communication in a practical theological sense is not a neutral concept; it is not supported by the general conviction that communication is a "must," since people simply cannot do without it. It is informed by the confidence that communication stems from God, who puts himself with his total being at the service of genuine humanity.

Therefore, when we speak about the communication of our faith, we may mean different things. I mention three possibilities: (1) The communication of faith is understood in terms of the communion be-

6. H. Kraemer, *Communicatie. Een Tijdvraag* (The Hague, 1957), p. 21.
7. Kraemer, *Communicatie,* p. 29.

tween God and humans; that is, we refer to a dialogue between God and people, for example, in prayer. The communion with God is seen as similar to the communication between people: God is a speaking God who enters into communion with us by speaking and hearing. (2) The communication of faith may, however, also be understood in terms of a purely interhuman discourse — as a dimension of the praxis of our faith. This refers to the interaction between people, for example, to the sermon as an address, or to a pastoral visit as a dialogue between two persons. These dimensions of the communication of faith must be judged on their own merits. And we must note that there are related scientific disciplines, such as rhetoric, communication theories, and psychological counselling, that focus on interhuman discourse. Practical theology uses the insights of those disciplines. (3) But a third aspect must be taken into account: the almost "sacramental" connection between interhuman discourse and divine-human discourse. The uniqueness of practical theology emerges at this point (in the third section below, we shall see that this connection can take different forms). I regard interhuman discourse as a medium of the discourse between God and us, but it is also possible to see interhuman discourse as a sign that points to divine salvation. The remainder of this chapter will explore these three approaches. I will begin by outlining a few aspects of the divine-human discourse; then I intend to discuss a few fundamental concepts from the linguistic side of communication; and, finally, I will deal with the connection between interhuman discourse and divine-human discourse.

The Interaction between God and Humans

Let's first pay attention to our communion with God. There is a close analogy between this kind of intersubjective relationship and the interhuman discourse. Th. C. Vriezen is of the opinion that the term *interaction* "describes in a superb way the relationship between God and humans; it presupposes a relationship between several persons, which is expressed in certain mutual actions."[8] He sees the core of God's reve-

---

8. Th. C. Vriezen, *Hoofdlijnen der theologie van het Oude Testament* (Wageningen, 1966), p. 191.

lation in the Old Testament as communication; God approaches people and enters into a genuine communion with them: "This is the essence of revelation, to bring about an interaction between God and the human being."[9] This communication takes places in a variety of forms: through the Spirit, through the Word, through visions, but also through mediators of this revelation. Vriezen regards this relationship of communion as the basic model for the entire biblical testimony. The main issue is the reality of the direct spiritual communion of God, of the Holy Spirit, with human beings and with the world.[10] This implies that faith itself, as communion between God and humans, may be viewed as a form of communication. This is probably most clearly expressed in prayer and in liturgical praxis. G. van der Leeuw defines liturgy as "an ecclesiastically instituted form of the interaction between God and man." This interaction, he continues, presupposes two parties — God and a human being. "It is a movement; it goes back and forth. God speaks and we respond. We speak and God responds. But the answer does not follow the question with total, automatic certainty. The answer must be a matter of expectation."[11] The interaction or communication between God and humans is thus of a peculiar kind, because the divine subject does not present himself in the same manner as the human subject.

From a philosophical perspective, Nicholas Wolterstorff has desired that we understand the discourse between God and humans not primarily in terms of revelation but rather as analogous to the "speech act." The Bible presents God as the speaking God, the God who gives promises and demands obedience. The transfer of knowledge is not the primary issue in this kind of language-based interaction. When we make a promise, we assume certain responsibilities with regard to another person. The trustworthiness of the one who promises is an important aspect. When we make a request, we ask someone for something: trust and compliance are the appropriate responses.[12] On this basis Wolterstorff develops a model of "divine discourse" (the title of his book) as analogous to interpersonal communication.

9. Vriezen, *Hoofdlijnen der Theologie,* p. 229.

10. Vriezen, *Hoofdlijnen der Theologie,* p. 171.

11. G. van der Leeuw, *Liturgiek* (Nijkerk, 1946), p. 15.

12. Nicholas Wolterstorff, *Divine Discourse: Philosophical Reflections on the Claim that God Speaks* (Cambridge, 1995), p. 35.

Thus, believing in God includes a divine-human discourse that is analogous to interhuman communication. Of course, there are also differences. It is an analogous, not an identical, form of communication. God is not present to us in the same way a fellow human being is. Moreover, there is a clear asymmetry between God and mankind. God is not at our disposal, and we cannot force his presence. This has to do with God's freedom and sovereignty. Is it still appropriate, then, to speak of a discourse between God and humans? How does God speak to us? When we name God, does God really hear us? We will see in the next chapter that the discourse between God and the human being does, in fact, often resemble interhuman communication. In that sense we may regard the interhuman discourse as an intermediary. In our discourse with others we name God, and his presence is thereby mediated. We also experience his presence in the ministry of the Word and the sacraments. In our pastoral and diaconal service, the signs of salvation are made visible. And thus, under certain conditions, divine salvation is represented in the interhuman discourse.

But why should we see communion with God as a form of dialogue? Wouldn't it be more appropriate to suggest that we do indeed experience something of his presence, but not in any direct way? That is, God does not directly address us, and there is no dialogue. We limit ourselves to what we experience "here below" and recognize no direct communion in terms of language-based interaction. This would still leave us with some experience of God; we would still see some signals and traces of God, but we may halt at these human experiences. It is primarily a matter of the presence of God in us, and of our discourse with our own experiences (intrapersonal), that we may express and share with others in interpersonal discourse. This, then, is what I would see as communication of our faith.

How do we deal with such questions? Allow me two remarks. I do not say that faith consists of an uninterrupted, actualized discourse between God and human beings. But we do have to face the question of whether faith can be understood as an actual dialogue and communication with God. Are there instances, even if they are isolated moments, when we may speak of a genuine interaction that goes back and forth? Can we say, God speaks to us and we speak to God? I believe that the answer is in the affirmative. God is a speaking God who makes himself known in his promises and commandments, which is how he speaks to us. And we explicitly address God in our prayers and our songs of praise. For a theological basis, I refer back to *iustificatio,* the justification of the sinner (Chapter 3). God acquits us and we appropriate this acquitting judgment to ourselves. Second, I point to the praxis of prayer. One of the key aspects of prayer is that we call God by name. We call upon his Name, confident that this Name also expresses the mode of his presence. When we call on God as the Holy One, or the Compassionate One, we characterize him as the Other to whom we can relate. At the same time, giving a name to God calls forth in us a particular attitude and a certain disposition — for example, one of dependence and trust. This positioning and defining of the subjects is in itself characteristic of the nature of prayer: someone speaking to God. And our prayer thereby becomes a speaking to God and not merely an intrapersonal discourse. Otherwise, our prayer would instantly become a form of meditation. Heiler thinks that prayer operates on two major presuppositions: (1) faith in the personhood of God, and (2) the assurance of his presence. Heiler adds that this gives prayer the structure of interaction, of communication. Prayer gives expression to our dynamic relationship with God; it is a way of rescue, an immediate touch, a personal bond, a reciprocal interaction, a dialogue, a "traffic," a communion, a unity between I and Thou.[13] It is no wonder, Heiler says, that prayer, as to its form, reflects interhuman social interaction. Prayer is a direct communion with God, analogous to interhuman social interaction. We also find this dialogue structure in an explicit way in Calvin's writings: prayer "is a communion of men with God by which, having entered the heavenly sanctuary, they appeal to him in person concerning his promises. . . ."[14]

Of course, this does not mean that there is, from our own point of view, a continuous *conscious* communion. But the reality and possibility of this communion is presupposed, and there are moments when it is consciously experienced. Yet the human subject will continue to meet alienation and doubt, negligence and indifference, rebellion, loneliness, and so on. There are all kinds of fractures in our communion with God. And in this very field of tension, the intrapersonal discourse plays an important role. In the preceding chapters I have entered a plea

13. Friedrich Heiler, *Das Gebet. Eine Religionsgeschichtliche und Religionspsychologische Untersuchung,* 5th ed. (Munich, 1923), p. 490.

14. Calvin, *Institutes* III.20.2.

on behalf of the subject-side of our faith, of the realization that our intellectual powers are engaged in the "exercise" of our faith. God's speaking and God's actions, indeed, manifest a constant movement from "above" toward "below." They also have their impact "here below" — in the human self, in tradition, and in culture. It does not always come straight from above, but also from within, where it was sown and where it grows. We contemplate God's Word, we keep the remembrance of Christ alive, we consider what the Lord has done, and we try to determine the will of God in our hearts. In that sense there is a good deal of intrapersonal communication of faith: the person's discourse with herself about God and God's salvation. This is also what we read in the Bible: "Why are you downcast, O my soul? Why so disturbed within me? Put your hope in God, for I will yet praise him, my Savior and my God" (Ps. 42:11). But the real issue is whether there are, in this intrapersonal conversation and in the interhuman discourse, moments when we say, "Yes, now I hear God's voice," or "Now I am speaking with God!" For example, when this same Psalmist says, "Show me your justice, O God," or "Send me your light and your truth," these are utterances that are part of a direct discourse.

The Interhuman Discourse

Interhuman discourse plays a pivotal role in our faith praxis. In this section I wish to introduce some concepts and distinctions that are important for a theological discussion of the communication of faith. I will not go into great detail, but I want to mention those factors and distinctions that will play a role in later chapters.

Two Areas of Attention

The first area that calls for our attention centers on the intellectual resources of the human subject. Speakers and listeners meet in the communication process. In our speaking we express our intentions, hoping and expecting that others will understand us.[15] A speaker puts a cer-

15. Searle, *Mind, Language and Society,* pp. 144-46.

tain opinion or experience into words and sentences, and the listener is able, through noetic action, to comprehend this opinion or experience. The functions of the human mind play an important role in this process of speaking and understanding. We can exchange information and can understand each other, and in so doing the speaker and listener — the subjects — interact.

But communication is not just a process between subjects, which leads us to the second area that merits our attention: our relationship with the world we live in. I have already shown (in Chapter 1) that our intentionality is not merely an expression of our mind but that it is also directed toward an extra-intellectual reality. This referential dimension of the human mind and of language is extremely important in the communication process: it is the point where the truth content of our statements is expressed. In communicating we utter statements about the reality all around us; we argue that certain things or events are true or false.

These two aspects have a practical theological relevance. In theology that is anthropologically oriented, the experience and intention of the speaker play an important role in the communication process. Lindbeck calls this the *experiential-expressive* model and points to Schleiermacher as its spiritual father.[16] (When I discuss Schleiermacher in Chapter 6, it will become clear what this means for the praxis of faith.) The second element, the referential function of language, is of crucial significance when we talk about God. Do our concepts and images refer directly to God, or are they primarily intellectual representations? Do we, in the final analysis, find the point of reference of our religious language in ourselves, or do we point toward God? (I will return to these questions in Chapter 8 in describing empirical theology and in the Chapters 10 and 11 in discussing the anthropological model.)

Analytical philosophy, in particular, has fiercely debated the referential role of language, words, and concepts.[17] Although the meaning of words does not coincide with their referential function, our language does express something about reality. In sentences with a

16. George A. Lindbeck, *The Nature of Doctrine: Religion and Theology in a Postliberal Age* (Philadelphia, 1984), p. 16.

17. See my *Divine Simplicity*, pp. 36-51; see also P. F. Strawson, *Subject and Predicate in Logic and Grammar* (London, 1974).

subject-predicate structure, the subject refers to a certain person or thing, while the predicate expresses a particular property; in the complete sentence we intend to say that the subject we are referring to does have this particular property. Proper names, especially, and certain defining descriptions have a referential function.[18] There has been intense debate about the referential function of the predicate — what is the relationship between concepts and properties? — and this is where the conceptualists and the realists diverge widely.[19] The realists argue that, in the shaping of concepts, our minds follow the structure of reality, a structure that exists independent of our observation, while the conceptualists defend the view that the human mind brings structure to reality. We give shape to reality through our concepts. Precisely in the theological reflection on the communication of faith is the question of "God's referent" of decisive importance. (I will return to this in Chapter 11 in discussing the question of how we can speak about God in the communication of our faith.)

The Connection between the Hermeneutical and the Analytical Traditions

In investigating some fundamental concepts and distinctions in the area of interhuman communication as we analyze the communication of faith, we would do well to look at some of the insights offered by Paul Ricoeur. Ricoeur tries to establish a link between the continental hermeneutical school of thought, on the one hand, and the more Anglo-Saxon-oriented analytical philosophy, on the other hand. Regarding the issue of realism, I try to use some of the insights of the analytical school in my own analysis; but when we view matters from the perspective of theology and the social sciences, I recognize the value of the more subject-oriented hermeneutical tradition. Ricoeur is a thinker who can help us establish connections. In his discussions with the French structuralists, he remains faithful to the extralinguistic reality of the subject and of the world. He differentiates between *langue*

18. Keith S. Donnellan, "Proper Names and Identifying Descriptions," in *Semantics of Natural Language*, ed. Donald Davidson and Gilbert Harman (Dordrecht/Boston, 1972), pp. 356-79.

19. Alan Donagan, "Universals and Metaphysical Realism," in *Universals and Particulars: Readings in Ontology*, ed. Michael J. Loux (Notre Dame, 1976), pp. 125-55.

(language) and *parole* (speech): *langue* has to do with linguistics; *parole* has to do with the use of language in interpersonal communication. He describes *parole,* the language of our common usage, as "a means of mediation, a medium through which we approach reality; this is the fundamental referential aspect of language. At times we share our experience; that is the social aspect. At other times we express our inner self; that is the personal aspect. This mediation implies three things: the signifying, that is the process of referring to . . . (saying something about something), communication and expression."[20]

The remarkable thing about Ricoeur's thought is that the referential function flows via the speaker, and the intention of the speaker thereby receives the emphasis in the communication. "Discourse refers back to its speaker at the same time that it refers to the world. This correlation is not fortuitous, since it is ultimately the speaker who refers to the world in speaking. Discourse in action and in use refers backwards and forwards, to a speaker and a world."[21] In this way Ricoeur maintains the subjective element. The reference to the world is rooted in human experience and, in that sense, precedes language; thus it shapes the ontological condition of language. The intentional reference to something outside of language has its roots in a "more originary move starting from the experience of being in the world and proceeding from this ontological condition towards its expression in language. It is because there is first something to say, because we have an experience to bring to language, that conversely, language is not only directed towards ideal meanings but also refers to what is."[22] This clearly shows how Ricoeur attributes an independent significance to ontology: reality does not dissolve in language or in the mind.

With regard to interhuman communication, we have already noted two important dimensions: the intentionality of the human consciousness and the aspect of referent. Communication includes the total discourse of speaking and listening, talking and understanding, question and answer. What is involved in this process between speaker and listener? What is the secret of the transfer that takes place? The

---

20. Paul Ricoeur, "Contribution d'une réflexion sur le langage à une théologie de la Parole," *Revue de Théologie et de Philosophie* 18 (1968): 333-48.

21. Paul Ricoeur, *Interpretation Theory: Discourse and the Surplus of Meaning* (Fort Worth, 1976), p. 22.

22. Ricoeur, *Interpretation Theory,* p. 21.

miracle of successful communication is that the other person hears and understands what one has said. One is thus succeeding in transferring something from one sphere of life into another. I express something about myself, the other person understands it, and in so doing we share something. This results in a social connection that is characteristic of our human existence. But how does this communication take place? Ricoeur suggests that the dialogical structure of language allows for a breakthrough into the fundamental loneliness of every human being.

> By solitude I do not mean the fact that we often feel isolated as in a crowd, or that we live and die alone, but, in a more radical sense, that what is experienced by one person cannot be transferred whole as such and such experience to someone else. My experience cannot directly become your experience. An event belonging to one stream of consciousness cannot be transferred as such into another stream of consciousness. Yet, nevertheless, something passes from me to you. Something is transferred from one sphere of life to another. This something is not the experience as experienced, but its meaning. Here is the miracle. The experience as experienced, as lived, remains private, but its sense, its meaning, becomes public. Communication in this way is the overcoming of the radical non-communicability of the lived experience as lived.[23]

In our speaking we are able to transfer something from one sphere of life to another; but what we transfer is not the immediate experience itself (as an action of the psyche), for that is not communicable. But we do transfer its meaning. We believe, says Ricoeur, that the actual experience remains private, but its meaning can be externalized in language and can be transferred. The experience becomes public as propositional content, and this gives us the possibility of communication. The actual experience is not communicated, but rather its noetic expression.[24] And that noetic expression is caught and understood by the listening party. Therefore, a certain tension remains between the experience itself, the expression of that experience in language, and the noetic content of that expression. The last two elements represent the difference between

23. Ricoeur, *Interpretation Theory*, pp. 15, 16.
24. Cf. Wolterstorff, *Divine Discourse*, pp. 130-52.

the language statement (locution) and the content of what has been said (illocution). In the transfer and the process of comprehending we are mainly concerned about the illocutionary "loading" of a statement. The concrete action of uttering language is, as a moment of speaking, a passing event; but its illocutionary content is comprehended by our minds and, in a sense, continues to exist separate from the actual speech. Thus Ricoeur says that the words we utter are actualized as an event but understood as meaning; consequently, meanings are neither a matter of the psyche nor of languages, but a category *sui generis*. Ricoeur thereby avoids the view of Romanticism, on the one hand, which points to the inner life of the author as the source of meaning, and the position of Structuralism, on the other, which points to the text as such as the source of meaning.[25]

In our discussion of the communication of faith, we must focus on two particular aspects: (1) the expression of our consciousness, and (2) the referential dimension of discourse. The intention of the speaker plays a crucial role in the communication process. We are able to express an experience or thought in language, and others are able to understand what we say. In the praxis of faith this interaction and exchange are important, particularly in proclamation and pastoral work. But what exactly do we exchange or share with the other? Does a speaker express her subjective experiences in language and thereby transfer the noetic content to a listener? Ricoeur's statement seems to suggest that something is transferred from one realm of consciousness to another. Does this mean that, in the communication of our faith, we externalize our inner life or experiences and report them to the other? Ricoeur's statement shows his affinity with the continental-European hermeneutical tradition, which, to a large extent, can be traced back to Schleiermacher. This leads to an expressive communication model in the theological tradition that is geared toward the experiential aspect of faith. (What this entails for the praxis of faith will become clear in my analysis of Schleiermacher's views on the communication of faith in Chapter 6.)

Concerning the referential dimension of discourse, we refer to the reality we live in when we communicate. We say something about something; this is the ontological basis of our language and leads us to the

25. Wolterstorff, *Divine Discourse*, p. 152.

truth claim. Language and symbols enable us to establish a link with the world around us. In this connection we face an important question: What is the nature of that link and how does it function in our use of religious language? What, in fact, do we do when we utter the name of God? Do we refer to God himself? We cannot ignore this question in any discussion of religious communication. Thus a central question in our reflection on the praxis of faith is, How do we speak about God? The revelationary model suggests that God himself is the subject of words and actions, and that God may be identified as such, namely in the person of Jesus.

Human Discourse as Intermediary

This section will deal with the role of interhuman discourse in the communication of faith. The development, maintenance, and renewal of our life of faith take place in the form of religious activities, which imply a sort of interpersonal communication or social interaction. Practical theology has a long-standing tradition of focusing on activities such as pastoral work, preaching, liturgy, catechesis, and diaconate. Interpersonal discourse plays an important role in all of these activities, even though each particular activity implies a specific kind of interaction. While preaching is the delivery of a public address, the personal conversation is the basic form of pastoral work. Symbolic and dramatic expression, as well as ritual, plays a key role in liturgy; catechesis is a form of interaction based on learning processes; and the diaconate constitutes concrete social interaction. And even though we are dealing with specific and diverse activities, they are all forms of interpersonal communication. For that reason the sub-disciplines that study these various activities belong together in practical theology.

What I wish to emphasize is that interpersonal communication is a constitutive factor in all these activities that together shape, maintain, and renew our life of faith. Our faith is actualized and intensified through these forms of interaction. Or, to put it differently, our communion with God is actualized through interhuman discourse. Thus we may, in one sense, say that human words and actions result in communion with God (the divine-human discourse). We find, in the

Protestant tradition particularly, a reticence to link this interhuman discourse with the divine-human discourse: it might impinge on the sovereignty of divine revelation. And it might also restrict human freedom of choice and responsibility. Indeed, the Protestant tradition has rejected the direct causation of the one (i.e., communion with God) through the other (i.e., interpersonal communication). But what Protestantism in fact rejected was a magical or mechanical identification. And this has to do with the pneumatological understanding of faith praxis. Our communion with God is personal in nature and demands a sincere assent from us; therefore, it is always a matter of Word *and* Spirit, of Word *and* faith. The faith relationship implies a personal and mutual involvement of God and humans. God speaks and we hear, God promises and we trust; we pray and call, and God hears. This pneumatological approach to the relationship between God and humans does not in any way lead to a disconnect between the interhuman discourse and the divine-human discourse. If that were the case, it would deform and underappreciate the significance of Word and sacrament in the Protestant tradition. A pneumatological approach also leaves room for a linkage between interhuman discourse and divine-human discourse. If there were no such linkage, our interhuman speaking and acting within the communication of faith would become completely haphazard. For God would then be able to reveal himself in anything — or rather in nothing.

In this context, Firet refers to the human service as an intermediary. He points to those actions that are "directed toward the actualization and maintenance of the relationship between God and the human being, and the human being and God."[26] In other words, interhuman communication and social interaction play a mediating role concerning our communion with God. They may be described as ways of "coaching," as God uses the interhuman. Calvin believes that God's Word can come to us from the mouth of a fellow human being: "For, among the many excellent gifts with which God has adorned the human race, it is a singular privilege that he deigns to consecrate to himself the mouths and tongues of men in order that his voice may resound in them."[27] For both Luther and Calvin, this meant that hearing

---

26. J. Firet, *Spreken als een Leerling*, p. 32.
27. Calvin, *Institutes* IV.i.5.

the word of the gospel via the voice of another human being may be understood as a true word of grace from God.

The verbal, symbolic, and social interaction is thus an important intermediary in the communication of our faith. In theological terms we are dealing with "representation" and "application." Representation, making present, is taking place in the interaction. But what do we "make present"? Do we reveal something personal, such as an experience or opinion? Or do we "make present" God's Word, or God's promise, or God's salvation, or the forgiveness of sins? Do we represent a past event, for example, the acquittal by Christ, or rather a future event, for example, the delivery from death? All of these dimensions are included. Of course, it is not just a matter of "making something present"; more is at stake. It touches on our existence and the circumstances of our lives. The interaction is such that the addressee actually experiences something as salvation that comes from God.

There are different ways in which the linkage between inter-human discourse, on the one hand, and divine-human discourse, on the other, may be understood. I believe that the linkage is such that, under certain conditions, a statement made by a fellow human being may be understood as a statement from God. That's what happens, for example, in a liturgical setting: in the salutation, in the preaching of the sermon, and in the benediction. The connection receives a material and visual actualization in the administering of the sacraments. In church we do not just speak about God; we also speak on behalf of God. The sermon is not just instruction but also proclamation. In our conversations together we don't just share our experiences; we also encourage and comfort each other. This kind of intermediary speaking and acting presupposes a "double agency": a statement made by X is understood as a statement by Y. That in itself is not strange. It is very possible that a given speaker puts someone else's intention into words.[28] This usually is clear from the setting and context in which someone speaks. It is true, for example, of liturgy and the authority of the ecclesial office. This speaking on God's behalf is, of course, conditioned by certain agreements and rules.

Another important point must be noted. In the case of a "dou-

---

28. Ronald F. Thiemann, *Revelation and Theology: The Gospel as Narrated Promise* (Notre Dame, 1985), p. 106; Wolterstorff, *Divine Discourse,* pp. 37-57.

ble agency," it is essential to clarify on whose behalf a statement is made or to whom it refers. This is a crucial aspect in the communication of faith. When a statement is made on God's behalf, it is important that God is first defined — so that another person knows of whom we speak. Moreover, this act of definition and description already has a definite effect. And this is of major significance because the interaction takes place, in effect, between the one to whom I refer and the addressee. For this reason, the reference to God and the narrative identification of God play a critical role in this view of the communication of faith. Whether or not an addressee understands a "speech act" about God as a word from God depends on the definition and description of God.

We may look at interhuman communication from yet another vantage point, that is, in terms of an ethical and religious appreciation of interpersonal communication as social interaction. Van der Ven opts for this approach regarding the communication of faith. His theological thinking is such that he sees interhuman communication as a sign indicating God's salvation. Since the quality of life is to a large degree determined by social interaction, the latter may be evaluated in terms of good and bad. On the basis of this normative-ethical approach, Van der Ven develops an eschatological-theological theory of faith communication. (I will work this out in greater detail in Chapter 7.)

Having sketched in outline the main themes concerning the communication of faith, I will focus in the following chapters on some fundamental practical theological models. They will provide a reconstruction of how a practical theological theory may be developed from the angle of the communication of faith. I will pay special attention to the relationship between human discourse and communion with God. Chapter 6 will deal with Schleiermacher's proposal: I devote a separate chapter to Schleiermacher because he is the one who brought practical theology as a distinct discipline to development, and he is still a weighty influence in the discipline. Schleiermacher gives a central role to the human heart in the communication of faith: for him, religion is anchored in the human heart, and the communication of faith drives the circulation of our religious experiences and thereby ensures the development of our faith. After that, in Chapter 7, I will deal with the hermeneutical-communicative model, which has been the dominant paradigm of practical theology from the 1970s onward. I will pay special attention to Van der Ven, one of the key representatives of this school of thought.

CHAPTER 6

Schleiermacher: Faith as Expression

This chapter on Schleiermacher is to be read as an intermezzo. This book is built on a number of themes, and I do not devote a full chapter to the ideas of any one thinker — other than in this chapter. Why make an exception for Schleiermacher? First, Schleiermacher's proposal clarifies what is involved when we opt for an anthropological approach to religious life. He gives a dominant place to spiritual life in the praxis of religion, and he knows how to put the experiential dimension into words. The language he uses to describe faith and the atmosphere he evokes differ from the climate of Chapter 4 above, but there are also similarities. Schleiermacher is also interested in the "indwelling" of salvation.

The difference — and this is the second reason for this chapter — has to do with the way the "otherness" of God enters the discussion. The human mind is the point of departure and forms the basis for our speaking about God. Schleiermacher's theology does not allow for the alternative — that is, to start from God's speaking, from God's self-revelation. Schleiermacher's views are thus a typical example of an anthropological approach. It is important to begin by unpacking his position, which will allow us to get a better insight into the unique character of this approach and to see what it means for the communication of faith. Schleiermacher is a good example of expressive communication, and the hermeneutical tradition can, to a large degree, be traced back to him.

The third reason I want to investigate Schleiermacher for a full chapter is that he challenges and stimulates my own thinking. He is able to value the human subject in the praxis of faith in such a way that the mystical and pietistic dimension becomes visible and can be described. Yet Schleiermacher is not concerned with the individual and solitary subject. As a matter of principle, he deals with the human being in communion, with the human being who is addressed. But I am also of the opinion — and this is my quarrel with this theology — that the transcendence of God is so absolute that God disappears behind the horizon of what is knowable. (I will discuss this especially in Chapters 10 and 11.)

Existential Discourse and the Person's Inner Self

Schleiermacher argues that the expression of faith — and this includes the intention to communicate and share the faith — is an integral part of the life of faith.

> Once there is religion, it must necessarily also be social. That not only lies in human nature but also is preeminently in the nature of religion.[1]

The fact that we want to communicate our experiences with others is not something of secondary importance. It would be unnatural to contain within ourselves what has been generated within us. The more intimately we have been touched, Schleiermacher says, the stronger is the urge to discover something similar in others. How would a human being

> . . . keep to himself the influences of the universe that appear to him as greatest and most irresistible? How should he wish to retain within himself that which most strongly forces him out of himself and which, like nothing else, impresses him with the fact that he cannot know himself in and of himself alone.[2]

There is not only a strong urge from within to share something with the other, but religion itself is accompanied by the sense that no single

---

1. Friedrich Schleiermacher, *On Religion: Speeches to Its Cultured Despisers* (Cambridge, 1988), p. 163.

2. Schleiermacher, *On Religion*, p. 163.

human being can ever experience its full significance. Thus there is an interest to be complemented by the other.

> This is how mutual communication organizes itself; thus speaking and hearing are equally indispensable for everyone.[3]

We are thus confronted with a reciprocal sharing, and this means that we are always involved in a process of speaking *and* hearing. Even though Schleiermacher gives full attention to human subjectivity, it does not lead to solipsism; the religious subject is never the isolated individual. From the very beginning the emphasis is on communion with the other and on the totality of which we are a part. Religious communication is unmistakably a reciprocal communication. Moreover, it is always provisional in the sense that a greater treasure, which we have not yet allowed into our inner beings, is hidden somewhere.

This reciprocal communication finds its best expression when people talk together. Schleiermacher was a person who appreciated good company and good conversation. Personal experiences, originating in the encounter with people, were important to him. Nicol says that for Schleiermacher the existential dialogue with others was, in the Romantic tradition, an occasion of religious experience. The existential conversation offers the possibility of a mutual appreciation of the inner life of the other. It is well known that Schleiermacher often had intimate conversations, particularly with women, in the Berlin establishments.[4] Nicol quotes from one of his letters: "It is deeply entrenched in my nature, dear Lotte, that I will always find it easier to converse with women than with men; for there is so much in my heart that they [men] seldom understand."[5]

But what actually happens in a conversation, and what does the inner self reveal? This leads us to a crucial point in Schleiermacher's theology. In his lectures entitled *On Religion* he says that the *universum* is revealed in the inner life, that inner things enable us to know the outer things. The universal, the transcendent, the infinite, the divine — all are revealed *in* the finite, *in* our hearts. We experience eternity *in* time, infin-

---

3. Schleiermacher, *On Religion,* p. 164.
4. Martin Nicol, *Gespräch als Seelsorge. Theologische Fragmenten zu einer Kultur des Gesprächs* (Göttingen, 1990), p. 32.
5. Nicol, *Gespräch als Seelsorge,* p. 32.

ity *in* the finite, the transcendent *in* the immanent. That is the principle of identity of Romanticism. The divine is revealed in the world, and the world is contained in God.[6] This leads Schleiermacher to make this statement: "Let us repair to humanity, that we may find the material for religion."[7] Humanity is the key to the universe (the divine). He says in his dogmatics that piety consists in "becoming aware of ourselves as utterly dependent, or, what is the same, as in a relationship with God."[8] It would be incorrect to think that in Schleiermacher's thought the divine originates in the human. It does reveal itself in the human, but there is also a movement from the outside to the human's inner being. The only thing we can say about this is that we experience the impact of it — and no more. "All intuition proceeds from an influence of the intuited on the one who intuits, from an original and independent action of the former, which is then grasped, apprehended, and conceived by the latter according to one's own nature."[9]

In any case, it is clear that our inner self is the place where we become aware of our dependence and where we experience the immediate presence of God. Schleiermacher writes in one of his letters that his religion is a religion of the heart through-and-through; but it is not only of his own heart, since it also shines forth in relationship with the other.[10] He emphasizes the indissoluble connection between religion and interpersonal communication in a paraphrase of Genesis 2. Before the creation of woman, man was alone with nature. At that point there was not yet a condition for genuine life.

> Since the deity recognized that his world would be nothing so long as man was alone, it created for him a partner, and now, for the first time, living and spiritual tones stirred within him; now, for the first time, the world rose before his eyes. In the flesh and bone of his bone he discovered humanity, and in humanity the world; from this moment on he became capable of hearing the voice of the deity and of answering it, and the most sacrilegious transgression of its

6. Cf. Paul Tillich, *Perspectief op de protestantse theologie van de 19ᵉ en 20ᵉ Eeuw* (Utrecht, 1967), p. 132.

7. Schleiermacher, *On Religion*, p. 120.

8. Schleiermacher, *Der christliche Glaube* (Halle, 1830), par. 4.

9. Schleiermacher, *On Religion*, p. 104.

10. Nicol, *Gespräch*, p. 35.

laws from now on no longer precluded him from association with the eternal being.[11]

In his encounter with another human being — in love and through love — the first person discovered religion. Therefore, the following three components are always linked together: the universe, the person's inner self, and fellow human beings. In the loving encounter with another human being, the person becomes aware of his own self, of the world, and of God. Yet Schleiermacher does not let the interhuman encounter coincide with communion with God. Communion with the other person functions as a bridge.[12]

Both Tillich and Barth point out that the identity principle of Romanticism influences Schleiermacher's view of religion as feeling.[13] Religion should not be defined in terms of theoretical knowledge or moral action, but as a feeling of absolute dependence. Nonetheless, the word "feeling" is misleading: it is not the same as sentiment, nor is it a psychological label. Its meaning is closer to the concept of intuition — of immediate awareness. It refers to the awareness of the divine in an unmediated way, prior to any rational understanding, at a point where it is not yet possible to distinguish between subject and object. It is the presence of eternity within time. It is not a subjective ocean kind of feeling, Tillich says, though, unfortunately, many have interpreted it as such. "This led to a related unfortunate misunderstanding in the churches in Germany, for when religion was preached as feeling the male section of the German churches stopped going to church. . . . The young people and the men were not satisfied with feeling. They expected the sermons to reflect sharp reasoning and ethical relevance. When religion was reduced to feeling and weakened through sentimental songs — instead of the great ancient hymns, which contained the religious power of the divine presence — people lost their interest in the churches."[14]

The fact that this feeling cannot be clearly defined is the cause of this confusion. Schleiermacher believed that the core of religious life

11. Schleiermacher, *On Religion*, p. 119.

12. Cf. Nicol, *Gespräch*, p. 35.

13. Tillich, *Perspectief*, pp. 155-64; see also Karl Barth, *Die protestantische Theologie im 19. Jahrhundert*, vol. 2 (Hamburg, 1975), p. 379.

14. Tillich, *Perspectief*, pp. 157, 158.

cannot be worded conceptually, for that would lead us into the domain of metaphysics. But neither is this feeling identical with action. Its essence lies not in thinking, nor in acting, but in contemplation and feeling. By this he intends to say that it is prior to any analysis and any theory. It is an inner awareness of an exceptional event, which in fact only exists in the individual's receptive commitment. When detached from that primary and intuitive action of the inner self, it disintegrates.

> That first mysterious moment that occurs in every sensory perception, before intuition and feeling have separated, where sense and its objects have, as it were, flowed into one another and become one, before both turn back to their original position — I know how indescribable it is and how quickly it passes away. But I wish that you were able to hold on to it and also to recognize it again in the higher and divine religious activity of the mind. Would that I could and might express it, at least indicate it, without having to desecrate it! It is as fleeting and transparent as the first scent with which the dew gently caresses the waking flowers, as modest and delicate as a maiden's kiss, as holy and fruitful as a nuptial embrace; indeed, not *like* these, but it *is itself* all of these. A manifestation, an event develops quickly and magically into an image of the universe. Even as the beloved and ever-sought-for form fashions itself, my soul flees toward it; I embrace it, not as a shadow, but as the holy essence itself. I lie on the bosom of the infinite world. At this moment I am its soul, for I feel all its powers and its infinite life as my own; at this moment it is my body, for I penetrate its muscles and its limbs as my own, and its innermost nerves move according to my sense and my presentiment as my own.[15]

This quotation shows that, as far as Schleiermacher is concerned, the principle of distance and separation does not apply to the domain of religion. No duality, but identity. God is in the here and now; God is in the depths of everything. That is the Romantic belief of being mutually present in the other. Though I believe we must ask Schleiermacher some critical questions with regard to religious epistemology, I must also admit — and appreciate — that this model provides ample scope for a rich, mystical, and imaginative religious experience. The experien-

15. Schleiermacher, *On Religion*, p. 113.

tial aspect of the moment exceeds any expression in words by far. This existential experience as it is lived, we have heard Ricoeur say, remains private, but its meaning can be communicated. In this he agrees with Schleiermacher. The experience itself contains an actualizing moment: "I know how quickly it passes away. It is as fleeting and transparent as the first scent with which the dew gently caresses the waking flowers, as modest and delicate as a maiden's kiss. . . ." But it is movement and activity; or, to put it more accurately, there is both passivity and activity. "I lie on the bosom of the infinite world. At this moment I am its soul, for I feel all its powers. . . ." It brings vitality and activates.

The Inequality in Communication

The preceding paragraphs show that, in Schleiermacher's model, religious experience and religious communication are indissolubly connected to each other. We become conscious of ourselves, the world, and God in the encounter with the other. Exchange and reciprocity are central themes in religious praxis, and these aspects also embody its communal character. In fact, we should say that, in Schleiermacher's proposal, interpersonal exchange and communion are both equally original *(ursprünglich)*.[16] When we give expression to what touches and fascinates us, and we sketch this in images and imaginative language, it becomes accessible to others. And from this intention to express flows the desire to share it with others.

The word *darstellen* (to make present) is important to Schleiermacher: it includes the notion of externalization, but also of representation and actualization in the present. Communication unfolds the inner self in such a way that others gain access and are themselves stirred in their own hearts. *Darstellung* has an actualizing function, both for the hearer and the speaker. But it must be spontaneous and free and may never be accompanied by force or intentional pressure. For it is in the free interaction between expression and recognition that, as this takes place, the relationship between people receives its form. Thus the core of Schleiermacher's view on praxis is that com-

16. Wilhelm Gräb, *Predigt als Mitteilung des Glaubens. Studien zu einer prinzipiellen Homiletik in praktischer Absicht* (Gütersloh, 1988), p. 205.

munion finds its structure in the circulation of expression and reception.

Concerning the way religious life is expressed, we might suggest that the state of our inner selves — as yet undefined in itself — receives expression in certain articulations via our body language and gestures (for example, in the mimicking of our facial appearance). This enables us to observe via our senses another person's joy or distress, for example; yet this expression would remain extremely limited if we were to refrain from using speech and language. It would require a degree of intelligibility and communicative skill if we wish to communicate something adequately. Without language the inner life would eventually become mute. Schleiermacher believes that Christianity presupposes communication through language, for how would the Savior be able to have an impact on our lives if he were unable to communicate his self-consciousness by means of human discourse? Christianity has always been spread through proclamation. But *Darstellung* does take place via human discourse in an appropriate style: poetic, rhetorical, and *darstellend belehrend* (teaching through expression).[17]

However, religious communication within faith communication requires an element of leadership. Schleiermacher bases the need for leadership on the dialectic between an activity that is mainly productive, on the one hand, and an activity that is primarily receptive, on the other.[18] This dialectic is needed to create the "circulation of religious interest." Hence it is no surprise that he refers to practical theology as the *Umlauf*-method (circulation-method).[19] The interaction between the producing and receiving activity generates communion and at the same time activates religious life.

On this issue of Schleiermacher's practical theological reception, we encounter rather diverse interpretations. Bohren discovers in Schleiermacher's thinking certain culturally determined power structures that ground the ecclesial power in the civil distinction between *Gebildeten* (educated people) and *Ungebildeten* (uneducated people), which is, in effect, a sanctioning of the new aristocracy of the nine-

17. Schleiermacher, *Der christliche Glaube*, par. 15.2.
18. Schleiermacher, *Praktische Theologie*, pp. 16, 49.
19. Friedrich Schleiermacher, *Kurze Darstellung*, ed. Heinrich Scholz (Darmstadt, 1993), par. 268.

teenth century — the educated citizenry.[20] Bohren thus highlights the inequality of power in the communicative process that is apparent in Schleiermacher's distinction between clergy and laity. Bohren, instead, pleads for the *begabte Gemeinde* (a gifted church). Gräb, on the other hand, hardly comments on the role of leaders and praises Schleiermacher for his view of reciprocity in interpersonal communication, which connects the social and the personal.[21]

The interesting thing is that both aspects are present in Schleiermacher's thought: the reciprocity between people as well as the inequality that is an unavoidable aspect of leadership activities. Looking at it from a historical perspective, we should note that Schleiermacher's experiences in the Moravian Brotherhood continue to have their influence: "I wish I could draw you a picture of the rich, luxuriant life in this city of God when its citizens assemble, all of whom are full of their own power, which wants to stream forth into the open, all full of holy passion to apprehend and appropriate everything that others might offer them."[22] This is the ideal of free expression that allows the sentiments of the inner self to come into the open. In our analysis of the role of the clergy, we should also keep in mind that Schleiermacher, as a child of the Enlightenment, strongly supports the autonomous and free expression of faith. Moreover, he presupposes an active role of the laity in the interaction between clergy and church members: "The true purpose of religious communion is, therefore, the circulation of religious interest, and the clergyman is only an organ in the body."[23] But this does not take away from the fact that there is a fundamental inequality within the community. The *Kirchenleitung* (church leadership) evolves from the old dualism between *den Hervorragenden und der Masse* (the elite and the common people).[24]

What exactly is the nature of this inequality? Schleiermacher sees two kinds of inequality in the Christian community. The first is absolute and concerns Jesus Christ, the founder of the Christian faith, whose uniqueness Schleiermacher underscores:

---

20. Rudolf Bohren, *Das Gott schön werde* (Munich, 1975), p. 169.
21. Gräb, *Mitteilung*, pp. 201-12.
22. Schleiermacher, *On Religion*, p. 165.
23. Schleiermacher, *Praktische Theologie*, p. 65.
24. Schleiermacher, *Kurze Darstellung*, par. 267.

Christianity proceeded from Christ and was in Him. All others must, in comparison with Him, be rated as zero. There was an absolute inequality, for the entire creation proceeded from this.[25]

Schleiermacher gives ample attention to the Incarnation in his dogmatics, showing how crucial the person of Christ is for him. As a community of faith we relate to one unique person, and through our faith in Jesus the Redeemer we share in the Christian community.[26] Christ lives in a total God-consciousness, and thus his life has an *urbildliche* (archetypal) meaning — the total God-consciousness becomes incarnate in a historic person.[27] At the same time, Christ has a *vorbildliche* (model function) dignity, for he is the mirror by which we become aware of our own shortcomings. Thus there is in Christ a unique origin, while he also has a religious impact; and in that sense there is an absolute inequality between Christ and us.

But there is another inequality that is the basis for leadership activities. The apostles play a *leitende* (leading) and productive role with respect to the community. Initially, they were the closest to Christ, but their activity was only a temporary stage. Over time the idea of the community became more central. Yet, as time goes on, there is a new inequality: the distinction between leaders and the masses. Schleiermacher points to *Bildung* (education), where expertise in languages — and thus knowledge of the original sources — is an important aspect. We express our faith primarily through language, and not everyone has the same language skills.[28] He does not provide any further argumentation, thus leaving us with the impression that he is imposing on organized Christianity the view of an educated citizenry that was current at the time. There is a need for leadership, and the well-educated theologian plays a significant role. Knowledge of the ancient languages, Bohren declares somewhat hyperbolically, becomes a symbol of power. It is remarkable that Schleiermacher's explanation for the need for leadership is not based on *ministerial* motives of mediation between

25. "Christianity finds its origin in Christ, and was in Him. All others are zero in comparison with Him. There was an absolute inequality, for all of creation went forth from this point." Schleiermacher, *Praktische Theologie*, p. 13.

26. Schleiermacher, *Der christliche Glaube*, par. 14.

27. Schleiermacher, *Der christliche Glaube*, par. 93.

28. Schleiermacher, *Praktische Theologie*, p. 15.

Christ and the church but becomes purely a matter of *Bildung*. Ministers and theologians have developed a certain erudition, and on that basis they assume a leadership role. That role is necessary, for thereby religious circulation is maintained and piety is strengthened.

The Task of Practical Theology

Leaders should not only have well-developed communication skills but must also actively participate in the life of the church themselves. "The clergyman," says Schleiermacher, "lives in and with his church, and knows the religious life of the church from within."[29] From personal contact with the church, leaders know about people's needs. In addition, they must have a personal communion with Scripture and fill a leadership role in that respect. These two dimensions, close contact with the church and familiarity with Scripture — and in that order — are very important for Schleiermacher because of his conviction that clergy must first possess something themselves before they can share anything with others. This is because communication proceeds from the leader's own self-consciousness.

We help each other become faith partners through this exchange, which is a circular process of speaking and listening, sharing and understanding. Interpersonal human discourse has the potential of becoming the Word of God; that is, it can stimulate and activate our inner selves in such a way that we become conscious of our bond with God. It is not some businesslike "something" that is transferred in interpersonal communication, but it has to do with something very personal; it is about one person's sharing with the other. In Schleiermacher's view, human subjectivity is fully present; or, to put it even more strongly, we cannot communicate apart from the subject. In other words, it all passes through the subject, and we may even say that it originates in the subject. Thus we see that, first of all, communication has an expressive character: we share what we first experienced ourselves. Apart from that expressive character, another aspect is important: the level of the interaction. Everything is involved in the interaction between one human being and the other, not only the content of

29. Schleiermacher, *Praktische Theologie,* pp. 240, 241.

what is said but also the way it is said. Content and form are no longer distinguishable; body language, feelings, and context all play their role.

All of this is closely linked to Schleiermacher's view of faith. Faith develops as the consciousness of God in the human self: in the communication of faith this God-consciousness is transferred from the consciousness of one person to that of another. Viewing it from that perspective, we can understand why Schleiermacher constantly refers to *Selbstmitteilung* (self-communication) and *Selbstdarstellung* (self-presence). The main function of the church service, he says, is an edifying activity based on "the sharing of the pious self-consciousness to the extent that this can be expressed in thought."[30] This term "thought" is not to be primarily understood in terms of cognitive abilities and discourse, but rather in terms of the poetic and the artistic. The term *Selbstmitteilung* implies that one's total being is involved: we share our own God-experience. The *Darstellung*, as I have explained above, is part of the dialectic of productive activity and open receptivity. The relationship between those who produce and those who receive is, according to Schleiermacher, a sharing that proceeds from the former to the latter, and in such a way that what is shared becomes the Word of God.

> This sharing of the self can only take place through the stimulating impulse of the *Selbstdarstellung*, while the analogue movement, caused by the one who shares in the one who responsively receives, becomes a power which incites the same movement.[31]

However, the sharing of the self must meet a certain condition, for we are dealing with an activity of the Holy Spirit, and the Spirit takes everything from Christ. What we share must agree with Scripture, and we must be able to defend it as *Schriftgemäss* (according to Scripture). Schleiermacher says that genuine Christians not only want to keep inside themselves what is in agreement with Christ, but want to develop it further. And we can only share that which is from Christ and dwells in us.

"To the domain of practical theology belong all rules of art that pertain to leadership activities."[32] This concerns, particularly, the exe-

---

30. Schleiermacher, *Kurze Darstellung,* par. 280.

31. Schleiermacher, *Der christliche Glaube,* par. 133.1.

32. Schleiermacher, *Praktische Theologie,* p. 17; cf. Schleiermacher, *Kurze Darstellung,* par. 260.

cution of these activities. We may well ask, how does this leadership actually take place? Schleiermacher speaks of the technique that allows the church to function and to be perfected (the term "technique" is to be interpreted as a manual that indicates how something can be realized).[33] This implies that these leadership activities do not follow a haphazard scheme but are characterized by a professional rationality. It is not a matter of impulsive action but a professional competence in line with certain rules, for which guidelines can be provided. Take, for example, the sermon as an expression and sharing of devout self-consciousness. We can develop a theory of homiletics to the extent that we regard the sermon as an art and a skill; in that sense, practical theology is the *theory* of praxis. Schleiermacher distinguishes between activities that target the community and those that target the individual. Liturgy and homiletics belong to the first category, while pastoral work fits into the second category. It is remarkable that pastoral work is subdivided into catechetical and pastoral activities, probably because catechesis deals with a smaller group in the church rather than with the entire church.

Thus the leader must have experience and skills in two areas: he or she must be a good theologian, one who is familiar with religious life and with the fundamentals of the Christian faith, and he or she must also have communicative qualities. Armed with these qualities, he or she must be able to act purposefully. Schleiermacher adds a typical nineteenth-century idea regarding that purposefulness. The strategy has to do with the inequality between the present historical reality of the church and the ideal of perfection we strive for. The church definitely has its shortcomings, and everything can be improved. But with what can we compare the present imperfect reality of the church? This is where idealism comes into the picture: the ideal is a goal that we say must be reached, while at the same time we cannot say with any certainty that it ever will be reached.[34] This ideal motivates us toward purposeful action. We often find this dialectic between *Idee* (idea) and *Erscheinung* (appearance) in older publications by German practical theologians — when they wrote about the way the church acts.[35] How-

33. Schleiermacher, *Praktische Theologie,* p. 25.
34. Schleiermacher, *Praktische Theologie,* p. 18.
35. Theodor Albert Liebner, "Begriff, Gegenstand und Einteilung der praktischen

ever, we should note that theologians do take account of the content of revelation in their concept of the *Idee:* it is a philosophical category that includes revelation in Christ as well as eschatological expectation.

The goal of the activities of the leaders is the edification of the church members and the nurture of spiritual life (Schleiermacher uses the term *Seelenleitung* [nurturing of souls]). However, this does not imply the assigning of a central role to the individual. Due to the communicative structure of our life as a community, the individual and the communion are closely connected. But the development of the person and progress in spiritual life receive all the attention. The leaders are motivated by their desire that "all people become good and perfect Christians; when that goal is reached . . . *Seelenleitung* will no longer be needed."[36] But as long as we fall short in self-knowledge and possess an impure will, this leadership activity will be needed; and as long as it is needed, its execution must be adequate and meticulous. Concerning the practical execution of the activities of the leaders, Schleiermacher speaks about the "purity of the medium." Interpersonal communication must be adequate, that is, according to "the rules of the game"; and it must not contradict the fundamental views of theological reflection. Both conditions must be met.

> No method should be of such a nature that it conflicts with the academic and ecclesial *Gemeingeist* (communal spirit); not of such a nature that it weakens the Christian foundation or abolishes the *Gemeingeist* of the church.[37]

As to "the rules of the game," Schleiermacher refers to rhetoric, poetry, painting, and architecture. For example, we must use rhetorical skills if we want to express a certain conviction, while we also use the principles of eloquence. When we insist that faith is shaped and nurtured by preaching, the listener must be able to properly understand the preacher, for the effectiveness of the preaching depends on the *Reinheit der Darstellung* (clarity of expression). The clarity, or purity, of the *Darstellung* is of critical importance if we want to have a certain ef-

---

Theologie," in *Praktische Theologie. Texte zum Werden und Selbstverständnis der praktischen Disziplin der Evangelischen Theologie,* ed. Gerhard Krause (Darmstadt, 1972), p. 55.

36. Liebner, "Begriff, Gegenstand und Einteilung," p. 39.
37. Liebner, "Begriff, Gegenstand und Einteilung," p. 39.

fect. But a sermon that is preached in accordance with "the rules of the game" may not always bring the desired result. We are looking for an impact on the heart, Schleiermacher says, and that is something other than merely satisfying the *Darstellung*. Neither can we say that the *Darstellung* is only a means toward an end; for the means should contain nothing that conflicts with the desired result in any way. Thus the medium we employ must be suitable for the transmission of our faith. We cannot separate the form of interpersonal communication, and the way it is shaped by leaders, from its content. Or, to phrase it another way, the relational aspect and the content cannot be disconnected. We must cultivate the purity of interpersonal communication if we want to give a stimulus to the proper functioning of religious circulation.

Summary and Conclusion

Schleiermacher's abiding significance in the discipline of practical theology lies primarily in the domain of the communication of faith. In conclusion, I want to focus on two areas that demand our attention. The first area concerns the inherent link that he establishes between interpersonal discourse, on the one hand, and the faith experience, on the other. Here Schleiermacher provides some fundamental insights that earn our positive appraisal. Second, Schleiermacher offers a typically anthropocentric approach to the praxis of faith. Concerning the subject-element of faith, he has a one-sided emphasis on the inner self. As a result, faith receives a noncognitive status. As far as the object-side of faith is concerned, his position leads to a nonreferential speaking of God, which reduces the God-concept to an anthropological category.

As we look more closely at discourse and faith, allow me to comment further. We have seen that, according to Schleiermacher, human discourse has the structure of a reciprocal exchange. We are concerned with speaking *and* understanding, production *and* reception. Thus he does justice to the dynamism of faith praxis, while at the same time pointing to communality and mutual involvement as key values of our faith. The reciprocal discourse is fundamentally human, and spiritual life is totally embedded in interpersonal communication. Practical theology, as a theory of praxis, deals with interpersonal communication of religious praxis, in the conviction that this communication aims to stimulate and develop our spiritual life. Pursuing and developing a theory about interpersonal discourse is thus an essential part of practical theological studies. How does the process of speaking and understanding (the interaction) take place within the various praxis domains of religious life? A number of dimensions play a role: (1) How does the activity of the leaders take place, and what part do authority and power structures play in it? (2) How do the person and personality of the leader function regarding the interaction? Schleiermacher is correct in pointing out that the entire person participates in the faith communication. (3) Which theoretical presuppositions from other disciplines have an impact on the theoretical reflection concerning the praxis domain? For instance, what theory of learning has an impact on catechesis? What theory of discourse on the pastoral conversation? What rhetorical theory on homiletics? (4) Does the interaction happen in a way that accords with matters of faith? If we value the freedom of the individual, will this freedom also be respected in the interaction process?

We cannot detach communication as a medium from religious circulation as a spiritual phenomenon. Even though Schleiermacher speaks about the "technique" of leadership, his theological writings tend to focus quite explicitly on content. His thinking boils down to the fact that a religious process gets started in the manner of an interpersonal discourse. The goal is not just pure communication but also an effective impact on daily life. Classical religion focuses on communion with Christ, and Schleiermacher uses such traditional theological terms as "new birth" and "sanctification" in this connection. The communion with Christ takes shape in the communicative process. It is realized through human mediums, but conversion and faith are the result of the divine power of the Word; it depends on what Christ himself does. In that sense, there is no difference between us and Christ's disciples.

> It is always the priority of this same divine power of the Word . . . which leads to conversion and faith. The point to stress is only that the *Selbstdarstellung Christi* is now mediated by those who proclaim Him; but since they belong to Him as organs of his body, and since therefore the working proceeds from Him, it is essentially something He does.[38]

38. Schleiermacher, *Der christliche Glaube,* par. 108.5.

The dynamic influence of what Christ does brings the feeble and slumbering God-consciousness to development and produces renewal in the human heart. Even in his soteriology, Schleiermacher thinks in a firmly anthropological way; the important thing is what happens in human self-consciousness. Through communion with Christ the natural abilities are more and more attuned to perfection and the redemptive nature of the Savior. As a result, a new life is developed, and in this context Schleiermacher uses the dogmatic terms "new birth" and "sanctification." The tension between the "old man" and the "new man" remains, but the emphasis is placed on the *genesis* of renewal, in which penitence plays a significant role. When the Christian faith is put into words, the emphasis is on terms that point to Christ *in nobis*. But the notion of justification is not entirely absent. Schleiermacher views justification as the new and perfect relationship with God, in which we are liberated from the self-consciousness of our guilt.[39] Otherwise, the process of conversion and renewal would become an unbearable burden.

Then there is the second point: the noncognitive status of faith and the nonreferential speaking of God. Schleiermacher is opposed to a purely rational and moral approach to faith, and he anchors spiritual life in a feeling of unconditional dependence. In so doing, he positions religion in the hidden recesses of the human consciousness, in an undivided center of the person, where the kinds of distinctions we normally use in our dealing with the world and people around us do not apply. It almost seems as though this undivided center transcends the knowable, just as God is transcendent. We must speak about it in a preliminary way, for the very moment we turn it into a conceptual framework, we are no longer at the actual source. This extreme form of transcendence makes the transcendent absolute. No concepts are available, and language is thus inadequate to communicate it. In this Schleiermacher is a child of his time: during the Enlightenment era God increasingly became the unknowable Absolute, the *Universum,* while faith in God, in terms of the attitude of humans, received the extreme status of unconditional dependence. In this scheme the faith relationship loses the concreteness of the relationship between an I and a Thou. A concrete relationship enables us to respond to the question of who the Other is

---

39. Schleiermacher, *Der christliche Glaube,* par. 107.

and who we are ourselves; cognitions then play a definite role. Schleiermacher, however, is so afraid of the criticism of metaphysics that he wishes — from an apologetic perspective — to provide a safe haven for God and faith. God is not a metaphysical being, nor an object of our knowledge, and faith is not something rational. In this way Schleiermacher tries to keep the liberal modernism of the *Vernunft-religion* (rational religion — Hegel) at a distance. Faith, he says, deals with a relationship with an "infinite totality."

> [B]ut while brooding over the existence of this god before the world and outside the world may be good and necessary in metaphysics, in religion even that becomes only empty mythology, a further development of that which is only the means of portrayal as if it were the essential itself, a complete departure from its characteristic ground.[40]

This approach has had a strong influence on modern theology, particularly in the twentieth century on Paul Tillich, and more recently on theologians such as Gordon Kaufman and David Tracy. Regarding our faith in God, this has resulted in a symbolic and metaphorical speaking about God. I cannot deal with these considerations in any further detail in this chapter, but I will return to them in Chapters 10 and 11.

40. Schleiermacher, *On Religion*, p. 105.

CHAPTER 7

Salvation: Sign and Word

The Hermeneutical-Communicative Paradigm

As the action-theoretical paradigm was being developed in the last quarter of the twentieth century, reflection on the communication of our faith received a powerful impulse in the discipline of practical theology. In line with the thought of the social philosopher Habermas, the concept of *communicative action* comes into use. Although this means that human action now becomes the primary object of practical theology, it also means that, via the concept of communicative action, interpersonal communication also receives ample attention. It takes into account very clearly that human beings are always embedded in social, political, economic, and cultural structures. Practical theology focuses on the question of "whether and how this communicative activity within the conditions of the church and other societal institutions occurs, whether and how it should and can be improved."[1]

Gerben Heitink emphasizes that practical theology, as a discipline of crisis, has a practical aim: the improvement and renewal of communicative action. Gert Otto points out that the influence of Habermas is understandable, since interpersonal communication is something we all constantly participate in. He believes, moreover, that the term *Herrschaftsfreie Kommunikation* (nonauthoritarian communication) refers to something that has yet to be fully realized.[2] This utopian desire receives an eschatological focus in the practical theological

1. Van der Ven, *Practical Theology,* p. 40.
2. Otto, *Grundlegung,* p. 215.

reception: it reaches out to a quality of communal life that we hope for and long for. On the other hand, it is from the vantage point of the ideal situation that we can criticize the present. This allows practical theology to become a critical theory of praxis. Peukert, in particular, has contributed to this theological-eschatological interpretation, and Van der Ven has pursued it as well.

But interpersonal discourse, which is expressed in the concept of communicative action, is not the only approach in the action-theoretical paradigm. A supplementary kind of thinking becomes apparent in the interest in hermeneutics. This should not be surprising, for written and oral texts play an important part in religious praxis. The term "text" often refers to Scripture and tradition, and the hermeneutical approach is particularly directed toward the meaning and interpretation of texts. "What Christians actually do," Dingemans says, "is in principle inspired by the gospel of Jesus Christ, as it is transmitted to us through texts from the past that are reinterpreted for the present."[3] Dingemans is somewhat critical of the action-theoretical paradigm. He suggests that it is too much preoccupied with the social sciences and therefore tends to approach praxis too much from the angle of action, while we should also pay attention to the underlying intentions and the theological frame of reference. He argues that this would receive more justice in the broader approach of the alpha-disciplines, and would also permit a more serious inclusion of the biblical tradition. In the modern use of hermeneutics in practical theology, the following question has center stage: How can texts from the past have something meaningful to say in the present?

Friedrich Schweitzer is of the opinion that texts from the tradition cannot automatically be treated as authoritative for the present: "The concept of hermeneutics compels us to think of the challenge . . . of interpreting and disclosing the tradition from the perspective of the present."[4] That is, starting from the questions and needs of the present, we begin our dialogue with Scripture and tradition; and via this exchange, which is directed by the actuality, we arrive at a plausible judg-

---

3. G. D. J. Dingemans, *Manieren van doen. Inleiding tot de studie van de praktische theologie* (Kampen, 1996), p. 48.

4. Friedrich Schweitzer, "Praktische Theologie und Hermeneutik," in *Paradigmenentwicklung in der Praktischen Theologie*, ed. Johannes A. van der Ven and Hans Georg Zieberz (Kampen/Weinheim, 1993), p. 30.

ment. Practical theology, it is thought, deals with two poles: the Christian tradition and the specific actions in a concrete praxis. This practical theological methodology implies two basic notions: interpretation and correlation. Dingemans tries to establish a bridge between the two.

The main question of this chapter is: What contribution does the hermeneutical-communicative paradigm make in the development of a theory of faith communication? I wish to look explicitly for the theological content of the theories that are developed and for the theoretical arguments that are used regarding interpersonal discourse.

The Religious View of Discourse

I will discuss the hermeneutical-communicative approach by referring to some publications by the Dutch practical theologian Johannes van der Ven, who is the main proponent of this theoretical strain and has defended his views in a consistent way. In this chapter I will not spend time discussing his view of practical theology as empirical theology (that will be part of the next chapter's discussion of how we may speak of God). Here we will deal with his ideas about the communication of faith in the action-theoretical paradigm. I will confine myself mainly to *Practical Theology: An Empirical Approach* (German edition, 1990; English edition, 1993) and *Ecclesiology in Context* (1993). Even though there is only a three-year period between the two books, there are a few minor differences: (1) *Practical Theology* is primarily action-theoretical in orientation, while the issue of semiotics is central to *Ecclesiology*. This results in a stronger emphasis on the linguistic aspect of interpersonal discourse in the latter book. (2) *Practical Theology* exudes the atmosphere of a wildly spreading pluriformity, with all the conflicts that may entail. Van der Ven emphasizes the need to carry on a dialogue between all the divergent opinions and is adamant that no decision be forced on us by some authoritative intervention, which would be unworthy of a faith community. Thus he gives strong priority to consensus in his view of communication. This has shifted somewhat in his book *Ecclesiology*: "The loss of societal plausibility makes continuous religious communication a necessity, both internally and externally."[5] The church is no

5. Johannes A. van der Ven, *Ecclesiology in Context* (Grand Rapids, 1993), p. 63.

longer self-evident and thus must legitimate itself and introduce the topic of divine salvation. In this context he furthers expands on the relationship between interpersonal communication and religious communication. (3) In *Practical Theology* the theological implications of the communication process follow a trajectory of rather complex reasoning: Van der Ven arrives via the ethical aspect of the communicative process at a theological motivation that is inspired by the *basileia*-symbol. In *Ecclesiology*, Van der Ven opens up salvation from God for discussion in a more direct way. Furthermore, it is remarkable that both studies have a diaconal focus as their underlying intention.

The Hermeneutical-Communicative Foundational Pattern

Van der Ven's first aim in *Practical Theology* is to show that hermeneutics and communication are fundamental notions in the church's praxis. In praxis, he says, the main issues are "the verbal and non-verbal interpretation of written and spoken texts and their verbal and non-verbal communication."[6] From this perspective we are able adequately to describe the basic functions of the church. The function of the *kerygma,* for example, must be understood as the interpretation of texts and as communication, with the use of the instruments of modern rhetoric and the psychological learning processes. The basic function of the liturgy may be viewed from the same hermeneutical-communicative perspective, but rather embodied as ritual. "The central focus of liturgy, especially the eucharistic liturgy, is after all on texts and their interpretation. . . . The ritual activity can be seen as the dramatic symbolization of the hermeneutic of these texts and the process of their communication."[7] Furthermore, with respect to *koinonia* and the *diakonia,* Van der Ven believes that the hermeneutical-communicative perspective reveals an important notion: the orientation and inspiration has much to do with the constant reading and interpreting of texts from the Christian tradition (and other religious traditions) and the ongoing communication of their meaning. The interpretation of these texts should not be an academic pursuit but an

6. Van der Ven, *Practical Theology,* p. 40.
7. Van der Ven, *Practical Theology,* p. 42.

activity that is characterized by engagement. From concrete need we turn to inspiring texts. We cannot work with the homeless or asylum seekers, with foreigners or marginal youth, he says, without telling, interpreting, and repeating stories.

Strangely, Van der Ven does not deal with the question of how interpersonal discourse operates in the various basic functions of the church, at least not in *Practical Theology*. He does not explain how interaction, via language and ritual, mediates salvation. The question of how we can speak of a *common* discourse in a pluriform context, rather than of the mediating role of the discourse, occupies a central place. He analyzes communicative praxis in terms of the conversations people have about faith; and he investigates the conditions for a communal discourse about divine salvation. Communication must fill certain normative conditions if people are to come together in discourse, says Van der Ven; and he borrows these normative conditions, without any further argumentation, from Habermas: equality, freedom, universality, and solidarity.[8]

According to Van der Ven, it is characteristic of contemporary hermeneutical praxis that texts no longer have one single meaning. There is an enormous gap between the original text and the present situation of the hearer or reader; yet these texts address us and we derive meaning from them. But we can no longer accept a meaning that has been handed down from the past. It is only in the dialogue between then and now that we can derive a possible meaning for the present from an ancient text. Further, situations and contexts in the present are so diverse that even viewing them from a current perspective does not allow us to speak of one single meaning. We are faced with a plurality of interpretations and inevitable conflicts between interpretations. This issue, Van der Ven argues, must become the object of our study; in other words, pluralism and conflict are the central themes in communicative praxis. Van der Ven does not believe that doctrinal authority or ecclesial hierarchy are viable options.

Communication is, first of all, an exchange between the participants in a conversation. This exchange does not only involve cognitions; the affective dimension and the intentions of actions also play a role. We not only wish to share something with the other; we also

8. Van der Ven, *Practical Theology,* p. 60.

wish to be understood, and we hope for the other person's agreement, if possible. In any case, we must be prepared to try to understand the perspective of that other person. Van der Ven goes one step further, insisting that ultimately our understanding of the other should lead to an agreement, a consensus between participants. This ultimate aim is usually beyond our reach, which then calls for reconciliation.

Moral and Religious Appraisal

Van der Ven follows another line of argumentation that concerns his view of social interaction. He realizes that communication fails more often than it succeeds. We are extremely vulnerable in interpersonal interaction, and numerous factors leading to that failure come into play: (1) Matters that are related to the receiver and/or the sender. We may fail in our assessment of reality; and it's also possible for us to mislead or manipulate the other. (2) There may be an incongruity in our use of language and symbols. It's possible that the illocutionary loading of a statement differs from what the speaker intended. When someone describes a religious experience, and that is subsequently understood as prescriptive, something has gone wrong in the communication process. This is also true when someone makes a metaphorical presentation that is then taken to be literal or factual. (3) Van der Ven also points to social relationships and involvements between people. Do we actually have the ability to establish a symmetrical communication? This depends, among other things, on the self-image of one participant over against that of the other. Inequality of power and other forms of dependence may hinder symmetrical communication. (4) The cultural, political, and social contexts in which conversations take place determine their limits to some degree. Dialogue in a church community is determined, at least in part, by inequality in knowledge, verbal skills, social positions, and so forth.

What we need to emphasize is that we cannot simply declare that we face limitations in our communicative action and leave it at that. We need to find ways, Van der Ven says, to push against these limitations and to transcend them. This leads him to a normative reflection on praxis, which, in summary, allows him to arrive, via the intermediate step of ethics (establishing norms for communicative action), at a

theological motivation to help people transcend these potential failures time and again. This is also where we find the link to reconciliation. Unfortunately, Van der Ven's argumentation is at times unneces-
sarily complex, and his dependence on Habermas is irksome rather
than helpful. The complexity of his argumentation can be blamed on
the underlying idea that a theological argument can only be valid if the
road is first paved by a way of reasoning that is generally accessible.[9]
Via ethics and via Habermas, Van der Ven eventually arrives at the
basileia-symbol. I don't share the kind of thinking that looks for such
foundations; and he remains absolutely unclear about why he adopts
the normative *principia* for the communicative endeavor from Habermas — equality, freedom, universality, and solidarity. Is Habermas's approach universally accepted? Is his authority self-evident? Van der Ven
has to go to a lot of trouble to show in his theological analysis of the
basileia-symbol that Habermas's *principia* are in accordance with the
central motives of the *basileia*-symbol.

Aside from these jumps in the argumentation, however, Van der
Ven's thinking is clear. He wishes to prove that communicative action has
an ethical as well as a religious dimension. The interaction between people
is to be evaluated — as social interaction — in terms of good and bad, but
also in the religious terms of salvation and evil. I agree with that point of
view. A communicative action theory without a worldview and without
religion is in a sense incomplete, Van der Ven says, because without them
the fundamental dimensions of communicative action cannot find their
fulfillment. We may use the normative principles of power-free communication, but what guarantee do we have that we are not pursuing an illusion? Is universal solidarity ever possible to put into practice? This is
where we encounter questions of worldview and religion: "The commitment to freedom, equality, universality, and solidarity that is intrinsic to
all real communication necessarily demands absolute universal liberation
and reconciliation in the religious sense."[10] And thus the heavy theological notions of liberation and reconciliation demand attention; for communicative action, in the final analysis, is about salvation and doom. And
from that perspective, Van der Ven is able to interpret interpersonal communication, particularly its social dimension, as a sign of God's kingdom.

9. Van der Ven, *Practical Theology,* p. 68.
10. Van der Ven, *Practical Theology,* p. 62.

Consequently, the social — and thus the ethical — dimension of the interaction between people can become a sign of God's salvation. This is the theological perspective on communication. It is noteworthy that Van der Ven makes a rather direct link between interhuman communication and such heavy theological notions as reconciliation and liberation. He points to the exodus from Egypt and Jesus' death as liberating and reconciling acts.[11] What happens is that he ascribes a religious meaning to interpersonal communication: communicative action becomes a sign of salvation. He seems to say that, from a Christian perspective, we derive inspiration for wholesome communication from the expectation of the coming divine kingdom. But due to the obstinacy of suppressive evil in and around us, we must always rely on the reconciliation and liberation that came in Jesus. Moved by his life and death, we have the courage to tackle irreconcilable differences, and we cherish the hope that we can live together in harmony. In other words, faith provides the ultimate motivation and inspiration concerning communicative action, and faith invites us to live in wholesome communion.

Signals of Divine Salvation

In his book *Practical Theology,* Van der Ven offers an action-theoretical reconstruction of religious communication in which three things stand out: (1) Social interaction has logical priority above the interaction through language. (2) He postulates, via the ethical approach, the need for a religious definition of reality. (3) Spiritual life is ultimately the motivating factor in our intentional pursuit, through our actions, of the best possible communication — communication where reconciliation between people is the crucial issue. I believe that this is an optimal interpretation of Van der Ven's ideas from a practical theological point of view. It is clear that this action-theoretical paradigm has a further impact on the reconstruction of religious communication and that Word-revelation does not occupy a central role in theological reflection.

---

11. Van der Ven, *Practical Theology,* p. 62.

The Semiotic Angle

The relationship between the communication-theoretical insights and the theological insights is somewhat different in *Ecclesiology* from what we find in *Practical Theology*. Regarding communication, in *Ecclesiology* Van der Ven finds his orientation in semiotics, and he uses some of the terminology of Peirce. In the triangle of *sign, denotatum* (that to which the sign refers), and *interpretant* (the interpreting person), the dialectic between the sign and the *denotatum* is of special significance. Initially, Van der Ven seems to take a very broad view of the concept of a sign: it may include words, phrases, texts, poems, and so forth, but also all kinds of nonlinguistic phenomena, such as body postures, artistic expressions, and so on. But a closer look makes it clear that Van der Ven again hardly touches on the dimension of language but mainly pursues various social phenomena. Using semiotics, he tries to clarify the dialectic between social and religious phenomena. People who believe may experience a particular reality around them as religious: that is, they may see social phenomena as religious signs or appreciate events and phenomena from the outside world as divine salvation. It seems to me that the word "appreciate" is more appropriate than "interpret" because it expresses a value judgment and does not so easily lead to the faulty conclusion that we are the actual source ourselves. Van der Ven describes this process of creating religious meaning as follows:

> The social phenomena in the church (sign) refer to God's salvation *(denotatum)*, at least to the person who sees it as a sign *(interpretant)*, on the basis of conventions which are embedded in the religious tradition (codes).[12]

What does Van der Ven see as the *denotatum,* the salvation that comes from God? With the support of Schillebeeckx — besides Vatican II, one of his most authoritative theological sources — he seeks to define it using terms such as "reconciliation," "forgiveness," "return," "communion," and "freedom." But everything may, in effect, become a religious symbol: the greeting ceremonial in a worship service, the circle around the altar, the bread and wine, the liturgical garments, and so forth. The

12. Van der Ven, *Ecclesiology,* p. 107.

core thought is that social phenomena in the church operate as religious symbols. The religious dimension is not added, but may, because of its sign-characteristic, be regarded as salvation from God. However, the fact that something operates as a religious symbol is not arbitrary; for the sign is embedded in the religious tradition, in the historical process that attributes religious meaning. Thus are religious meanings exchanged in religious communication.

Evaluation

I offer a few remarks regarding this reconstruction.

1. Van der Ven hardly differentiates between human discourse through language and the other signs and symbols. But, if it is indeed true that something can only function as a sign when it has been defined as such (in a mental act), then it seems to me that these symbols, if they are to function as such, are dependent on the word as the communication medium. Signs and symbols must be named and defined. To me, this would mean that in interpersonal discourse the priority lies with language and in faith with the Word.

2. Within the context of the Roman Catholic tradition, it is relatively easy for Van der Ven to link the dialectic of the sign and the *denotatum* to the sacrament, particularly with regard to the way the church functions. Thus the church itself points to the salvation that comes from God, because the church participates in the foundational sacrament: Jesus the Christ.

3. But the sacramental dimension is not primarily directed toward the historical revelation in Jesus Christ. There is, of course, a connection. This dimension is the *exemplum* of ultimate salvation, but the sign-character of the sacrament is first of all directed toward the present experience, toward phenomena in the reality that surrounds us. The sign also receives a strong eschatological meaning: it points forward to the kingdom of God. It is characteristic of Van der Ven's view that the sign and the signified almost converge. The reality around us may become a sign: we may experience nature as a gift from God, or love among people as a

signal pointing toward God's love, or a liturgical gesture as God's protection. Salvation becomes present in these ways. Communication between people may likewise become a religious sign; it may point to communion with God. But these things remain signs, and a sign is not the thing itself; it is not identical with salvation. It points to it, is directed toward it. The church is the sacrament of this salvation. "The ultimate reality that is its origin and base is not the way other realities are, for it is a beckoning and receding perspective: the kingdom of God."[13] We can only speak of it by focusing on one aspect and viewing it from one particular perspective. But ultimately the sign and the object that is signified *(denotatum)* converge in the human being, the *interpretant,* who observes signals of salvation in the reality that surrounds us and says, "I see something of God." Perhaps she even says, "This is God."

4. If we look at it from a theological angle, it is not surprising that Van der Ven prefers an immanent-eschatological concept of God over a more theistic view of God, in which the externality and otherness of God are more clearly pronounced. The religious is anchored in phenomena or events in reality, and it is in a religious experience of reality that these phenomena or events may become signs of God's salvation. Thus, for example, the love between people may be experienced as a sign of divine salvation; in that sense, God is both immanent and eschatologically transcendent.

The Paradigm of the Speaking God

My reconstruction of the communication of faith differs somewhat from Van der Ven's model. The difference is not that I do not support a reciprocal relationship between communication-theoretical and theological insights. The distinction is based on the primacy of the word in discourse. Protestant theology regards the communion between God and the human world primarily as a "word-communion." This has two consequences: (1) The logical priority in the faith relationship is found in God — that is, God addresses us as a speaking

13. Van der Ven, *Ecclesiology,* p. 166.

God. (2) Human discourse becomes the intermediary of this divine speaking.

Seen from a biblical-theological angle, the prophetic tradition plays an important role in Protestantism. In the praxis of the church, the ministry of the Word takes priority over the ministry of the sacraments, even though there is a strong connection between the two. This focus on the spoken word also implies, from a rhetorical perspective, that the desire to convince people and the desire to bring them to change and renewal are part of the faith communication.

Promises and Commandments

The unique feature of the Christian faith is the conviction that God is a speaking God. The relationship that expresses itself in our faith is characterized by the fact that God speaks, while we listen and respond. Particularly in the prophetic tradition we find direct divine-human discourse. Since there is an interpersonal relationship, we ascribe personal properties to God: God is full of compassion and emotion — and is loving; God reveals his will; God chooses and calls, sends and comes; God enters into communion with us, knows us, and knows our motives. That God is a speaking God comes from the fact that promises and commandments play an important role in the divine-human relationship. God speaks to us and promises his salvation. As the speaker, God is totally involved in this, for his faithfulness is the guarantee of the fulfillment of those promises. And in his speaking God also indicates where we find the quality of this salvation: those who obey the commandments share in his salvation. His speaking may therefore also be a judgment, when we ignore the commandments. God's justice is at stake, and there is no salvation without justice.

The fact that God is a speaking God also implies that there must be a social community. When someone begins to speak, it is with the intention of creating communion. This explains why the word-revelation is accompanied by the notion of the covenant. We discover this in the Old Testament at two critical moments: God calls Abraham, promises him his blessing, and establishes a covenant, thus making a commitment to Abraham; likewise, God speaks to Moses on Mount Sinai and gives his commandments, often referred to as the "Ten Words."

This is the establishment of a covenant, accompanied by a series of blessings and curses. The following statement underscores that the giving of the law at Mount Sinai was primarily a word-revelation: "Then the Lord spoke to you out of the fire. You heard the sound of words but saw no form; there was only a voice" (Deut. 4:12).

Both the Old and New Testaments link the existence of the created world with God's speaking: "And God said . . . and there was . . ." (Gen. 1). "In the beginning was the Word, and the Word was with God, and the Word was God" (John 1:1). The Bible presents God's speaking as powerful and effective: "For he spoke, and it came to be" (Ps. 33:9). The word is closely linked to the act. While our human speech is at times only a verbal sign, God's speaking represents his real presence. "Speak to us yourself and we will listen," the people of Israel say to Moses, "but do not have God speak to us or we will die" (Exod. 20:19). This is why God speaks to humans via a human voice, through the mouth of one of the prophets or through the mouth of Jesus. Jesus repeatedly said that he was not speaking his own words but that they came from God. Albrecht Beutel says that in the Bible the interaction between God and human beings is presented as primarily *solo verbo*.[14]

The Prophetic Tradition

In the prophets we often meet expressions such as "thus says the Lord" or "the word of the Lord came upon me," and so on. Often these prophetic events are accompanied by dreams, visions, and special circumstances, but the word-revelation is the core and what is said is transmitted as human testimony by the prophet. We can distinguish three stages: the words God spoke directly to the prophet; the verbal relaying of God's word in the words of the prophet; and finally, the written word of the prophet. If the word is central, then the element of being a witness is also important. When we hear the word, we have no option but to speak that word, even when it seems to conflict with reality. The calling of Jeremiah is a classic example: he says, "The word of the Lord came to me"; then he mutters in protest, "I do not know how to speak; I am only a child." But "the Lord said to me, 'Do not say, "I am only a

---

14. Albrecht Beutel, "Sprache und Religion," *Pastoraltheologie* 83 (1994): 12.

child." You must go to everyone I send you to and say whatever I command you'" (Jer. 1:4-7). Then we get to hear something close to a revelation in Jeremiah's heart: "The Lord reached out his hand and touched my mouth and said to me, 'Now I have put my words in your mouth'" (v. 9).

We are not told how a prophet recognizes that it is God who is speaking to him. We can see it as a form of inspiration, but in such a way that the prophet receives the word that comes to him. What counts is the voice behind the voice of the prophet — inspiration as the divine breath. We can clearly see this in the vision in which Samuel is called. God calls him during the night, and Samuel at first thinks it is Eli's voice. But Eli's suggestion helps him discover that this is God calling, and Samuel then responds, "Speak, for your servant is listening" (1 Sam. 3:10). When Samuel tells Eli the next morning what God has said to him, Eli accepts it as a word from the Lord. The prophet becomes the intermediary with respect to God's speaking; he speaks on behalf of God.

The word-revelation is more than an interpretation of events. It is sometimes suggested that faith is simply a perspective on certain events: it begins with certain phenomena or events, so the argument runs, and we interpret these retrospectively as having religious meaning. But there seems to be more reason to see God's speaking to humans, during and after the event, as a direct communication with us. When Moses is keeping his father-in-law's flocks in the desert and notices the burning bush, he hears God's voice at the same moment. The angel of the Lord appears as a flame in the burning bush, and God calls, "Moses, Moses!" He responds, "I am here!" God then reveals himself as the God of Abraham, Isaac, and Jacob and says that he has noticed the plight of his people in Egypt. God dispatches Moses to the pharaoh to ensure that the captive people may depart. But Moses brings up all kinds of objections to God's commission. They all boil down to the fact that he doesn't have a shred of evidence that he has indeed been called; he can only say that he has heard the voice of God. The priority lies in God's speaking and in his plan to liberate his people — and the signs that are to follow. I believe that it is thus incorrect to regard revelation primarily as event-plus-interpretation. This would not do justice to the independent status of the prophetic word-revelation.

This Old Testament background also puts its stamp on the New Testament testimony. "In the past God spoke to our forefathers through the prophets at many times and in various ways, but in these last days he has spoken to us by his Son" (Heb. 1:1). The Gospel of John, in particular, emphasizes that Jesus speaks the words of God. He lives in close contact with the Father and focuses his life on the will of the Father: "My food is to do the will of him who sent me" (John 4:34). But Jesus is not presented as one of the prophets; there is a discontinuity with the Old Testament prophets because, as the incarnate Word, he is unique. Jesus is preeminently the Word of God. And he is not so merely as the spoken word, but also as action, as the effectuating force in human existence — the deepest and most essential word. Jesus is the Word in the positive sense as the fulfillment of true communion and obedience, but also in the negative sense as the bringer of the doom message that the communion is in disarray and there is injustice. Jesus stands in the center as fulfillment and origin. The prophetic witness leads to Jesus, and the apostolic witness issues from him. He is the personification of the promise and the commandment: in him the Word has become complete human reality, and the communion between God and man has been fully realized. In that sense, as far as communion with God is concerned, in the person of Christ we encounter a new situation. From Pentecost onward the apostles bear witness to the salvation that has come in the beloved one. The community through the Word is now anchored in the communion with Christ.

The Gospel as Word and Promise

Karl Barth tried to clarify this uniqueness of Jesus Christ as the Word of God by drawing three concentric circles: Jesus Christ himself is the core, embodying the direct and original speaking of God as *revelation;* he is surrounded in the next circle by the *witness* of the apostles and prophets; the third circle is that of the *proclamation* of the church, which is, of course, regulated by the witness of the prophets and apostles.[15] Barth keeps Word and act closely connected. The action-

15. Barth, *Church Dogmatics* I/1, p. 145.

character indicates that the word is not just the expression of the person but also implies a change of the *Umwelt* caused by the person. At the same time, the word-character indicates that we feel addressed by it and are personally engaged. The idea of the Word of God points to a reality where God and humans are involved as speaking and acting persons. For Barth, the notion of the Word of God is ultimately grounded in the conviction that God speaks; this implies, he says, that the speaking has a spiritual dimension. God makes himself available and addresses the human spirit in such a way that we can hear and understand. The notion also implies, according to Barth, that the element of personality is presupposed, and thus provides for a relationship from person to person. Based on this, he is able to identify God's Word with the Son of God, Jesus Christ.[16]

It is essential, at least in the Protestant tradition, for this emphasis on the word to continue in the New Testament community and in the church. The speaking God also calls us to a living communion with him, and God does that by inviting us to a life in communion with Jesus Christ. Thus there is a new situation: Christ is the true embodiment of communion with God; in Christ we are incorporated, that is, the church is a Christ-community. But the Old Testament background does continue to exist: God is a speaking God, and word and response, promise and trust, gift and obedience remain the key elements. In that sense, the promise of Abraham did not lose its power when Christ came (Gal. 3:17). We now see God in Jesus Christ, but the entire Old Testament background continues to echo this. The structure of promise and faith remain valid in the church. Christ is the Word of God, and this means that he is not someone or something standing on his own, in isolation. He is the message that must be believed; he is the speaker who is not without hearers; he is the head of the church, which is his body. Where we find the Word, Luther says, we find the God who promises, and there we must also find the faith of those who accept the promise.

> God has never entered into a relationship with people — and this is
> still the case — other than through the word of promise. And, re-
> versely, we may be sure that we will never be able to enter into a rela-

---

16. Barth, *Church Dogmatics* I/1, p. 137.

tionship with God other than through the way of faith in the word of his promise.[17]

Word and promise remain closely linked: the gospel is the good news *pro nobis*. God's speaking continues after the historical revelation in Jesus Christ. After his resurrection, Jesus charges his disciples, "Go into all the world and preach the good news to all creation" (Mark 16:15). "It is impossible," Berkhof says, "that the firstfruits can remain a single individual." For that reason, the concentration on the one person who represents us is followed by "the centrifugal movement of the winning of people, of the spreading of the renewal among people everywhere."[18] The New Testament witness has both an apostolic and a missionary character; the kerygma proclaims Jesus Christ and shouts that the kingdom of God has arrived. In that sense it is apostolic: it always refers back to its source. But the testimony also contains the element of recruitment: it invites us to share in communion with Christ, and it is an appeal to penitence and remorse. Proclamation points to the past, to what took place. But it also has an impact on what follows in history; it urges people to change and to seek renewal. The apostles bear witness but also admonish (Acts 2:40), and they try to persuade their hearers. The intention to persuade is not foreign to the Word of God. Remember the addresses and letters of Paul. During one of Paul's speeches (Acts 26:28), King Agrippa says to him: "Do you think that in such a short time you can convince me to become a Christian?"

Conclusions

I now want to draw five conclusions about the communication of faith.

1. The fact that God is introduced as a speaking God also implies an emphasis on the divine initiative. God is the subject of the speaking and the acting; God comes to us in his Word, his promises, and commandments. In the faith relationship the logical priority always lies with the divine subject. My discussion of the *iustificatio* in Chapter 3 al-

17. Martin Luther, *De babylonische gevangenschap van de kerk; Brief aan Paus Leo X; De vrijheid van een christen,* Dutch translation by C. N. Impeta; introduction by W. J. Kooiman (Kampen, 1959), p. 40.
18. Berkhof, *Christian Faith,* p. 325.

ready indicated how deeply this is rooted in the Protestant concept of faith.

2. If communication through language is so central to the divine-human discourse, it also implies that faith is to be defined as a relationship between persons. The faith communion presupposes personality and subjectivity — both on God's side and on our side. It is a matter of speaking and listening, promise and faith, commandment and obedience. It is precisely because of the role of language in communication that we may define faith in terms of a relationship between God and human beings.

3. A speaker looks for an audience. The one who created humans in his image and likeness wanted to create communion. And it is linguistic communication that creates a social structure. When I promise something to someone, the other must have reason to trust that I will keep my word. If I make all kinds of wild promises but never keep them, my promise will not have much value. In making a promise, we become part of the equation ourselves, for we say to the other, "You can count on me, and I ask you to trust me." We occupy a normative position in discourse: we assume the operation of certain values and are prepared to uphold them. In other words, a speaker has both rights and duties.[19] It is remarkable that this social structure is inherent in the divine speaking, namely, the notion of covenant.

4. There is a special relationship between language and so-called institutional facts. Language is used to describe things, but also to constitute them. When a magistrate says, "I declare you husband and wife" or other words or phrases to formalize a marriage, a new situation has been created. The words have the power to constitute this new situation. When a president says, "We declare that we now are at war with you," a totally new situation has been created. John Searle says that such declarations have the illocutionary purpose to "change the world by suggesting that the change has already been effected."[20] And the justification of the sinner, as divine imputation, must also be regarded as declaratory. The Word of God as promise possesses the same declaratory connotation: it is the pledge that God will judge the world from the perspective of his desire that the world be saved. The Christian

19. Wolterstorff, *Divine Discourse,* pp. 75-94.
20. Searle, *Mind, Language and Society,* p. 150.

faith understands this in the sense that God looks at us in Jesus Christ, in whom God has fully revealed his kingdom. The apostolic witness as Word of God thus contains the promise that this reality is valid. And God asks for faith, that is, he wants that reality of the promise to be at work in our lives.

5. The divine-human discourse is analogous to the discourse between people. This means that our experience in interpersonal discourse allows us to imagine how our communion with God may come about. In this respect, Schleiermacher is correct in his view that we are able to hear the voice of God since we associate with fellow human beings. Even though God is present in a different way, this does not mean that we cannot enter into some sort of dialogue with God, for example, through prayer. On the basis of speech-act theories, Wolterstorff has developed a model in which God's speaking is understood as *double agency discourse,* where God sees interpersonal discourse as "deputized discourse" or "appropriated discourse." God may speak through human witnesses (e.g., through prophets), just as a president may be represented by a diplomat. The words of the one may be taken as the words of the other; we may also regard it as declaring assent to someone else's words. When someone makes a motion during a meeting, we may support the proposal by seconding it. In so doing we share in the responsibility for the motion. Or we may say, "I fully agree with what she has said or written." These are forms of appropriated discourse, and in this sense God may use human testimonies and events. But whatever may be the case, it is important — from a practical theological point of view — to realize that language has a mediating role in the communication of faith, and that this mediating function is not illogical.

A Comparison

What, then, is the result of my reflections on Van der Ven's thought? I believe that he does not do full justice to the subjectivity of God. When he says that a social event in the reality that surrounds us (usually) becomes a sign of God's salvation, the divine subject only enters the picture as a perspective from which things may be viewed but not as the center of consciousness and activity. In addition, God is less explicitly represented as a person, while this is an important facet of a speaking God. In Van der Ven's paradigm, the human being becomes the one who attributes meaning, albeit in the context of the tradition. This is because humans cannot provide solitary and arbitrary religious interpretations, since they are bound to religious conventions that are embedded in tradition. Nonetheless, humans are the prime element in the creation of meaning, while in linguistic discourse, at least as I have described it, humans are primarily the receivers, while God provides the meaning. The model of the speaking God more explicitly points to God's externality and priority.

This brings us to yet another issue: the particularity of the Christian tradition. What role is attributed to Christ in this creation of meaning? Van der Ven does mention Christ, but mainly with respect to motivation and inspiration prior to the act, and when he deals with the ultimate expectation and the critical (final) judgment. Remarkably enough, he hardly touches on the relationship between Christ and the religious sign. He discusses the sacramental nature of the church, but not the sacrament as such. As a result, the relationship between Christ and social phenomena in the reality that surrounds us remains rather vague. Do those things that become religious signs — that is, what emerges in our reality, such as love between people, reconciliation, social justice — do these things get their significance from Christ? And is there, in that sense, also a line from the past — from the divine revelation — to the present? It would appear that Van der Ven, as a "modern" theologian (a theologian rooted in the Enlightenment), tries to work with universally accepted criteria in his discussion of religious signs, and then subsequently attempts to absorb in this what is peculiar to Christianity. But that leads me to ask: Doesn't the sacrament as a sign have a unique character since it represents Christ? Whether we want to interpret the basic function of the church by means of categories of language or sacramental categories, in either case we cannot get away from the fact that salvation is mediated in and through Christ's work.

I believe that Van der Ven fails to give due attention to this theological normativity. Why is it always necessary to refer back to a norm? That has to do with the conviction that a unique *disclosure* of salvation took place in the revelatory discourse of the Old and the New Testaments. And since that reality still has an impact on the lives of people and on the things that happen in the world, the gospel spreads through the world by way of human discourse. This interpersonal discourse is indeed something very vulnerable, subject to perversion and misrepresentation. Unfortunately, another human measure does not exist.

Consensus and Dissensus

We have seen how Van der Ven puts great emphasis on striving toward consensus. He creates the impression that communication should eventually lead to consensus — via exchange and mutual understanding. It is not of material importance whether he derives this idea from Habermas and ultimately from the Enlightenment ideal of critical rationality, or whether it coincides with the Catholic aim of reaching an ecclesial consensus. But we should add a few remarks from the perspective of linguistic discourse. We know from rhetoric that human discourse must be viewed as persuasive discourse.[21] Kenneth Burke suggests that the key idea consists of "the use of words by human agents to form attitudes or to induce actions in other human agents."[22] The attempt to convince others is not foreign to a speech-act as such. It proceeds from the desire to create community, but certainly also from the realization that change and renewal is a precondition for any adequate form of communion. The intention to persuade has to do with the values one wishes to pursue.

I want to clarify this further. For many of us, "rhetoric" carries a negative meaning. We tend to think that it has to do with the unnecessary and enticing embellishments of language, with conscious misleading, with verbal abuse of power. But one can also maintain that rhetoric is based on a realistic view of life; often there is more dissent than consensus. In reality we find irreconcilable differences between people — in the areas of ethics, politics, and religion. And there are many instances where we cannot explain the different opinions on the basis of a common goal or a shared interest. Opinions and thoughts may remain diametrically opposed. In our post-Enlightenment era, we have

21. Cf. Richard R. Osmer, "Practical Theology as Argument, Rhetoric and Conversation," *The Princeton Seminary Bulletin* 18:1 (1997): 50.
22. Kenneth Burke, *A Rhetoric of Motives* (Berkeley, 1969), pp. 41, 43.

distanced ourselves more and more from the idea that all our convictions should ultimately converge in a common, rational, and universal value system. An entire nation may err, a scientific consensus may be overturned by a paradigm shift, and deceit may be a matter of strategy. In our modern society we see not only consensus but very often disunity, opposition, conflict, disagreement, separation, and division. The so-called common denominator is fragmented, and we experience exclusivism at least as much as we do inclusivism. In fact, doesn't the interaction between people presuppose a certain degree of inequality and differentiation? Isn't it kept going by attraction and repulsion, by opposition and challenge?

It would thus appear that the attempt to convince or persuade the other presupposes a certain plurality in thought. In any case, there is the realization that bonding and community do not happen automatically and that a transformation may be needed if genuine communion is to be attained — a change in attitude or insight. This explains why in interpersonal dialogue we try to convince others of our own values, opinions, and ideas. We try to bring others to the point where they will act in a way we desire or adopt a lifestyle we prefer. We do not hesitate to load our choice of words with an affective charge and to provoke their emotions. The classical distinction in rhetoric consists of the *logos,* the *pathos,* and the *ethos,* which the speaker uses to persuade his audience. But this does not take away from the fact that, in order to convince someone in a sincere manner, we must meet a few conditions: (1) take the other person utterly seriously and respect the free consent of the other, (2) believe that change is indeed possible, (3) be convinced that this change is beneficial to quality of life and to a mutual relationship.

The intent to convince implies an interest in the other and a desire to share something with the other. If we remind ourselves for a moment of the speaking of God, which we described earlier, and of the apostolic witness, we clearly discover a dynamic, performative effect. The Word of God aims toward change, turning around, renewal. I would not say that Van der Ven denies this. But I do think that he places too much emphasis on consensus as the criterion for truth and deals with dissensus in too harmonizing a manner. We can read that, for example, in his definition of religious communication, which is, he says, "the exchange of religious meanings, aimed at the development of an understanding and agreement within and between the participants and with religious tradition, in the perspective of religious reception, response, and reaction."[23] By "reception" he means the awareness of being addressed by God; by "response" he means the turning toward God, such as in prayer; and by "reaction" he means reaching out to other people in order to share the significance of faith. I would say that religious reception, response, and reaction are the goal of religious communication rather than a perspective. Van der Ven seems to suggest that the primary goal consists of mutual agreement and consensus.

23. Van der Ven, *Ecclesiology*, p. 56.

CHAPTER 8

How Do We Speak of God?

Practical theology deals with the concrete praxis of faith. In the previous chapters we have dealt with two important components: faith as it is present in the lives of people and the communication of faith. And we have found a close link between these two components: faith is itself a relationship, a communion, and it is expressed by means of interpersonal communication. But we are still faced with an important question that must be worked out in detail: How do we speak about God? In Part IV, I will offer two reconstructions of praxis that will, each in its own way, provide a picture of the reality and activity of God. In this chapter I would like to investigate a few preliminary questions of practical theology.

The Development of Practical Theological Theory

Practical theology occupies itself with concrete faith practice. We have defined this praxis as a relationship between God and the world, in which God is the speaking and acting subject. That brings us to this question: Can we clarify this further by enlisting theology? Or, on the other hand, should we remain silent about God? How do we deal with this issue?

A first — and rather obvious — answer is that practical theology seeks to develop a theoretical framework, which is one of the most important aspects of any academic discipline. The theoretical framework gives us insight into parts of reality and allows us to establish certain links. Practical theology is a discipline that focuses on practice, and for this study we have defined this practice as the praxis of faith. Compared to other theological disciplines, practical theology actually has a rather restricted domain of research: it studies the life of faith and the communication of faith. But that is clearly a very complex reality; for faith is embedded in the mental and psychosocial structure of human existence, and faith and human interaction are closely interwoven in the communication of faith. However, this complexity is not in itself a reason to abandon the creation of a theoretical framework. On the contrary, the more complex the field of study, the more urgent is the need for analysis of the various factors that play a role in this field and of the connection between them.

An Interdisciplinary Field of Study

Because our faith is embedded in our everyday life and in interpersonal communication, the study of practical theology demands an interdisciplinary approach, that is, one that takes into account the results of other sciences in its analysis and reflection.[1] As we reflect on our faith, we are also confronted with the human being as a spiritual and social being who uses language (all areas studied in the humanities and the social sciences). Thus it stands to reason that we, in our practical-theological reflection, make use of the findings of the humanities and social sciences. Yet, practical theology remains a theological discipline: the conceptualizing in the development of the theory is such that the basic concepts emerge from reflection on our faith tradition, which is the starting point for interaction with other disciplines. Theology is not an addendum to some sociological, psychological, or philosophical theory; though it has its own mandate, it must take note of the results of other disciplines at the same time — but not in the sense that practical theology simply follows the other sciences. Rather, practical theologians must think in terms of a critical correlation: critical in the sense that practical theology defines, on the basis of its specific understanding of praxis, the domain of inquiry, the nature of reality in this domain, and knowledge about this domain. When a theory is developed, the specific nature of the reality is recon-

1. Van der Ven, *Practical Theology,* p. 101.

structed, and a theological theory will deliver a reconstruction that is different from a psychological or sociological theory. In a theological reconstruction, the reality of religion is not primarily approached as a social or psychological phenomenon, but as the praxis of faith. Other academic disciplines may do the same, may do so on the basis of their own theoretical framework — on the basis of their psychological and sociological theories, for example. But practical theology reconstructs on the basis of a theological theory.

What is a theological theory? This question does not allow for one unambiguous answer; for example, it also applies to psychological theories. We may approach the reality of the human psyche from a behavioral, biological, materialistic, or constructivist angle. Each of these perspectives relies on distinct presuppositions, resulting in different reconstructions of the reality and knowability of the human self. A theological reconstruction of faith praxis is founded on the uniqueness of religion; that is, religion is not explained in terms of social cohesion or psychological development. Faith is to be approached from the point of view of its intrinsic meaning; it is to be determined from the perspective of establishing which data are relevant and how these data should be described and analyzed. As scientists, we always look at data on the basis of a theoretical framework, and the data we observe have an impact on our theory — even during the act of observation. This is not only true of theology but of all other human sciences.

Therefore, we cannot reconstruct a concrete aspect of praxis without any biases or values. The theoretical framework that is the basis for our observations already carries some presuppositions, such as theoretical axioms, as well as particular values and interests.[2] Since faith is an integral part of life and is intimately linked to our intellectual abilities and our psychosocial life, it will hardly surprise us that we can study faith from a number of very different perspectives. Faith is a phenomenon that belongs to our inner life; but it is also part of our psychological discourse, and it plays a role in the domains of society and culture. It is not difficult to imagine that there may be a world of difference between the perspectives and interests that inform the way we study faith.

2. Nicholas Wolterstorff, *Reason within the Bounds of Religion* (Grand Rapids, 1976), pp. 59-66.

Internal and External Perspective

The difference between a theological study of faith and an approach through the social sciences has at times been presented as the difference between an internal and external perspective. It has been suggested that the theological approach accepts the claims of faith, whereas an external perspective places these claims between brackets in its approach. It is argued that a theological approach is marked by personal involvement and engagement, while the social science approach would tend to be objective and at a distance. But this distinction is far from perfect, for it should be clear from the outset that the so-called external perspective also operates with certain theoretical presuppositions regarding the field of inquiry. The notion that using an external perspective serves as a guarantee for objective research is a fiction. It is very possible that this "external perspective" will filter out some important aspects. For example, the axiom *etsi deus non daretur* (as if there were no God) functions as just such a filter, and the result is that an essential factor, namely, the activity of God, is not considered. From the point of view of the human sciences, it may be relevant to put a filter on scientific inquiry, since the human sciences primarily study social reality. But from the angle of a theological study, it would be utterly strange if we were to ignore one of the central dimensions.

On the other hand, it is difficult to maintain the position that the internal perspective contains elements that are foreign to a scientific inquiry, while the external perspective reckons with generally accepted scientific insights. We may well wonder whether any domain of study can boast of generally accepted scientific insights. For isn't it true that theories provide a specific reconstruction of reality — and for that very reason are bound to differ? Do behaviorism and social constructionism share the same foundation? Associating a theological approach with an internal perspective does not lead us to conclude that other approaches depart from generally accepted axioms. Does an external perspective, in actual fact, exist? Whether theology takes as its point of departure a conviction that cannot be rationally defended — faith in the reality and the activity of God — calls for yet another discussion, which I cannot go into at this point.[3]

3. I refer to the philosophical discussion about foundational issues. See, e.g.,

How Do We Speak of God?

Etsi Deus non daretur?

That there is a degree of overlap between theology and the other human sciences can be explained in terms of the very nature of faith. We have already concluded that faith plays an important role in relationships between people. It is clear that the social sciences concentrate their attention particularly on what happens between people. Social theory views social order and society as human products. Sociologists do not study society from the perspective of a divine order but as a reality that is created and may be changed by human beings. Moreover, they also proceed from the assumption that there is a dialectical relationship between human beings and society.

Peter Berger described this very succinctly: "Society is a dialectic phenomenon in that it is a human product, and nothing but a human product, that yet continuously acts back upon its producer. Society is a product of man. It has no other being except that which is bestowed upon it by human activity and consciousness. Yet it may also be stated that man is a product of society."[4] When we view religion from this sociological perspective, it implies that we study religion — particularly the function of religion in society — as an empirical science, that is, as if there were no God *(etsi deus non daretur)*. This is quite logical from the point of view of the social sciences, which deal with the social dimension and would also study faith and religion from that angle. But it still depends on whether we leave space for the reality that faith may be seen as an authentic relationship between God and the world. Berger says that "sociological theory (and, indeed, any other theory moving within the framework of empirical disciplines) will always view religion *sub specie temporis,* thus of necessity leaving open the question whether and how it might also be viewed *sub specie aeternitatis.* Thus sociological theory must, by its own logic, view religion as a human projection, and by the same logic can have nothing to say about the possibility that this projection may refer to something other than the being of its projector."[5]

Alvin Plantinga, "Reason and Belief in God," in *Faith and Rationality,* ed. Alvin Plantinga and Nicholas Wolterstorff (Notre Dame, 1983), pp. 16-93; see also Wolterstorff, *Reason within the Bounds of Religion,* pp. 24-51.

4. Peter L. Berger, *The Sacred Canopy: Elements of a Sociological Theory of Religion* (New York, 1969), p. 3.

5. Berger, *The Sacred Canopy,* p. 180.

But not everyone is prepared to leave it at that. The idea that human beings themselves are the makers of religion — because of a latent need or a natural desire — is the basis for the critical stance toward religion that developed during the Enlightenment. In any case, the social sciences do not explain religion on the basis of its own intrinsic value but associate it with societal and social interests, idealizing or mental disturbances, or a perverted lust for power. Marx believed that the concept of mankind as the maker of religion lays the basis for the criticism of religion. Religion originates from self-consciousness and from a sense of self-worth, which humanity has either lost or has not yet attained. However, Marx does not detach the human being from his world; he is always concerned with the world of mankind, the social reality, and the state. This social reality gives birth to religion, which Marx happens to see as a wrong self-consciousness because the world itself is wrong.

Scientists approach religion more and more from an atheistic perspective, partly as a result of increasing secularization. With respect to practical theology, both a strong emphasis on an approach through the social sciences in the final decades of the twentieth century and a process of secularization have contributed to a devaluation of theological self-consciousness. Inspired by the theories of the social sciences, scientists suggested that the axiom *etsi deus non daretur* should also be applied to practical theology if it desired to be a scientific form of theological study. But practical theology has always been conscious of the fact that it has an independent status vis-à-vis the social sciences. For faith is its primary object. The question remains whether it has arrived at a reconstruction of the praxis of faith on the basis of its own specific theological responsibility.[6]

The Empirical Proviso: God-Language as Perspective

Van der Ven defines practical theology as empirical theology. On the one hand, he wants to say that practical theology studies actual praxis,

6. See Friedrich Schweitzer, "Practical Theology, Contemporary Culture, and the Social Sciences: Interdisciplinary Relationships and the Unity of Practical Theology as a Discipline," in Schweitzer and Van der Ven, eds., *Practical Theology: International Perspectives*, pp. 307-21.

and he uses empirical methods for this study that he has borrowed from the social sciences; on the other hand, he also wants to underscore that practical theology, in contrast to the social sciences, is in its research structured by theological theory. Van der Ven considers this aspect crucial, since the creation of theological concepts is the ultimate task of practical theology. The interdisciplinary nature is manifest in the fact that the empirical methods are derived from a discipline other than theology. Does this have consequences for the domain or the object of the inquiry? I would say that it does to the extent that what is being studied must be open to empirical research. This leads Van der Ven to conclude that the direct object of theology is not God but faith: God may be the direct object of faith, but not of theology. God can only be the object in an indirect way — to the extent that people believe they experience God. The object of the inquiry is found in the reception of the religious experience, the response in prayer and liturgy, and the reaction of people toward others. "Only in and through these multiple forms of reception, response and reaction and not outside of them is God indirectly accessible to theological research. The assumption is nonetheless that through this reception, response and reaction one at least draws nearer to God, that God's healing presence can be fragmentarily touched through them. These three elements can be empirically investigated, just as they can be studied by literary, historical and systematic means in theology."[7] The fact that God is indirectly accessible leads Van der Ven to the conclusion that God is himself "perspectivistically" present in a salvific way in the context of this reception, response, and reaction. We may say that we feel that God speaks to us, but the inquiry cannot go beyond this human reaction. Human ideas about, experiences of, and reactions toward God are empirically accessible, but God himself is not.

This empirical approach has met with all kinds of objections. It has been argued that it is a reductionist approach to faith, for not all aspects of faith praxis can be understood in empirical categories. How does this view deal with the mystery character of faith? Isn't it true that the mystery of God's presence in our life cannot be measured by this kind of inquiry? Van der Ven does not deny that we face a mystery when dealing with the topic of faith, but he still believes that our inquiry, however fragmentary and imperfect it may be, does provide us with

---

7. Van der Ven, *Practical Theology,* p. 104.

some insight. He insists that this empirical research from a theological perspective will reveal something of this mystery: "For however true it is that we are faced with this mystery about God and humanity, and however reluctant, fragmentary and imperfect our approach to it may be, nothing prevents [practical] theology from discovering, unraveling and revealing some aspect of this secret. And to those who think that this goes too far, I would like to say that nothing keeps [practical] theology from studying aspects of faith in the mystery of the human being and God."[8] This gives expression to the positive conviction that faith is important in human life and that it manifests itself in concrete forms. As a researcher, Van der Ven is curious about the actual content of faith praxis, and he believes that practical theology must study faith praxis. He does not deny that social science studies of the way religion functions also have great value; but that kind of research is informed by a social science interest and not by a theological interest. Practical theology studies praxis out of theological interest; consequently, it looks at the issues of content, which are closely associated with a specific faith tradition, by means of a conceptual framework that belongs specifically to that tradition.

Is Practical Theology Empirical Theology?

The question is not whether a study of praxis belongs to the *proprium* of practical theology. As a study of praxis, practical theology focuses its attention on a praxis domain and endeavors to chart that praxis in a responsible manner. Van der Ven himself has done an impressive job with his quantitative research and has thus contributed to the development of practical theology. Yet a discipline that studies praxis without empirical research may also contribute to an increase in understanding of the praxis field; however, this requires a solid knowledge of, and involvement with, the praxis domain. Thus it would be wrong to say that practical theology as an academic discipline coincides with empirical theology. This is certainly not the case internationally. But we may correctly conclude that empirical theology has given a strong boost to practical theology as a study of praxis.

8. Van der Ven, "Pastorale protocolanalyse I," p. 489.

We need to do some further thinking about whether the concept "empirical theology" is a fortunate term; it does provoke discussion, but it is also somewhat confusing because it tends to suggest that the research methodology, as it concerns the conceptual framework and its theoretical development, is determined by empiricism. We can see this inclination in Van der Ven. He pays a lot of attention to thinkers of the school of empirical pragmatism, and religious experience is the central concept in his analysis of faith praxis.[9] The *a priori* result is a particular structure in the approach toward praxis. There is no metaphysical or theoretical framework that describes faith in God as an interactive relationship between the divine and the human subjects. The reality of faith is understood and analyzed from the standpoint of the human subject, and the element of the divine object remains a matter of perspective. There is no framework that allows for a presentation of God as a speaking and acting subject.

Contrary to those who believe that religious faith is incapable of any conceptualization and quantification, Van der Ven maintains that he proposes a "moderate conceptual realism."[10] This formulation is rather vague and careful, but the essence is clear. Our human conceptualizing is not fully detached from reality. If that were the case, knowledge of reality would remain entirely impossible. The "moderate" nature is apparently in the fact that there is not a complete identification between concept and reality, but only "an aspectual identity."[11] I will go into greater detail when I deal with these underlying issues in Chapter 11, but I cannot avoid mentioning a few things here. I have no doubt that there is no complete identity between our understanding and the external reality; in most cases we only find a partial identity. My idea of what it would mean to be a cabinet minister of economic affairs, for example, would only partially coincide with what it actually means to be a minister of economic affairs. The reality is, no doubt, more complex that my understanding of it. But is that only a question of aspect? Possibly it is — in the sense that I understand certain aspects of it. But the "perspectivistic" notion seems less suitable.

But there is something else in Van der Ven's thinking that should

9. Van der Ven, *Practical Theology,* pp. 9, 10.
10. Van der Ven, "Pastorale protocolanalyse I," p. 489.
11. Van der Ven, *Practical Theology,* p. 131.

be noted. The question is whether we can know anything about things that are characterized as "mystery," for this is what we encounter in faith praxis. Can we know anything about our inner self, about the presence and reality of God? Doesn't every form of conceptualizing fail at this point? Van der Ven is correct when he says that there is even a degree of conceptualizing in these areas. For conceptualization is a prerequisite for knowledge, which means that in our reflection on, and analysis of, the praxis of faith — and thus when we are dealing with realities that are mysterious (such as human beings, God, and interaction) — we are confronted with a conceptualization of reality. Thus the question is whether this conceptualization allows for an understanding of reality. Do our concepts cover that reality? Can we actually know something of that reality? Wouldn't that be at variance with the mystery character?

Is God Only a Matter of Perspective?

I agree with Van der Ven that we can acquire knowledge of the reality of faith. We will not discover the full secret, but we will unravel aspects of it (which explains the term "moderate conceptual realism"). But the word "moderate" seems to create more confusion than clarity. (I will go a step further myself in Chapter 11, where I will defend the idea that our concepts do indeed link up with reality, and not only with human reality but also with divine reality.) Practical theology is not only concerned with knowledge about human faith but also with knowledge of the activity and presence of God, which I believe is incorrect to ignore as we seek to develop a practical theological theory.

This brings me to the term "perspectivistic." Van der Ven suggests that God is only spoken of in practical theology in a perspectivistic manner; he also uses the word "indirect" in this context, thereby driving a wedge between faith and theology. For he proposes that God can be the object of faith but not of (practical) theology; the faith of people is the object of practical theology, and that is open to empirical research. This leads to God's being reduced to a matter of perspective. When we take a closer look, this "moderate" conceptual realism now takes on a new meaning. Contrary to an identity between concept and reality, at least in certain aspects, we must now accept that concept and reality are connected by way of perspective. In other words, concepts from practical theology are directly related to the reality of faith and do only indirectly refer to God. The human being is the direct object of theology, while God is the indirect object — to the extent that God is present in the human experience and reactions. I believe that this corresponds with Van der Ven's opinions on the sign-character of salvation: something in reality points to the salvation God provides, and this sign is "perspectivistic." Van der Ven believes that empirical theology deals with signs, and that something of God becomes visible in those signs.

But it is questionable to detach human faith in this way from the reality of God. Is this distinction between God as the object of faith and the indirect object of theology tenable? Let us start with faith. There are people who believe in God; they have, I would assume, at least some knowledge of God. Is it direct knowledge? When God makes himself known in a discourse of speaking and acting, we encounter God in that discourse: we encounter God as the subject of word and action. We learn about God from his words and acts, his promises and commandments. Is that direct or indirect knowledge? It is indirect in the sense that, just as in the encounter with other people, we acquire knowledge about intention and character from the words that are spoken and from the activities we perceive. But it is direct in the sense that we meet the actual person. If this were not so, we would be incapable of knowing any other person. Do we know other people "perspectivistically"? I don't think this is an appropriate label. In our interpersonal interactions, knowing the other is linked to whether or not we have frequent intimate contact with the other and with the other's trustworthiness. In some cases we say, "I really got to know her." Faith in God has the same structure, and in some instances we may indeed speak of a real knowledge of God.

Let us move on to practical theology. Is God the object of practical theology? In other words, are God's words and acts the object of practical theology? Looking at the domain of our inquiry, the praxis of faith, we must say that faith understands itself as the reciprocal relationship between God and the world. We are dealing with an intersubjective communion. Theological reflection aims at the description of the domain of study from a theological angle, and this includes the reality of God and his salvation. But in the faith praxis of the church this also includes the mediation of this salvation by the church. In that sense it would seem correct to say that God's speaking and acting are the object of practical theology.

In the study of praxis, the testimony of God's speaking and acting is an important component, that is, we assume in our theological conceptualizing that the communion with Christ and with God has a real content. Of course, we are relying on statements made by human beings. But the point is that people don't merely refer to themselves in their statements; they also say something about God and his salvation. When we experience Christ's grace in Word and sacrament, we are not just dealing with our own experience as an experience, but also with the object of that experience. We are dealing with Christ in historical revelation and with him as the risen Lord. These are realities that faith knows as real. And as we "do" theology, we define those realities and the impact they have. Theology as an academic discipline, therefore, presupposes a metaphysical reconstruction of reality. This is what makes the term "empirical" confusing: it suggests that the reality that is being studied must fall within the confines of the empirical. But does the human self fall within the confines of the empirical? Can we empirically determine that another person has a soul, or has intellectual functions?

In our practical theological endeavors we use methods derived from other sciences. In a study of praxis there are many instances where the methods of quantitative and qualitative research used in the social sciences are quite helpful. Whether or not we speak of empirical methods in these cases has little relevance. The particular nature of practical theology is not based on the method used but on the theological conceptual framework.

A Hermeneutical Proviso:
Faith as Human Interpretation

The study of practical theology in the last few decades of the twentieth century has felt a strong impact not only from the action-theoretical paradigm but also from the hermeneutical tradition. This latter school of thought is represented in America by Don Browning and in Europe, for example, by Heitink, Dingemans, and Schweitzer.[12] It concerns an

12. See Friedrich Schweitzer, "Practical Theology, Contemporary Culture," pp. 307-21.

approach toward praxis that has a certain intuitive plausibility but is not always placed in a clear theoretical framework. The difficulty is in the strong reliance on a philosophical current of thought from within the Continental European tradition, which is applied to a practical theological setting.[13] In itself this is not objectionable, but it is at times difficult to discover how the argument runs and to understand what relationship there is between theological and nontheological motives.

The notion of interpretation has assumed a central role in practical theology. The dominant idea is that reality is always an interpreted reality: we always observe things within a particular interpretative framework and should not have the illusion that we acquire knowledge about "objective reality." Dingemans describes the point of departure as follows:

> Every hermeneutical theory will start with stating that there is no "Archimedic point" from which the world may be interpreted without bias or uncertainty. There is no absolute ontological or objective, nor any absolute anthropological or subjective certainty to be found.[14]

The presupposition is that there are no objective facts. Facts are always facts-for-the-individual or facts-within-the-human-horizon-of-understanding. Reality does not consist of a state of affairs, something that lies before us, but of something that a person understands in a particular way. Objective knowledge does not exist, for there is a multitude of possible interpretations, depending on the context within which the person understands.

Hermeneutics deals particularly with the way human understanding functions within the context of history; and thus history is primarily seen as history of the mind. Humanity itself shapes life as it develops historically; subsequently, humans are able to understand their own history. We owe this possibility to the specific ability of the human mind to place ourselves in the position of others. This ability allows us to acquire knowledge about the past. The human sciences, in particular, analyze the process of the social organization and historical development of mankind.

13. Gerben Heitink, *Practical Theology*, pp. 178-200.
14. Dingemans, *Manieren van doen*, p. 150.

The Principle of Reciprocity

The dimension of an ongoing history also plays an important role in the practical theological reception of hermeneutics. This leads to a constant reciprocity between tradition and the present; and this tension is the basis from which praxis is analyzed. "The field of inquiry of a practical theological hermeneutic," Schweitzer says, "is determined by the fact that, on the one hand, it includes the Christian tradition, while, on the other hand, it also embraces contemporary religious expressions, or expressions associated with religion."[15] This structure is quite clear in Dingemans's work; there is no question of any absolutely trustworthy access in the process of acquiring knowledge: "Constantly interpreting and standing in the tradition of interpretations of truth claims, and listening to the judgments of the interpreting communities in which we find ourselves . . . most people discover enough certainty to remain in balance in their lives."[16] We are part of on ongoing process in the development of humanity — without any firm point where we can get our bearings.

It does not become clear where the reciprocity is precisely located. It is a dialogue between the normative culture, on the one hand, and the tradition of the faith communities, on the other (with the stories of the biblical tradition in the background) — a dialogue that must proceed without norms.[17] "We test existing interests, needs, rules, roles, customs, rational insights and ideas that have developed over time to see whether they conform to new insights and the interpretation of our sources."[18] I believe that this implies a continuous regression. We bring experiences of the present or, to put it differently, interpretations of the world around us into dialogue with the interpretation of our sources. It remains unclear whether these sources have themselves been interpreted already on the basis of our newly acquired insights or can still function as a critical "over and against." The regression lies in the fact that one interpretation may cause or

15. Schweitzer, "Praktische Theologie und Hermeneutik," p. 33.

16. Dingemans, *Manieren van doen,* p. 164.

17. Dingemans, "Normativiteit in de praktische theologie," in *Lijden en belijden. Over de Derde Gestalte van het Antwoord,* ed. J. H. van de Bank and R. Brouwer (Zoetermeer, 1993), p. 57.

18. Dingemans, "Normativiteit in de praktische theologie," p. 57.

produce the other, which means that there is no longer any question of a critical dialogue. It does not really become clear that the dialogue contains a "critical" moment and that there is an "opposite" partner in the process of interpretation. For the human being continues to be the *interpretant,* and Dingemans fails to indicate where in the reciprocity we might find a criterion for our testing and how such a criterion would function.

Correlation

Following in the steps of Browning, Dingemans combines his hermeneutical approach with a correlational theology. Browning suggests that this correlation has to do with the plausibility of religion in modern society. If religion is to have any meaning in modern culture, the Christian faith must be translated into generally accessible concepts and experiences. Browning believes that the crucial point of the correlation is found in the practical-ethical significance of Christian communities. Because of this point of departure, if it wishes to be plausible in modern life, the praxis of faith must enter into a continuous dialogue with the interpretations of the Christian message, on the one hand, and the interpretations of and experiences in contemporary culture, on the other.[19] In this method of correlation, Dingemans says, there is no unambiguous point, neither in the objectivity nor in the subjectivity. Dingemans further explains the correlation as a form of interaction between God and the world, between revelation and experience.[20] God and his revelation are absorbed in the ongoing process of history, and they meet us in the contours of streams of interpretation. So once again we perceive that there is no absolute point where we can get our bearings. We are wrapped up in the historical process of culture, of which our faith praxis is also a part. Values are, at least to some extent, variable things that may be superseded by historical developments. In any case, they are subject to a complex process of change. "Even God himself," Dingemans argues, "is subject to a process of

19. Don S. Browning, *A Fundamental Practical Theology: Descriptive and Strategic Proposals* (Minneapolis, 1991), pp. 44-46.
20. Dingemans, *Manieren van doen,* p. 157.

change, while he remains true to himself. God is new every morning, without letting go of his original intentions."[21]

The Identity of Faith

In spite of everything, Dingemans's twofold model of reciprocity, which is based on his hermeneutics and his method of correlation, does not quite succeed. There is a strange — yet perhaps fortunate — inconsistency in his theology, for he says: "Faith in actual fact rests on a particular, fundamental interpretation of reality that lacks a rational foundation."[22] Apparently, there is a foundation after all that is not subject to any constantly progressing interpretation and needs no further argumentation in order to be plausible. That is where we find the identity of the Christian faith, the foundation of the Christian faith, the basic characteristic that determines the distinction between Christian churches and all other associations: the confession that Jesus is the Christ, that Jesus is Lord. But can this be something that needs no further interpretation? At this point Dingemans suddenly introduces the idea of archetypal experiences, or foundational interpretations, or archetypal understanding. But if this particular idea allows for an exception to the rule that interpretation is everything, we may well ask whether the rule itself has not been falsified. Apparently, Dingemans cannot ignore the question of identity in the end — and consequently the question of normativity.

In my view, this means that we cannot simply approach the praxis of faith from a hermeneutical angle. There is no doubt that the Christian faith is a historical religion and that historical transmission plays an important role in the Christian faith tradition. God makes himself known in the history of Israel and in the life of Jesus. And Dingemans rightly observes that professing that Jesus is the Christ determines the identity of the Christian tradition. Historical revelation plays a crucial role in the ecclesial mediation of salvation. We fall short in our analysis of the praxis of faith if we try to explain that process of salvation mediation solely in terms of the cultural-historical tradition. Dingemans

---

21. Dingemans, *Manieren van doen,* p. 161.
22. Dingemans, *Manieren van doen,* p. 167.

makes an exception in the ever-continuing interpretative process for the confession of Jesus as Lord because divine salvation is revealed in the person and life of Jesus. This is the event that the Christian communion confesses to be the once-for-all realization of the revelation and salvation of God. The revelation of this salvation is not our interpretation but is found in the words and acts of God. This brings us to a totally different dimension of reality: the metaphysical reality of the communion between God and the world, which implies that God addresses the world in word and deed. Practical theology is a theological discipline that studies this reality. We will see in Chapter 11 that it is essential for the divine subject logically to precede the human subject. And there we shall once again discover that the axiom of an all-encompassing human interpretation is inadequate.

The Search for God in Practical Theology

We find a tendency in empirical, as well as in hermeneutical, practical theology to approach the reality and the presence of God in the praxis of faith indirectly. As a result, the theological nature of practical theology is less pronounced, and the difference in the approach to religious praxis by the human sciences is somewhat obscured. The following chapters will explicitly deal with the search for God. The reasoning will be that we cannot adequately analyze the praxis of faith from a practical theological perspective if we reduce God to ideas and imaginations about God, or to human experiences of God, or to "God" as a religious symbol in a social-cultural system of meaning. The revelation of God and his salvation — and its presence in our world — belongs to the domain of practical theology. This in no way places the human world outside the field of inquiry; for it concerns the praxis of faith — and in that sense the praxis of people. But faith itself has an inner dynamic that must be analyzed on the basis of our communion with God.

Chapters 9 and 10 will deal with two reconstructions, each of which approaches God in its own way. The first approach emphasizes the revelatory perspective, God's movement toward the world. In the second approach, the anthropocentric perspective, the center of gravity is situated in anthropology, putting the full emphasis in our speaking of God on human experiences and ideas about God. In the first model the divine subject makes himself accessible in human reality, while in the second model the human subject becomes the central pole of the faith praxis. Both models will be clarified when we look at praxis in pastoral work and homiletics. I have intentionally selected these subdisciplines because proclamation plays an important role in the revelatory model and because pastoral care has seen a significant development in the anthropocentric model. In Chapter 11, I will deal in a thematic way with some of the problems in the underlying assumptions behind the two models.

PART IV

Reconstructions of Praxis

CHAPTER 9

The Revelatory Perspective

The Theological Structure

Jüngel tells us that we must understand Barth's position regarding the knowledge of faith in such a way that our knowledge of God becomes, in fact, part of the doctrine of God.[1] We would expect to see that knowledge of God is the human knowledge we have of God. But Barth turns it around: knowledge of God is primarily the knowledge that God has about himself. Barth begins, not from anthropology, but from the doctrine of the Trinity. God knows himself. God is the subject of his own being; God is subsequently also the subject of his becoming-to-be-known; finally, God is the subject of our knowing of him. The human subject is able to acquire genuine knowledge about God, not because of anything humans do themselves but only because God makes himself accessible. Our knowledge of God is part of the doctrine of God, says Barth, "because it can only consist in a representation *(Darstellung)* of the being and activity of God."[2]

> God is *gegenständlich* (objective) and therefore He can be truly known. He encounters man. He encounters him in such a way that man can also know Him. He encounters him in such a way that in that encounter God is and remains God and thus raises man up really to be a knower of himself. But that this is the case is wholly and utterly God's own being and work, which man can only follow.[3]

1. Eberhard Jüngel, *Gottes Sein ist im Werden*, 4th ed. (Tübingen, 1986), p. 54.
2. Barth, *Church Dogmatics* II/1, p. 32.
3. Barth, *Church Dogmatics* II/1, p. 32.

Our knowledge of God has been included in God's movement toward man. This same movement is also included in the notion of the Word of God. God enters the sphere and the reach of people by proclaiming his presence and by entering into a relationship with humans. "God speaks; He claims; He promises; He acts; He is angry; He is gracious. Take away the objectivity of this He, and faith collapses, even as love, trust and obedience."[4] This view of the relationship between God and the world emphasizes two dimensions: in the first place, it is a free act of God and not a self-evident relationship; secondly, humans do not have God at their disposal in any way. Nevertheless, humans get to know God in this *Gegenständlichkeit* as God really is. God does not hold back in any way; God identifies himself fully with what he has revealed.

In this concept God is the object of human knowledge, but he is not an object in the same way that other objects are. God is a subject who freely chooses to make himself present. He becomes present in the act of his revelation, and he cannot be known apart from this act of grace.[5] There is an undeniable actualistic element in this epistemology: it only happens when God makes himself known, and human subjects cannot record or retain this in their inner selves. The possibility of knowing God is restricted to God's self-revelation, which prevents any embedding of the knowledge of God in anthropology. However, it is about genuine knowledge, for God is revealed in phenomenal reality. He binds himself to the realities of time and space. "God is objectively [*gegenständlich*] immediate to Himself, but to us He is objectively mediate."[6] That is, God meets us in the *Gegenstände* (objects) of the world of phenomena. Humans thus stand before God in an indirect way; God encounters us in the signs of this world, and these hide him at the same time. Revelation is simultaneously a hiding. Thus Barth, like Van der Ven, emphatically speaks about God in the reality that surrounds us. The difference, however, is that it is not man but God who is the *interpretant*. In the revelation of God, as well as in the knowledge about God, God remains the *unaufhebbares* (unremovable) Subject. Nothing in reality has the power to point to God in itself, but God chooses to

4. Barth, *Church Dogmatics* II/1, p. 13.
5. Barth, *Church Dogmatics* II/1, p. 23.
6. Barth, *Church Dogmatics* II/1, p. 16.

use something that becomes the instrument of his presence. We cannot choose the *Gegenstände,* but we do acknowledge God in the *Gegenstände* he has decided to choose.[7] It always concerns events and situations in which God reveals himself, and in that sense God is known in his works.

I believe that Barth's concept of revelation contains an enormous tension. On the one hand, he wants to indicate that God makes himself known in the world of phenomena, and that God is fully present there; on the other hand, he wants to give full due to God's freedom and subjectivity by emphasizing that God does not coincide with his revelation. The revelation retains its sign-character. And even though God makes himself fully known in his revelation, it nonetheless remains his second *Gestalt.* But for us the revelation remains the primary form in which we know him. However, Barth tells us to refer back to God's primary *Gegenständlichkeit* as the Trinitarian self-consciousness. This means that God chooses in freedom to reveal himself. God decides to be present in the phenomenal world. And even though God reveals himself completely, it remains a divine initiative over which humans cannot and may not have power. This referral — and seen from our human perspective it is indeed a referral backwards — to the primary *Gegenständlichkeit* in the Trinitarian self-consciousness functions as an undergirding of the divine freedom in revelation. Because of this referral to the divine initiative behind revelation, which becomes visible in revelation, Barth continues to speak about a paradoxical identity between God and his revelation.

So we participate indirectly in the knowledge of God. God comes forward in a reality that is distinct from him; God hides in a world that is not identical with him. Barth says that revelation is a sacrament, that is, God becomes present through the creaturely world.[8] The outlines of God are, as it were, drawn for us. The *Realgrund* of this is the human nature of Christ; in unison with the eternal Word, that createdness becomes a sign of God.

> Because the eternal Word Himself became flesh, because the revelation of God took place once and for all in Jesus Christ, we know the

7. Barth, *Church Dogmatics* II/1, pp. 17, 18.
8. Barth, *Church Dogmatics* II/1, p. 52.

same revelation of God wherever it is attested in experience and rec-ollection.[9]

This presents us with a normative criterion: God is revealed to us in Je-sus Christ, and we know God fully in Jesus. And there is a retrospective continuity from Jesus Christ backward to the history of the people of Israel and a forward continuity to the apostolate and the church that was founded by it. Jesus Christ's humanity is the first sacrament, and this puts Jesus on a pedestal as a unique person.

It is clear that this model emphasizes God's movement toward man. But does it do justice to human subjectivity? Doesn't this posi-tion human beings completely in God and in Christ? What remains of the human "over against" God in the relationship? I will evaluate the revelationary model on the basis of Eduard Thurneysen's view of the pastorate and Karl Barth's view of homiletics.

Proclamation in the Pastorate

What are the consequences for our understanding of faith praxis? Thurneysen, more than anyone else, has pointed to the crucial conse-quences for practical theology. In the praxis of the church, he says, we are concerned with the proclamation of the Word of God. "The event of the proclamation of the Word of God is the real object of all prac-tical theology."[10] Thurneysen does not restrict himself to preaching in the worship service, but views the Word of God as a living, concrete word that enters our human existence. It is the repetition and re-newal of the word of the first witnesses: their story is a continuing story that continues to come to us as a new word. Practical theology focuses on the *Akt dieses weiterlaufens des Zeugnisses* (act of this ongoing testimony).[11]

This has far-reaching consequences for the way we understand praxis. In this model all practical theological disciplines are brought under the umbrella of proclamation: that is, all sectors of the church's

---

9. Barth, *Church Dogmatics* II/1, pp. 53, 54.
10. Eduard Thurneysen, *Die Lehre von der Seelsorge* (Zurich, 1946), p. 9.
11. Thurneysen, *Die Lehre*, p. 10.

praxis — whether liturgy, catechesis, church growth, or pastoral work — are ultimately concerned with the proclamation of the Word of God. Praxis consists of many quite different activities, but proclamation holds center stage. Christ as the living Word puts his claim on our whole life, and we are touched in our entire person by that Word. Even pastoral work comes under the umbrella of proclamation, because it is in essence the declaration of the message to the individual. Therefore, pastoral work has no content different from the other forms of proclamation; the only difference is that pastoral work occurs in the private sphere.

Numerous objections have been raised to this kerygmatic approach to pastoral care. The psychotherapy-oriented model, which emerged subsequently, voiced as its major criticism the fact that the kerygmatic approach fails to due justice to the pastoral conversation as discourse. Scharfenberg even refers to the abuse of conversation in the kerygmatic model: his criticism concerns both the method of conversation as well as the content.[12] According to Scharfenberg, the pastoral dialogue must be open and equal; when the pastoral visit essentially becomes a proclamation of God's grace, the dialogue as such suffers. At that moment the conversation takes on an element of a sermon or of the liturgy, and he considers this a foreign element, since the *partnerschaftliche Gegenseitigkeit* (being as partners at different sides of the table) is crucial to any genuine conversation. Of course, there are different roles in the conversation, but Scharfenberg points out that a conversation is, as a matter of principle, nonauthoritarian in nature. He also stipulates that the freedom of the person receiving pastoral care has to be guaranteed. He suggests that this kind of conversation consists of discussion and deliberation, and it would be wrong for one conversation partner simply to address the other, or for one participant to enter the conversation with a predetermined agenda. "Any conversation that only serves as an occasion for communicating a predetermined message, which is, for example, related to the past and is supposed to be known and available, must be labeled authoritarian."[13]

Scharfenberg believes that pastoral work viewing itself as proclamation expects far too much from information transfer. "Proclamation

---

12. Joachim Scharfenberg, *Seelsorge als Gespräch* (Göttingen, 1974), p. 14.
13. Scharfenberg, *Seelsorge als Gespräch*, p. 19.

— the term points to the declaration of something that is certain, unchangeable, objectively predetermined, something that one of the participants did not yet know, and that is transferred to the other in a coercive and authoritarian way."[14] Aside from the distortion in this caricature, the problem is clear. Is it allowed to introduce a "foreign" reality into the conversation? Does that put an end to the conversation? On whose authority does it happen?

On the other hand, it is argued that a therapeutic approach to pastoral conversation fails to do justice to the dimension of faith. Tacke says that, in the therapeutic model, "the *Gottesrelation des Glaubens* (communion with God through faith) is embedded and dissolved in a relation of dialogue between the participants in the conversation. And this results in a *Divinisierung des Humanen* (divination of the human) and an anthropologizing of salvation."[15] The mediation of the gospel, where God as the source of salvation is the explicit theme, disappears beyond the horizon. Opposing the therapeutic model, Tacke maintains that the pastoral dialogue may also be understood in terms of *Glaubenshilfe* (assistance in faith). And faith, he continues, is a power that does not arise from the person himself but rather takes hold of the individual who is imprisoned in himself.[16] Tacke further refers to the justification of the sinner: God places us in the freedom of Christ. Tacke says that the pastoral conversation should indeed be free of any coercive element, but he fails to see how the proclamation of the justification of the sinner would be at cross-purposes with that.

The Pastoral Conversation

The following dilemma emerges from this preliminary exploration: it follows from the revelationary model that praxis is focused on the proclamation of divine grace, and this leads to the question of whether that is in tension with the nature of interpersonal conversation in the pastoral setting. Doesn't proclamation hinder free conversation? I will

14. Scharfenberg, *Seelsorge als Gespräch,* p. 26.
15. See Nicol, *Gespräch als Seelsorge,* p. 119.
16. Helmut Tacke, *Mit dem Müden zur rechten Zeit zu reden. Beiträge zu einer bibelorientierten Seelsorge* (Neukirchen-Vluyn, 1989), p. 112.

respond to that question and try to do justice to Thurneysen's theological position. But based on the discussion in Chapter 4, I cannot help but conclude that it is precisely his theological one-sidedness that puts him in a fruitless dilemma.

Let there be no doubt that Thurneysen sees the pastoral encounter as interpersonal conversation in the first place. His critics overlook the fact that both participants, the pastor and the layperson, are at the same level in their relationship to the Word of God. They talk together about God, and "both attempt in the conversation they have together to hear and speak the Word of God. . . . I say: both people!"[17] If this element is missing, there can be no pastoral conversation. So Thurneysen does not believe that the pastor possesses something that she then transfers to the other. Both are dependent on the Word of God, and together they listen to it. Hearing the Word and responding to the Word are the central issues, and each partner may thus serve the other.

The difficulty in a correct understanding of Thurneysen lies in the fact that the term "Word of God" as a theological concept entails a certain degree of abstraction. It is the word of grace with which God encounters us; it is the actual peace of Christ in which we are placed; it is the word of forgiveness of sins through which we effectively become new persons; it is the word that causes sinners to become recipients of grace.[18] The expression "Word of God" is an umbrella concept under which the sound of *iustificatio* is distinctly heard and the element of promise is distinctly present. If we do not keep these notions in mind, misunderstandings may abound. God's Word is first of all an activity of God himself; for both partners in the pastoral conversation, it is a "foreign" word, which they can only repeat. The entire conversation is preconditioned by the Holy Spirit, who makes the prophetic and apostolic Word new and makes it alive.

What I want to emphasize is that we should not criticize Thurneysen too quickly for identifying the Word of God with what the pastor says, nor for transferring the authority of the Word to the person of the pastor. Thurneysen does not confuse the interpersonal conversation with speaking about God. The Word of God may happen during the conversation, but it is not within human ability to make it

17. Thurneysen, *Die Lehre*, p. 98.
18. Thurneysen, *Die Lehre*, pp. 141-42.

happen. This is comparable to Barth's doctrine of revelation: we discover here a paradoxical identity of the conversation between people and the Word of God; the one does not automatically allow us to assume the other. This detaching from human capability is also clear from the fact that Thurneysen does not follow the Romantics' idea that speaking is primarily a mode of expression. He does not deny that man is a spiritual being endowed with the ability of speech; but he refuses to deduce from this the communication of faith, as Schleiermacher does. "The entire person, also the person endowed with speech, is subject to sin. In spite of his endowment with speech, he can no longer speak with God, nor hear the Word of God."[19] Thus the Word of God does not lie hidden somewhere at the bottom of the soul, from whence it can be resuscitated with the assistance of the Bible. It is a *verbum alienum* that can only be repeated.

A Rupture in the Conversation

With this background in mind, we may get a better understanding of the controversial idea of a rupture in the pastoral conversation. When he speaks of this, Thurneysen uses the image of a canyon cutting through mountains and separating the steep rock from the flat glacier. The entire pastoral conversation is intersected by such a line of rupture. The conversation is cut through, disturbed, broken, and overcharged by the sign of God's Word. This is the overhanging cliff that stays with us in the background: the judgment that has already been pronounced by God in his self-revelation. We might call it a *pre*-judgment. "The conversation is led to the point where it takes the major, pastoral turn towards this disturbance, this rupture, namely through the hearing of the Word of God."[20] According to Thurneysen, this rupture does not take away from the attentive and constant listening of the pastor. The pastor is completely tuned in to the concrete life situation of the client — to his or her social, psychological, and personal needs. But how could the conversation really be pastoral if a glimmer of the light of judgment and grace in Jesus Christ is absent?

19. Thurneysen, *Die Lehre*, p. 93.
20. Thurneysen, *Die Lehre*, p. 127.

The conversation takes place with the grace of God as presupposition, a grace that places life in a different and new perspective. It would be heartless if the pastor did not confront the client with this.

Grözinger believes that this idea of rupture — despite the misunderstandings it might evoke — in fact clearly indicates what is at stake in every conversation that seeks to help the other: the victory over what is empirically given and the taste of something new. If this does not take place, the conversation, says Grözinger, becomes a tautological waffle. But when there is a rupture, something new will come to light through that rupture. It does not appear from itself; it demands change. The rupture points to something unexpected, such as a work of art that opens the eyes to something unusual. When God enters our life, the old breaks into pieces and something new replaces what has been broken.[21]

It is characteristic of this approach, I believe, that the human being is addressed from God's perspective and definitely not the other way around. Thurneysen approaches humans on the basis of the *iustificatio* in Christ, with particular reference to the forensic act. For that reason the dialectic between sin and grace plays a central role in his anthropology: between God and humans lies not only creation but also the dark mystery of sin, which has so completely disturbed the relationship between God and humanity. But grace provides for the continued pronouncement of God's Word over the sinful person. "God's Word is in its very nature and from the very beginning a word of grace to the sinner."[22] When we thus find our point of departure in the God who reveals himself, we will definitely know what it means that humans live under the umbrella of God's grace. Forgiveness is not something to which we are en route, but it is something that is already bestowed on us. According to Thurneysen, if we want to know what our actual situation is, we only need turn to Jesus Christ. Our own experience is not decisive; what is decisive is who we are in Christ. This acquittal may be heard in the pastoral conversation, in which we carefully listen to the other person. From that perspective we may reach out to each other.

---

21. Albrecht Grözinger, "Eduard Thurneysen," in *Geschichte der Seelsorge in Einzelporträts,* ed. Christian Möller, vol. 3 (Göttingen/Zurich, 1996), p. 283.

22. Thurneysen, *Die Lehre,* p. 56.

God speaks to us. And I wish to add a second qualification — that Thurneysen's model is without any anchoring in the human subject. This is where we discover the one-sidedness of this model: there is not a single point of contact in the human being, neither in the natural sinful person nor in the born-again person. From beginning to end, it is from God toward man. The anchoring in the human subject that results in reciprocity, that leads us to knowledge, love, and discipleship, and that creates an inner renewal — all of this Thurneysen views with suspicion. He believes that an improper shift has taken place in the *Neuprotestantismus* (and also in Pietism) from God as subject toward humans as subject, with the result that humans have become the center. What God does is subtracted from what man experiences. "It is not primarily the work of God in man, but rather the work of man, namely his awakening to a new life, is brought to the front."[23] Sanctification becomes an independent theme, detached from justification. Thurneysen says that the attention shifts from the effects of justification, such as remorse and repentance, to a new act — of which man himself is the agent. In Pietism, human piety stands alongside divine activity, and Thurneysen is totally against that. Apparently, he is so wary of the self-elevation of the pious person that the human element remains the predicate of the divine activity. Christ is and remains the subject from which everything else proceeds.

The Sermon as Proclamation

The revelationary model emphasizes the sermon as the proclamation of the Word of God. The focus is not primarily on the sermon as a human public address (the rhetorical aspect), nor on the process of understanding on the part of the hearers (the reception). It is small wonder, then, that the communicative process as such receives little attention. The theological content is the most important aspect because the sermon is human testimony to a divine event. Barth has worded this very succinctly:

> Proclamation is human speech in and by which God Himself speaks like a king through the mouth of his herald, and which is

23. Thurneysen, *Die Lehre*, p. 62.

meant to be heard and accepted as speech in and by which God Himself speaks, and therefore heard and accepted in faith as divine decision concerning life and death, as divine judgment and pardon, eternal Law and eternal Gospel both together.[24]

The sermon is — in the form of a human public address — a proclamation of the kingdom of God, that is, of the rule of God as this was manifested in Jesus Christ. Proclamation is the announcement, the public declaration, the testimony of an event *(Ereignis)*. It is not a contemplation of this rule but a proclamation that it has come. In order to avoid any misunderstanding, we need to emphasize that the sermon itself does not coincide with God's speaking but is a human activity that is subservient to the Word. Barth himself later says that the sermon is "not itself the kingdom of God, the divine seizure of power. It makes known the fact that this has happened. It is the proclamation of Jesus as Lord, the giving of factual information and the summons to an appropriate attitude of repentance and faith."[25] Any attempt to equate the authority of the sermon or of the preacher with the Word of God must be strongly rejected. Moreover, this proclamation does not allow for any self-authorized interpretation: the servant is bound as a herald to the word of the king. Barth derived this metaphor of the herald from an article by Friedrich on the meaning of the word *kerusso* (to proclaim) in the New Testament. According to Friedrich, the issue is the rule of God, and the sermon is not an enlightening speech on the nature of God's kingdom; it is the proclamation of that kingdom. Referring to Romans 10:17 ("Consequently faith comes from hearing the message, and the message is heard through the word of Christ"), Friedrich emphasizes the fact that the sermon and the active presence of Christ belong together. A herald goes through the country and announces what the king has to say. Likewise, Friedrich says, the content of the message is not determined by the situation of the reader, nor by the knowledge of the preacher; it has been predetermined as the proclamation of the divine kingdom.[26]

The metaphor of the herald has had a strong impact on the Barthian homiletical tradition. It has been understood to signify that

24. Barth, *Church Dogmatics* I/1, p. 51.
25. Barth, *Church Dogmatics* IV/2, p. 208.
26. Friedrich, "Kerusso," in *Theologisches Wörterbuch zum Neuen Testament*, ed. Gerhard Kittel, vol. 3 (Stuttgart, 1938), p. 710.

the person of the herald is of little importance in the communication of the message, and that the herald has no reason to worry too much about the situation of the hearers; for what is at stake is the message, and both the messenger and the listeners play a subordinate role. And Thurneysen, of all people, has reinforced that idea. In an article dating from 1921 (in dialectical theology the phase of *diastasis* and criticism), Thurneysen fulminates against the suggestion that we can make the message understood and can facilitate its entrance into a person's life by human means. There is an unbridgeable gap, he says, between the Word of God and the word of the preacher. To be a witness is a tremendous challenge, and only God is able to let his Word sound through the word of a human. Only the preacher who realizes that no human being may take God's Word in his mouth is allowed to do so. The witness, as he speaks of life, must die to everything that is human.

Thurneysen then makes four recommendations: (1) No rhetoric! The sermon must steer clear of every form of rhetoric. The preacher does not speak from his own impulses but purely from a commission. The greatest preachers and prophets spoke in spite of their own inclinations and emotions. (2) No attempt to address the needs of the hearers! Do not be concerned about the psychology of the listener and so-called knowledge of the person who hears. The sermon is not intended to communicate life experiences or pious statements, nor is it intended to arouse experiences and feelings in others. What, then, is the purpose of the sermon? Its goal is *Gotteserkenntnis* (recognition of God) and *Gottesverkündigung* (proclamation of God). When the human experience is placed in the center, the divine only serves as a perspective on life; God is present only because of humans and thus becomes an idol. (3) The sermon is not intended to put people at ease and build them up, but rather to break them down! We must question everything about humanity *(im-Frage-stellen)*, and this we do by portraying the breaking through of the coming, entirely different, new world of God. (4) No constant variation in the preaching! The whole message and the same message must be given every Sunday, for the only concern is that we speak of God. Thurneysen fears that otherwise "God" becomes a *Begleitmelodie für das Menschliche* (accompanying melody for what is human).[27]

---

27. Eduard Thurneysen, "Die Aufgabe der Predigt," in *Aufgabe der Predigt*, ed. Gert Hummel (Darmstadt, 1971), pp. 105-18.

We should not judge the kerygmatic tradition on the basis of Thurneysen's polemical yardstick. But the idea of the proclamation of God's Word is indeed fundamental. The sermon is a human form of address, but in that address God himself speaks to us. Bohren calls the sermon *Namenrede* (naming God).[28] It presupposes divine revelation in Jesus Christ. And since the sermon is restricted to the *Woher* (from where?) and the *Wohin* (where to?) of the message, it cannot be an open exchange about all kinds of themes. Our preaching takes place against the background of the Incarnation of the Word and stands in the expectation of the kingdom of God.[29] Preaching occurs between those two poles. "The sermon is not a neutral activity, nor an action between two partners, for it can only consist of lordship on God's side and obedience on man's side."[30] That inequality is part and parcel of the sermon as proclamation, but we must not transfer that inequality to the relationship between speaker and hearer. Admittedly, this could present us with a major problem: Can we easily distinguish between the power relationship in which the kerygma presents itself and the balance of power in interpersonal communication? In addition, we must remind ourselves that the metaphor of the herald is rooted in a feudal social system. How can this function in a culture shaped by Western democracy?

The kerygmatic tradition has been criticized in recent homiletic literature for making the sermon too much of a one-way street — with very little room for reciprocity. But even though the revelationary model primarily beats a theological drum, this does not mean that there is no attention to the human side. The question is, how is the human being served? How does one see the world? In the sermon, so the argument goes, the circle of light that shines forth from revelation falls over the world, and we are addressed from this circle of light. Barth points out that the speaker must realize from the start that she or he addresses people in their ultimate existence, as it is founded in the remembrance of Christ and the promise of the kingdom. It is true for the people to whom the preacher speaks: Christ has died for you and has

---

28. Rudolf Bohren, *Predigtlehre,* 5th ed. (Munich, 1986), p. 90.

29. Karl Barth, *Homiletik. Wesen und Vorbereitung der Predigt* (Zurich, 1966), pp. 36-40.

30. Barth, *Homiletik,* p. 35.

been resurrected for you. This is the *Gemeindemäszigkeit* (congregational dimension) of the sermon. A preacher cannot open her mouth without realizing that God has already shown compassion for the people. This is the objective, sacramental, and metaphysical presupposition on which preaching rests.[31] This does not mean that the preacher places herself over against the people; the congregation itself is the subject of preaching and wishes to be addressed from the perspective of its foundation. The church expects to be addressed on the basis of this reconciliation and in the expectation of redemption. A preacher who fails to do so does not take the people seriously. And this proclamation is a word *senkrecht von oben* (straight from above). This word of grace gives life to the church. Barth adds that this does not imply that the preacher has no eye for the needs of concrete people. He sees love for other people as a precondition for the right kind of preaching. The concrete life situation needs to be part of the sermon. But — and this is the crux of the matter — the sermon is not an extension or an explanation of our experiences. The church is entitled to see life in the spotlight of God's grace and to see it approached from the expectation of the kingdom. Using all her tact and emphatic abilities, the preacher must dare to undertake this adventure.

Conclusion

What is our conclusion about the way we speak of God? In this model, the idea that we have access to human faith but speak of God only "perspectivistically" is not acceptable. Speaking of God is, in fact, the basis for all meaningful speaking about human faith. Or we might put it even more strongly: God's own speaking, not our speaking of God, lies at the basis of our faith and God-language. When we speak of God, we repeat the revealed Word. There is an order to this that is asymmetrical and transitive. Faith is rooted in the revelation of Christ, and the revelation of Christ is rooted in a Trinitarian decision. God, not humans, has the primacy in that order.

We also know this three-ness from classical theology, even though

---

31. Karl Barth, "Die Gemeindemäszigkeit der Predigt," in Hummel, ed., *Aufgabe der Predigt,* p. 168.

at that time the distinction did not apply as much to epistemology as to ontology. Anselm, for example, says that God created the world in accordance with an *exemplum* in God's own Spirit. The creation of the world is preceded by a conceptual expression in God himself. Anselm refers to this as the *locution:* God's pronouncing of the things God was about to create, a contemplation of the reality and of future things by God's Spirit. This is the highest reality, the exemplary reality. In created reality this *forma* is subsequently expressed *per similitudo.* And then there is the third step: in our human conceptualizing and in our knowledge, we are in turn dependent on that *similitudo* of the created reality. The creatures that are endowed with reason create in their mind an image of reality, but in that process they remain dependent on the created reality, while the created reality itself is dependent on God's *locutio.*[32] The relationship of dependence is such that God is the origin and creator, while humans stand at the other end as the receivers. In this intellectual process, God — and not man — is at the center.

Barth applies this same scheme in his theological epistemology.[33] In this approach the doctrine of God is the center, while the doctrine of humanity comes at the end. As we study this, it is important not to lose sight of the asymmetry. Faith in God is rooted in a relationship of dependence on Christ. The believer does not have Christ at his disposal. God may withdraw from our speaking, with the result that we and our language stand in a void. We can never put an equal sign between our speaking of God and God's words.

However, it is remarkable that the primary focus of proclamation is on *iustificatio.* It is a testimony to God's coming to us, while very little is said about the enlightenment of — and anchoring in — us humans (the indwelling of the Holy Spirit). This, I believe, has four consequences: (1) The relationship between our speaking and God's speaking is only dealt with in terms of paradox and dialectic. The sermon is a human word and a divine word at the same time. In the pastoral conversation we carefully listen to the other, while it contains simultaneously the word of grace. God is fully revealed in Christ, but God also remains

---

32. See my *Divine Simplicity,* pp. 97-122.

33. Barth has defined his epistemology not only in his *Church Dogmatics,* II/1, but also in his study on Anselm, *Fides quaerens intellectum. Anselms Beweis der Existenz Gottes im Zusammenhang seines Theologische Programms,* 2nd ed. (Zurich, 1958), p. 2.

hidden, continuously different and new. As a result, the human word and the divine word may also be played off against each other, and thus neither is subjected to a critical reflection. (2) Very little attention is paid to the anchoring of faith in the human subject. We have seen in Chapter 4 how human subjectivity comes into play in the divine-human relationship; but the revelation model hardly leaves any room for that. For fear of subjectivizing, this model has bent the themes from the *ordo salutis* toward the objective revelation in Christ. (3) Inter-personal discourse is not identified as a separate domain of inquiry for practical theology. That is another result of over-accentuating external revelation. If faith as a phenomenon in human life would receive more emphasis, there would also be more interest in the role of the human subject in the communication of faith. (4) The relationship between God and humans is solely expressed in Christological terms. Thus the creaturely relationship between God and humans, where the human being (as creature) is the image of God — and thus was created and made suitable for communion — is not worked out in any detail. The same is true of the pneumatological relationship, in which humanity comes to a community of renewal through the Spirit.

CHAPTER 10

The Anthropocentric Perspective

The Theological Structure

In preceding chapters I have repeatedly discussed how our faith is embedded in the world in which we live. Chapter 1 dealt with the functions of the human mind, Chapter 2 with the human subjectivity in daily life, and Chapter 3 with the concept of indwelling. That attention for the subject component of faith does not automatically lead to an anthropocentric model. However, we did meet a classical representative of this model in Schleiermacher, who thought of faith communication mainly in terms of an expression of our inner life. We encounter God in our immediate experience, in our awareness of absolute dependence. The cradle of the communication of faith, so the argument goes, is in our religious experience. And when we speak of God, there is only a subjective awareness of God. In contrast to Barth's, Schleiermacher's speaking of God is not primarily connected with the external but with the internal — with what happens inside the human subject. Even in Schleiermacher's thinking, though, there is a reality that exerts influence on us, and an "outside" is clearly presupposed (otherwise, there would be no question of religion). But the "outside" can only be spoken of from the "inside."

Strangely enough, there is also a certain similarity between Barth and Schleiermacher. Both speak of God in absolute terms: God is the wholly Other; in fact, God falls outside all our categories, and we cannot simply name God. Yet we must speak of God, and we do so within the confines of our human reality, that is, within the categories of time and space. This means, for Barth, that God makes himself *gegenständlich* (bodily present) in Jesus; for Schleiermacher it means that the *Universum* (the ultimate) is revealed in the human's inner self. Schleiermacher also holds Jesus in high regard, but mainly as the one who possessed the awareness of the divine in a special way. Both Barth and Schleiermacher speak of God as unknowable in himself: they consider the divine to be absolute. Both also recognize a movement back and forth between Christ and the human subject. In Barth's thought, the human subject finds his identity wholly in Christ, while Schleiermacher allows the human subject an independent place.

Another aspect that is related is the approach of faith praxis as religion. Barth underscores that religion is, in fact, *Unglaube* (unbelief). It should be noted, however, that in that assessment he primarily has the institutional church in mind. In an anthropological model, faith is primarily considered a human expression, and religion is seen as an aspect of human culture. John Hick points out that modern science has replaced the word "God" with the word "religion." Religion may even be the object of research in that people can study the history, phenomenology, psychology, and sociology of religion.[1] While classical theology concentrated on the existence of God — his attributes and activities — much modern theology investigates the meaning and role of religion in human life. It is not the reality of God that holds center stage, but the religious experience of people; not the truth of religious conviction, but the way faith functions in daily life. Small wonder, then, that the relationship of the human being to his or her social and cultural reality receives great weight. The relevance of religion becomes apparent within that context, and that context also brings forth materials to which religion offers meaning. Thus this model provides for an intensive interaction of the person with the reality around him or her.

God as Symbol of the Infinite

The approach that starts with humans as cultural-historical beings and with religion as a human expression has its consequences for our concept of God. The symbolic character of our faith language stands out, the imaginative abilities of the human mind receive high marks,

1. John Hick, *Philosophy of Religion* (Englewood Cliffs, NJ, 1973), p. 79.

and God himself disappears beyond the boundaries of our human existence because God is a symbol of a different order. We cannot refer to God as a subject to whom we can ascribe any well-defined predicates. We have already seen (in Chapter 1) that Tillich sees faith as a relationship of infinity, and God belongs to the pole of infinity.

> Whatever we say about that which concerns us ultimately, whether or not we call it God, has a symbolic meaning. It points beyond itself while participating in that to which it points. In no other way can faith express itself adequately. The language of faith is the language of symbols. . . . The fundamental symbol of our ultimate concern is God.[2]

This is a notion of God as the foundational symbol of faith; it amplifies the pole of the infinite and the unconditional. The reason Tillich gives for the idea that God can only be spoken of by means of symbols is that the absolute can only be made accessible through symbolic language. We have no concrete terms at our disposal. Faith is a relationship of infinity and does not refer to some subject that can be defined in concrete terms.

I cannot enter into an extensive discussion of the concept of symbol here, but I will mention two aspects that are relevant to what I want to say. First, a symbol points to something beyond itself; it brings us in touch with a deeper or higher reality. A symbol thus allows us to cross boundaries. Second, it is argued, the symbol reveals a dimension of that reality that would otherwise remain hidden. In a symbolical expression, therefore, we get in touch with reality through a method other than thinking in language. This is not just because the symbol permits us to tap into other dimensions of the reality that surrounds us, but also because the symbol appeals to specific layers of the human self, for instance, to our intuitive abilities. A remarkable aspect of this approach is the strong emphasis on God's transcendence, on the one hand, and the anchoring of faith in the human self, on the other.

Tillich uses the expression "ultimate concern" to point to the divine reality as well as to the human subject, who finds himself in an attitude of being ultimately concerned. It is difficult to determine

---

2. Tillich, *The Dynamics of Faith*, p. 45.

whether Tillich, with his "ultimate concern," focuses on the attitude of the religious person or on the object of the attitude. In other words, are we dealing with an anthropological category here, or is there also a theistic parallel? In his book *Dynamics of Faith,* Tillich does differentiate between the *fides qua creditor* and the *fides quae creditor.* The first expression refers to the central act of the personality; the second refers to the object toward which that act is directed ("there is no faith without a content toward which it is directed"). But that content is the symbolic world — the unconditional and infinite, beyond the opposites of subjective and objective. "In terms like ultimate, infinite, absolute, the difference between subjectivity and objectivity is overcome. The ultimate of the act of faith and the ultimate that is meant in the act of faith are one and the same."[3] The subject-object paradigm, as we know it from daily experience, disappears as we experience the unconditional. On the one hand, Tillich tries to do full justice to the mystery and transcendence of God, and thereby also to the character of faith. On the other hand, it will hardly surprise us that, in Tillich's line of thinking, religious symbols are anthropologically explained and are, just as are social and artistic symbols, understood in a nonrepresentative and noncognitive way. In such a case, there is no reference to a divine reality that is external to our human reality.

Making God's Transcendence Absolute

What are the consequences of this line of thinking for our speaking about God? I believe we are faced with a process of absolutizing God's transcendence: God becomes the *eigenschaftlose Absolute* (an absolute without properties). God is not a being, but is being itself; and we cannot speak about God in a pattern of subject and object. Tillich speaks of a "God beyond God," where words and concepts no longer apply:

> There can be no doubt that any concrete assertion about God must be symbolic, for a concrete assertion is one which uses a segment of finite experience in order to say something about Him. It transcends the content of this segment, although it also includes it.

3. Tillich, *The Dynamics of Faith,* p. 11.

The segment of finite reality which becomes the vehicle of a concrete assertion about God is affirmed and negated at the same time.[4]

In this way any language about God becomes utterly paradoxical and dialectical. God is so transcendent that he lives beyond what is utterable. When we speak of faith, Tillich says, we are at the boundaries of human possibilities, or, to put it even more clearly, faith *is* that boundary.[5]

We often meet this idea — that our speaking of God takes us to the limits of our human consciousness and of existence — in theological traditions following from Schleiermacher and Tillich, as well as in more recent variants. David Tracy emphasizes that we must realize that religious language and religious experience are always *limit*-language and *limit*-experience.[6] As in Tillich's thinking, this results in a separation between God-in-himself (as a transcendental idea) and our concrete concepts and images of God. Tracy differentiates between an abstract and absolute pole in God, on the one hand, and a concrete pole that is fully absorbed in the social-historical process, on the other hand. "When we affirm that God is dipolar, therefore, we affirm that God has both a concrete pole which is eminently social and temporal, an ever-changing, ever-affecting, ever-being-affected actuality, and an abstract pole which is well-defined — if "concretely misplaced" — by traditional Western reflection upon the metaphysical attributes of the Wholly Absolute One."[7]

We find this same separation in Gordon Kaufman: "God" as the "Ultimate point of reference," who is at the beginning of all things, and "God" as a religious symbol in the social-cultural system.[8] The idea that God stands at the limit, or is himself the limit, or is worshiped as an expression of the infinite by finite people — that idea carries with it a differentiation in God, a bipolarity. Kaufman says that the real referent of "God" remains inaccessible to us; it will always remain the unknown *X*, purely a "limiting idea." But the actual praxis of religious life leads us to a referent of God that is available, an imaginative construct

---

4. Tillich, *Systematic Theology,* vol. 1 (Nisbet, 1968), p. 265.

5. Tillich, *The Courage to Be* (London, 1955), p. 179.

6. Tracy, *Blessed Rage for Order,* p. 93.

7. Tracy, *Blessed Rage for Order,* p. 183.

8. Gordon D. Kaufman, *Theology for a Nuclear Age* (Manchester/Philadelphia, 1985), p. 34.

by which we allow ourselves to be led.[9] The images of God we do have access to, which are expressed in various metaphors, originate in the historical-cultural process; but they also indicate that God is an immanent power in the historical process. The symbol "God," Kaufman says, suggests a reality, an ultimate power that finds its development in an evolutionary process.[10] "God" as symbol is closely linked to the development of fundamental values in human life. Sallie McFague, in her book *Models of God,* argues from the angle of this theological model for a reconstruction of the classical concept of God. Metaphors about God, she says, say something about *our* concepts of God, but not about God himself. She appeals to Tillich and Kaufman for this conclusion.[11] And since these metaphors and symbols are part of the social-cultural reality, they can be deconstructed or reconstructed. Then she pleads for some new metaphors — such as mother, lover, and friend.

So we are faced with a somewhat paradoxical situation concerning our speaking of God. On the one hand, the transcendence of God is absolutized: the subject-object distinction that we use in our common speech does not apply. This means that we cannot refer to God as a subject of speaking and acting and that we cannot ascribe any predicates to God. Seen from our human perspective, God is the pole of infinity, an "ultimate point of reference." The downside of this, however, is that "God" — as religious symbol, as image we create as humans, as metaphor — fully participates in our human existence and becomes part of social-cultural life, and as such is subject to change. The result is that all our emphasis in speaking about God is on human experience. George Lindbeck points out that

> . . . whatever the variations, thinkers of this tradition all locate ultimately significant contact with whatever is finally important to religion in the prereflective experiential depths of the self and regard the public or outer features of religion as expressive and evocative objectifications (i.e., nondiscursive symbols) of internal experience.[12]

9. Kaufman, *God the Problem* (Cambridge, 1972), pp. 85-86.

10. Kaufman, *Nuclear Age,* p. 43.

11. Sallie McFague, *Models of God: Theology for an Ecological, Nuclear Age* (London, 1987), p. 37.

12. Lindbeck, *The Nature of Doctrine,* p. 21.

Under the influence of Englightenment Idealism, and particularly in the phenomenological-existentialist stream, Lindbeck says, the Kantian-inspired shift toward the subject is clearly present. Since God is no longer accessible to us humans, we are reduced to our images and experiences of God. As far as the communication of faith is concerned, the emphasis is now on our expression. We share our experiences, our observations, our opinions; we are able to make others partakers through the communicative process. We speak of God through our experiences, and thus always indirectly; the emphasis is on the subject-side, and there is no room for the object-side in any objective sense — but only symbolically. For that reason, this model is at times referred to as "expressive-symbolical."

The Expression of Faith through Preaching

Other than with the revelationary model, the anthropocentric model has not in recent years produced any theologians who themselves have combined the fundamental-theological and the practical-theological study of faith, except for Schleiermacher, the representative par excellence and founding father of the anthropocentric model. Tillich has certainly influenced the development of pastoral theology, especially with respect to incorporating the psychology of faith into pastoral work. Unlike Schleiermacher, however, he has not occupied himself with practical theology as a discipline. Looking at the concrete implications of the anthropocentric model in preaching and pastoral care, we encounter a wealth of tendencies and ideas that are defensible on the basis of this model. Indeed, it is a current of thought that, in a critical dialogue with Enlightenment culture, has embedded itself deeply in Western theology and the praxis of faith. The revelationary model had its central and unequivocal theme in the proclamation of God's revelation in Jesus Christ; but the anthropocentric model misses such an unequivocal theological basis. Human subjectivity plays a crucial role, which directs attention primarily to faith experience. It is true that this can be elaborated on in a number of ways. In the school of Schleiermacher, an important role is played by sentiment and feeling, while those who are inspired by Tillich pay closer attention to the cultural bias in the way faith is expressed. But let us now look at how this is expressed in preaching and pastoral care.

Expression of the Religious Personality

I will start with an older version of the anthropocentric model — one from the late nineteenth century. We have seen (in Chapter 6) that Schleiermacher considers the sermon as the communication medium of the pious self-consciousness. The communication of faith begins through the reciprocal exchange of faith experiences, and this interaction further stimulates faith and brings it to development. There is thus ample attention to humans as bearers of faith and as subjects of the exercise of faith. The anthropological anchoring continues to play an important role in the praxis of faith during the Enlightenment, and toward the end of the nineteenth century this receives a theological basis, particularly in liberal modern theology. Friedrich Nierbergall, a professor of practical theology in Marburg, is an interesting representative of this kind of practical theology. He believed that theology should broaden its inquiry and not look solely at the gospel as its object; human life should be included in its domain of study. The humanities have to be included so that preachers will not be helpless as they meets praxis. Nierbergall calls for classes in ethnology and psychology.[13]

The hearer becomes increasingly important in homiletics in this scheme. While speaking to a meeting of ministers in 1904, Niebergall posed the following question: How can we preach in such a way that we are relevant to the time in which we live? How can we do justice to modern humankind? By this he does not mean only that the wording of the sermon must be in tune with the times, but that it also must be in tune with the spirit of the age so that it can truly address the needs of the people. "The sermon," he says, is the public address of a

> . . . religious personality who has been called to that task, and who
> on the basis of his understanding of the gospel assists a religious
> community in finding an answer to their questions and needs and
> to find help.[14]

---

13. Friedrich Nierbergall, "Wissenschaftliche Grundlagen der Praktischen Theologie," in Krause, ed., *Praktische Theologie*, pp. 223-37.

14. Niebergall, "Die Moderne Predigt," in Hummel, ed., *Aufgabe der Predigt*, pp. 9-74.

This description emphasizes the subjectivity of the speaker as well as the subjectivity of the hearer. The speaker must not stop when he has read Scripture and provided a theological exegesis, but must shape the lives of his hearers. This presupposes that the preacher must know about the real interests of the people and must gain an understanding of the psychology and the social circumstances of modern people.

This approach is accompanied by a few theological shifts. In a critical sense, this implies the end of a literal inspiration of Scripture, and that has its consequences for preaching. One can no longer say, "It is written!" For Scripture is simply a collection of documents that "manifests an ascending line in expressing religious life."[15] Therefore, we should not ask what the Bible says in a particular instance, but we should try to discover what led the people to express themselves in the way they did. The Bible introduces us to the ancient world, with all the ideals and convictions that were part of it. Friedrich Niebergall believes that there is a positive way to deal with higher-critical exegesis. We have regained an interest, he says, in the religious person. And the Bible is not about doctrines but about people: "What freedom and what richness is in the motto: the Scriptures as the expression of a personal communion with God." Religious life receives its embodiment in people, and people are depicted in the Bible as historical beings. They embody the powers that are at work, as well as the ideals that are current, in a concrete situation.

But how do these historical personages of the past relate to the present? What authority can we attribute to the Bible? Are we back to the idea that a fixed period from the past appears to have some exclusive authority? Should we subject ourselves to this, sacrifice our freedom, and let go of our contemporary insights and ideals? First of all, Niebergall says that it is not clear whether we read our contemporary ideals into Scripture or whether we derive them from Scripture. Apparently, there is some sort of reciprocity. Something happens in our culture, and then we somehow find something in the Bible that throws light on it. As a result, we see Jesus as an embodiment of the social ideal under certain conditions, while at other times we see him as an embodiment of the ethical ideal. Nierbergall believes that we should not give past revelation an absolute status. If we fix God's revelation in the

15. Niebergall, "Die Moderne Predigt," p. 48.

past, we subject the present to a distant past; on the other hand, if we see no value in the past, the present becomes absolute and tyrannical. Niebergall prefers an analogous approach. What does something that was expressed in a particular way in the past ask of us in our day and age — in the context of our own contemporary situation?

> We believe we are entitled to shape our ideals in continuity with the foundational period of our religion, in accordance with our own needs and thoughts.[16]

Historical revelation remains important, for it shows us personalities who may enrich us. Preachers have the task of helping the church focus on these religious personalities as sources of faith who carry divine power, and thus to make listeners understand how God builds his kingdom and educates his people.

What is typical of this approach? (1) The attention to the concrete human person in whom religious life is expressed. (2) No final revelation in the past to which we must subject ourselves. (3) Reciprocity between present and past with regard to the significance of the Scripture for the praxis of the church.

An Expression of the Symbolic Consciousness

Let us now look at a late-twentieth-century model. David Buttrick holds a prominent position in American homiletics in the last quarter of the twentieth century. In his book *Homiletic*, he unfolds a theory of preaching in which human consciousness plays a crucial role.[17] Buttrick believes that in the salvation-historical tradition *(Heilsgeschichte)* preaching has overemphasized God's activities of the past, with the result that it has not adequately highlighted God's activities in the present. How can the modus of the past, he asks, be connected with the modus of the present? For our preaching, after all, addresses the person who lives now. Buttrick's second objection to the concept of salvation history is that we cannot speak of God's revelation in historical events; for these events must always be related to the human under-

---

16. Niebergall, "Die Moderne Predigt," p. 55.
17. David Buttrick, *Homiletic: Moves and Structures* (London, 1987).

standing of them. History, he says, is always embedded in a social consciousness.

> [W]e may begin to view God not so much as an actor in history, but
> as a "symbol source" or "image giver" to human social conscious-
> ness. Though there may be problems connected with such a theo-
> logical shift, they are surely more manageable than those con-
> nected with the idea of a God who acts in history and is on display
> in self-evident God-events.[18]

A symbolic orientation, Buttrick continues, will do much more justice
to the presence of God in the here and now. How does he view this? A
faith consciousness is formed through preaching, and a disclosure of
God himself takes place, which enables us to experience the actuality of
grace. Buttrick defines God as *Consciousness* and the revelation of God
as a disclosure of God that takes place by means of symbols that are derived from social life — a shift away from history toward symbolic consciousness. Establishing a link between God and human consciousness, Buttrick argues, will not automatically cause us to fall back into
the old subjectivistic theology. For we are dealing with the social consciousness that develops in the progress of history. But, he says, we are
concerned with "God-talk" in relationship to the structures of human
consciousness. Thus in our preaching we make full use of images, symbols, metaphors, and myths, since this allows us to have access to the
depths of the human soul as well as to the heights of the mystery of
God. Jesus Christ, Buttrick says, is the living symbol of God's love.

Metaphorical language is essential in any speaking about God;
for God is not available in the way other objects are. God is *Presence-in-
Absence*. We constantly experience God as being different; we are unable
to picture God without some human analogy, for example, God as a
shepherd, as a father, as a judge, and so forth. The comparisons are always derived from our social world, and they work in two directions: if
God is a father, then we are his children; if God is a ruler, then we are
his subjects. The relational images and metaphors are in part determined by the social roles that exist in a particular culture and time.
Metaphorical designations demand great care in our use of language

18. Buttrick, *Homiletic,* p. 115.

and in our theological judgment, for there is always the danger that we make God into an extension of our self-consciousness. But we have to take that risk, for there is no way to talk about God outside of this narrative consciousness. For the language of God's grace happens to be linked to social history and to our personal development. God becomes a part of the human world through analogy. But there is more. We also use amplification and negation, and this is necessary if we want to avoid making God too familiar. God is the majestic and lofty One, greater than humans and other than humans — the Holy One, the Creator of heaven and earth! We assign attributes to God that distinguish him from us humans; and we do so in an extreme way through the use of paradox.

Language, human consciousness, and the world around us are connected in this approach to our speaking about God. Language enables us to give names to the reality that surrounds us and to be aware of that world; it enables us to think and to establish links with the world around us. But the language of faith has a peculiar connotation: it is often narrative and has an evocative character. In faith, Buttrick says, we define the world as God's world, and we tell stories with a transcendental dimension. For ultimately the Christian faith derives its value from the character of Jesus Christ. The story of Jesus as living symbol makes it possible for us to look at the world with new eyes, from the angle of a new social order, and with the expectation of salvation for the people. The language of faith carries this consciousness of a new world into our human consciousness. Our preaching "renames the human world as a space for new humanity related to God."[19]

Therapy-Oriented Pastoral Care

Regarding this model, we need to say more about pastoral care than we did about homiletics. This concerns a kind of pastoral work in which pastoral psychology comes to development, and in which interpersonal conversation acquires a central role in pastoral praxis. Psychological insights play an important role in pastoral conversations; these conversations must help the person with whom the pastor is talking. Pastoral

19. Buttrick, *Homiletic*, p. 17.

care must have a healing dimension and must improve the congregant, just as is the case in a therapeutic session. Healing, growth, development, and renewal become important components in "client-centered" pastoral care. This school of thought is also referred to as "therapeutic pastoral care" because the model of conversation as *therapeuticum* — as developed in psychoanalysis — has its influence on pastoral care. When the element of therapy enters into the pastoral conversation, some clear distinctions are needed. Clinebell offers the following description:

> *Pastoral care* is the broad, inclusive ministry of mutual healing and growth within a congregation and its community, through the life cycle. *Pastoral counseling,* one dimension of pastoral care, is the utilization of a variety of healing (therapeutic) methods to help people handle their problems and crises more growthfully and thus experience healing of their brokenness. . . . *Pastoral psychotherapy* is the utilization of long-term, reconstructive therapeutic methods when growth is deeply and/or chronically diminished by need-depriving early life experiences or by multiple crises in adult life.[20]

These definitions tell us that the pastoral conversation will pay attention to (1) the crises and problems people are facing; (2) to the fact that these problems and crises may be rooted in blockades or inhibitions that may have originated in childhood or in later life; and (3) that methods of therapy may be used in the pastoral conversation to achieve healing. This presupposes knowledge on the part of the pastor regarding the connection between life experiences and psychosocial processes, and also a competence in methodical conversation.

In therapeutic pastoral care, healing contains a spiritual, but also a therapeutic, dimension. It doesn't merely consist of the proclamation of forgiveness of sin (as the theological expression of the faith dimension); but it receives concrete form in the interpersonal pastoral relationship. In a similar way, just as the personality of the therapist finds herself in a situation of transferral in the personal encounter with a client, the personality of the pastor also plays a significant role as he talks with people in his congregation. Pastoral care, says Tillich, "is based on the unconditional acceptance of the other, and the pastor must prac-

20. Howard Clinebell, *Basic Types of Pastoral Care and Counseling* (Nashville, 1991), p. 26.

tice this as he meets people." Otherwise, there will be no healing. "No self-acceptance," Tillich says further, "is possible if one is not accepted in a person-to-person relation."[21] Tillich's words here constitute a fundamental theological statement: faith is to be defined in terms of unconditional acceptance. He adds that this acceptance is not to be detached from the concrete interpersonal encounter; that is, the personal relationship between pastor and layperson is in itself an instrument of pastoral care. We learn from this that the interhuman relationship becomes an important link in the chain of pastoral care.

Tillich's Concept

This calls for further explanation. First, I want to say something about Tillich's approach, and second, about the embedding of faith in psychosocial life and its implications for the development of pastoral counselling. I will then return to Tillich's views regarding faith.

Tillich sees various polarities at the basis of the human psyche. He believes that human existence develops in the tension within a foundational bipolar structure: self and the world. A human being constitutes a unity in himself, but not as an isolated individual. The person becomes who he is in a constant interaction with his environment and with other human beings. For example, this is expressed in the polarities of individuality and participation.[22] On the one hand, human beings need self-assertion, self-determination, and individuality. We are unique individuals — incomparable. On the other hand, we belong to a larger something; we participate in society; we share with others; we form a community. As a human being, I face the challenge to be myself; but I should also have the courage to belong to a group. When this courage to be part of something larger is overemphasized in a radical way, I may become submerged in a form of collectivism (such as in communism). On the other hand, when the courage to be myself is radically extended, I lose all contact with the outside world in some extreme form of solipsism and existentialism. In the latter case, I as a human being am reduced to what I make of myself, and thus freedom is

21. Tillich, *The Courage to Be,* p. 157.
22. Tillich, *The Courage to Be,* p. 76.

absolutized (Sartre). The human being is only what he is *a se,* that is, from himself.

Tillich has described the twentieth century as "the century of anxiety," and he arrives at these polarities because of his analysis of human anxiety. In their existence, humans face the constant threat of non-existence: "Anxiety is the state in which a being is aware of its possible non-being."[23] We encounter this fear at the point where we experience infinity as our own infinity. Is has no definite object and is not intentional in itself. I can say that I am afraid of something, but fear, as such, is a sentiment of the self; it is not intentional. Tillich differentiates between three kinds of fear: fear of death, fear of the meaninglessness of existence, and fear of eternal damnation. All three are existential, that is, they are part of life and should not be considered as some neurological aberration. Tillich entitles his book about this anxiety *The Courage to Be,* for there is not only fear, there is also courage — the courage of self-assertion. "Courage does not remove anxiety. Since anxiety is existential, it cannot be removed. But courage takes the anxiety of non-being into itself. Courage is self-affirmation 'in spite of', namely in spite of non-being."[24]

In this self-assertion, human beings can assert themselves as either parts of an all-inclusive whole or as individual selves. But it remains a risky undertaking: the constant threat of nonbeing remains, for one can lose oneself and become an object among the multitude of things, or one can lose the world and live in the emptiness of oneself. Ultimately, Tillich seeks a religious foundation for this courage: it is rooted in a power-of-being that exceeds the power of the self and the power of the person's world — that is, it is rooted in *being* itself. Religion is existence in the grip of the power of being itself. Thus courage, says Tillich, has an open or hidden religious root. I will return to the theological definition of this religious root later.

Correlation

In his analysis of anxiety, Tillich uses the correlation method. He analyzes a phenomenon in the human realm with the help of anthropolog-

23. Tillich, *The Courage to Be,* p. 34.
24. Tillich, *The Courage to Be,* p. 59.

ical categories, and then he connects this with a theological explanation of that same reality. He does differentiate between the two, but that does not prevent him from jumping from one to the other; they are two sides of the same coin. He links the courage to be (as an anthropological category) with the courage to trust (as a theological category), the latter expression being the theological correlative of the first. In other words, it is the courage to accept that one is accepted, which pretends to be a contemporary interpretation of the old concept of the justification of the sinner. This correlation does indicate a clear connection between the life of faith and the way the human psyche functions. Faith is embedded in the development and in the dynamic of the psychosocial interaction. For that reason, according to Tillich, it is impossible to separate the religious sphere from the psychological sphere. This also implies that in our pastoral care we cannot detach our faith from the psychosocial sphere of life. Faith is part of the development that people experience (the life cycle) and is also negatively impacted by any aberrations or damage in the functioning of the human mind.

Developments in Pastoral Care

When pastoral care is approached from the angle of healing in this scheme, psychosocial recovery is undoubtedly part of the process of pastoral care. Our concern is to help the person return to wholeness, to see the restoration of elements of a life that have been damaged, disturbed, or alienated. To some extent, then, the work of the pastor thus begins to resemble that of the physician, the social worker, the probation officer, and the therapist. But the pastor, Sewart Hiltner says, has the special task of keeping an eye on the wholeness of the person; and this point of view attributes an important role to the pastoral attitude.

> Where impairment is due to negative feelings, whatever their nature, healing begins by acknowledgment, acceptance, understanding, and assimilation of those feelings, and not through encouraging bright thoughts, verbal encouragement of the right feelings, and the like.[25]

25. Sewart Hiltner, *Preface to Pastoral Theology: The Ministry and Theory of Shepherding* (Nashville, 1958), p. 111.

So it is essential for the pastor to be able to deal with any negative feelings — that she does not reject them but reacts with empathy. This attitude of acceptance is crucial in the pastoral relationship. The person of the pastor manifests God's accepting love in her pastoral habitus. In the here and now of the encounter, unconditional acceptance must become evident; it makes it possible for church members to give a place in their lives to their own feelings and to acquire a more positive self-image. Remarkably, after the passage quoted above, Hiltner refers immediately to both Freud and Tillich: he mentions Freud in connection with the role of the therapist, while he borrows the concept of unconditional acceptance from Tillich.

The anthropocentric model has played an important role in the development of pastoral care. The embedding of faith in psychosocial life receives ample attention in this model, which also allows for nontheological theories as a perspective on the professional activities of the pastor. As early as the 1960s, the ideas and training models of the American Clinical Pastoral Training were introduced in Europe. Faber and Zijlstra, in particular, have done pioneering work in this area.[26] Explicit attention has been given, since that time, to the training of pastors in how to conduct pastoral conversations, with emphasis on the role of the pastor in the pastoral interaction. Analyses of these conversations have often indicated that the pastor is unable adequately to deal with the feelings of the pastorant. Zijlstra has shown in his research that, during these training sessions, the pastor tends to become increasingly aware of the complexity of his own inner experiences and of the communication process.[27] Becoming aware of his own contribution to the conversation — and particularly of his own inhibitions and blockades — proves to be extremely important in the pastor's learning process. "It is far from easy," says Clinebell, "to relate to the depths of other persons. To do so is to come alive to their personhood — to their pain and potential, their emptiness or fullness, their unique blend of hope and despair. It is painful to relate to the depths of others because it inevitably exposes us to the dark rooms of our own inner world. Their emptiness reminds us of our own. Their anger and guilt cause

26. W. Zijlstra, *Klinische pastorale vorming. Een voorlopige analyse van het leer- en groepsproces van zeven Cursussen* (Assen, 1969).

27. Zijlstra, *Klinische Pastorale Vorming,* pp. 204-8.

ours to resonate."[28] A pastor who is unable to deal with his inner fears cannot help others.

Being-Part-Of and Being-On-Your-Own in the Christian Faith

The influence of this model reaches further than the pastoral conversation. The embedding of the Christian faith in psychosocial life is also noticeable in other aspects of the praxis of faith. Moreover, the Christian faith itself — as a relationship with God — may also be understood in terms of the polarity of the self and the world. If it is true that trust in God constitutes an important notion of the Christian faith, how does this faith relate to the "basic trust" we may have, or may not have, experienced in our childhood years? Is there reciprocity between basic trust and belief in God? If the interaction between the self and the world is so fundamental, it stands to reason that this will also play a role in religious instruction and education. Most people have been taught to believe in a socialization process as part of their education; indeed, we adopt numerous ideas, beginning in early childhood, from the community we grow up in — from the family, the school, the church congregation, and so forth. We listen to Bible stories, participate in children's clubs and youth work, receive a host of impressions during worship services and other church activities. We see what faith means to people around us — to parents, other educators, and friends. In that sense, faith is a social event: it is part of our communion with other people, and it develops through participation in social and institutional practices. And it is through this institutionalizing of the faith, Berger says, that it is transmitted from one generation to the next.[29]

On the other hand, faith is not just a matter of education and socialization. We must also pay attention to our own individuality, our own freedom and responsibility. The believer not only joins others along the road of convention and tradition but also arrives at her own judgment on the basis of personal experience and insight. Faith is also a form of individuation. Indeed, the community plays an important role in the Christian faith. Through baptism we are accepted institu-

28. Clinebell, *Basic Types,* p. 15.
29. Berger, *A Far Glory,* p. 170.

tionally into the new community. But this does not take away from the fact that we have to make our own choices, accept our own responsibilities, and make our free and independent judgments. Our faith may lead us to break away from old traditions and to embark on a new journey. Think of Abraham and Paul. They broke away from their old network, but they eventually entered a new community. In this process, however, there is a moment when the individual believer is entirely on his own. Berger refers to the "solitary believer," suggesting that this individuality is implied in the act of faith. This individuality and the possibility of making one's own decisions are deeply rooted in the social and cultural life of Western society. As part of that historical development, Protestantism has always emphasized personal conversion — a conscious individual choice and an inner renewal. Tradition, education, and participation in religious practices form no guarantee for a living faith. Living faith demands personal assent and conscious acceptance.

Tillich's Theological Foundation

Tillich defends a correlation between our psychosocial life and our religious life. What does this correlation look like? We have seen how the courage of self-assertion has a dominant role in the victory over fear. This courage is self-assertion in spite of the threat of nonbeing; and it is precisely at this crucial point, the "in spite of," where we can make the connection between the psychosocial and the religious spheres. The courage to conquer the threat of nonbeing expresses itself in us through the polarity of individualization and participation. From a religious perspective, the pole of participation finds expression in a mystical union, while the pole of individualization has to do with a personal encounter with God. Tillich believes that Protestantism has, in particular, focused on the pole of individualization: the courage of trust, of personal faith. Luther fought for the immediate I-thou relationship between God and man.

> Again and again [Luther] uses the word *trotz*, "in spite of." In spite of all the negativities which he had experienced, in spite of the anxiety which dominated that period, he derived the power of self-

233

affirmation from his unshakable confidence in God and from the personal encounter with him. According to the expressions of anxiety in this period, the negativity his courage had to conquer was symbolized in the figures of death and the devil.[30]

Tillich suggests that the Reformation broke with the semicollectivism of the Middle Ages. Luther's courage was certainly not the courage to be-part-of. His courage to trust was a personal courage, a courage rooted in the I-thou relationship with God. The church and the church councils were unable to give him courage. Says Tillich: "When the Reformation removed the mediation and opened up a direct, total and personal approach to God, a new non-mystical courage to be was possible."[31] Thus the emphasis is placed on the individual human self in the encounter with God as a person. Seen from a religious angle, the focus is on the courage of faith as the courage of confidence; but — and this is the religious dimension — it is not trust in oneself. In fact, the Reformation points to the opposite: we can only begin to have trust in our own existence after we have stopped relying on ourselves. This element also clearly expresses the theological meaning.

> In the center of the Protestant courage of confidence stands the courage to accept acceptance in spite of the consciousness of guilt. Luther, and in fact the whole period, experienced the anxiety of guilt and condemnation as the main form of their anxiety. The courage to affirm oneself in spite of this anxiety is the courage which we have called the courage of confidence. It is rooted in the personal, total and immediate certainty of divine forgiveness.... In the Lutheran formula that "he who is unjust is just" (in the view of the divine forgiveness) or in the more modern phrasing that "he who is unacceptable is accepted" the victory over the anxiety of guilt and condemnation is sharply expressed. One could say that the courage to be is the courage to accept oneself as accepted in spite of being unacceptable. One does not need to remind the theologians of the fact that this is the genuine meaning of the Paulinian-Lutheran doctrine of "justification by faith" (a doctrine which in its original phrasing has become incomprehensible even

30. Tillich, *The Courage to Be,* p. 152.
31. Tillich, *The Courage to Be,* p. 154.

for students of theology). But one must remind theologians and ministers that in the fight against the anxiety of guilt by psychotherapy the idea of acceptance had received the attention and gained the significance which in the Reformation period was to be seen in phrases like "forgiveness of sins" or "justification through faith." Accepting acceptance though being unacceptable is the basis for the courage of confidence.[32]

This brings Tillich to the core of the Protestant conception of faith: the justification of the sinner. But he explains this view of faith in terms of general anthropological categories — courage and anxiety — which reveals his apologetic method: he defends the possible meaning of religion in nonreligious terms. But the correlation, which he presupposes, also leads to a degree of identification: the one is like the other. This has two consequences: (1) The "courage to be" carries with it the necessity of transcendence; it always has either an open or hidden religious root. (2) The notion of a personal God is overshadowed by a more general concept of transcendence — being itself, the unconditional. This is where Tillich speaks of the "God beyond God," God beyond the subject-object distinction. And here again the paradox reigns supreme: "Each of these paradoxes drives the religious consciousness towards a God above the God of theism."[33]

Conclusion

In speaking about God in the anthropological model, I arrive at the following conclusions.

1. In contrast to the revelationary model, the logical priority in the anthropological model is not in the fact that God himself speaks. The point of departure is in the human realm: we speak of God in *limit-language,* and we experience God in *limit-experiences.* God is only indirectly accessible, and our speaking of God is embedded in a symbolic order that results from a social-cultural process.

32. Tillich, *The Courage to Be,* pp. 155, 156.
33. Tillich, *The Courage to Be,* p. 177.

235

This model does not lead us to speak of God as the subject of speaking and acting; God is not referred to as an actor. As a result, more attention is given to the function and meaning of the word "God" than to any description of the referent of "God." In other words, what is at stake is the meaning of religion and not so much the truth of God's salvation. In addition, this approach puts great emphasis on divine transcendence *(Deus semper maior!)*. This absolutizing of the transcendent also implies that faith becomes primarily an experience of transcendence, which reinforces the mystical dimension of religion.

2. In the anthropological model the emphasis is on the human subject, and the cardinal point is the attention to the embedding of faith in the psychosocial life. Other than in dialectical theology, there is no rupture between a theological and anthropological description of faith. This has two consequences: (a) the concrete challenges we face in life are an integral part of the theological reflection; and (b) interpersonal communication becomes an explicit theme as a constitutive factor of the praxis of faith. It is hardly surprising that the nontheological dimension of the practical theological inquiry is well developed in this model.

3. The problem with this model is the identification of the psychological with the religious. In Tillich the correlation is more than a matter of analogy: the one is not like the other; it is identical with the other. In any event, Tillich does not sufficiently differentiate between the faith relationship (the divine-human relationship) and the self-world relationship. Even though the two relationships have the same formal structure, it does not make them identical. Tillich jumps too easily from one domain to the other, from the psychological to the theological, from psychology to pastoral care, and from unconditional acceptance to the justification of the sinner. There is a close connection between these various domains, but there is also a transition from the one to the other. Faith, as a relationship with Christ, has the structure of an I-thou relationship, but it cannot be identified with the I-thou relationship in social interaction. The faith communion is symbolically expressed through baptism, and that symbol is closely linked to the idea of the justification of the sinner. Despite the interweaving of those domains, there is also a transition from one

236

to the other. Faith, as communion with Christ, has the structure of an I-thou relationship; but it cannot be identified with the I-thou of social interaction. The communion of faith is symbolically expressed in baptism, and this symbol is closely linked to the concept of the justification of the sinner. St. Paul says: "We were therefore buried with him through baptism into death in order that, just as Christ was raised from the dead through the glory of the Father, we too may live a new life" (Rom. 6:4). Baptism, as an expression of the Christian faith, places us in a new polarity: between old and new, between death and life, between sin and acquittal. Our faith makes us aware of the polarity of salvation and damnation, which awareness comes via communion with Christ. Of course, this new polarity becomes intertwined with the polarities of social interaction: God's salvation dwells in the people. But it also diffuses itself, for faith pretends to bring renewal and change. But there remains a difference: justification is a divine, not a human, judgment. Therefore, there can be no identification of the psychological with the religious, for this would mean that we would dissolve the divine into the human, or the converse — deify the human.

CHAPTER 11

A Plea for a Discussion of the Foundations of Practical Theology

What Is the Central Theme?

We have seen that spiritual life is centered in the relationship between God and the human being, and this relationship can be expressed in various ways. The revelation model assigns logical priority to God: God makes himself known; God initiates the encounter and realizes the communion. There is a movement from God toward humans, and this sequence alone produces salvation and life. This movement is the root of the doctrine of grace and provides the foundation for the justification of the sinner: God declares human beings free and imputes the righteousness of Christ to them *(imputatio)*. God exists *extra nos* as a subject of speaking and acting.

Things differ somewhat in the anthropocentric model. Human subjectivity — whether or not in relationship with the surrounding social reality — constitutes an important point of orientation in the praxis of faith. In this reality people experience signs of salvation that point toward God. One might say that human reality forms the domain within which our religious life occurs. The light of God's salvation enters through the gaps of our existence and stirs desire and hope, but we can only speak in preliminary ways about God. God is part of a different reality, but we can imagine him. God is at the limit of our human existence, and our human experience allows us to speak of him in only a tentative way, not with finality. God is transcendent and only indirectly accessible.

The anthropocentric model is mainly shaped by the philosophy of the Enlightenment, particularly by Kant, who believed that God cannot be an "external object," at least we humans can't know him as such, because he does not fall within the conceptual framework of human knowledge. But Kant says that human knowledge has the tendency to want to proceed beyond that limit; as a result, "God" functions as a transcendental idea, as the regulating Idea.[1] This philosophical school of thought has been a major factor in the development of a climate in which God is presented as an indefinite and metaphorical entity. Not a God who concretely speaks and acts, but an infinite God who is far beyond us; not a God with a revealed identity, but "God" as the human Ideal. The concept of "God" stands for the highest ideal, but a beckoning perspective that cannot be fully reached in our human existence.

My argument in this study has been based on the thesis that the life of faith consists of an actual relationship between God and the human world. This intersubjective relationship presupposes that both God and humans are subjects of consciousness, speaking, and acting. In this reciprocal relationship the one subject addresses the other: God addresses people, and people turn toward God. This relationship can only be a living communion if God is indeed known by us as a subject of speaking and acting. What is at stake is that God manifests himself as subject of speaking and acting, and that we recognize and know him as such.

I will now concentrate on this theme, investigating it from two perspectives. First, I will do so from the central theological view that God is a speaking God. I have described in Chapter 7 how God is presented in the prophetic tradition as the speaking God who addresses humans as the Word. I will now return to this and will further argue that, if we understand the Word as promise, this will imply that God is prior to man. Second, I will engage in a critical dialogue with the neo-Kantian absolutizing of God's transcendence. I will defend the proposition that we refer to God himself and that, through our stories and descriptions, we identify him as the God of Israel and the father of Jesus Christ.

---

1. Immanuel Kant, *Kritik der reinen Vernunft (The Critique of Pure Reason),* Wilhelm Weischedel/Wissenschaftliche Buchgesellschaft edition, *Kant Werke,* vol. 4 (Darmstadt, 1975), pp. 563-64.

The Promise and Trustworthiness of the Speaker

Assigning a central role to the Word and the promise in our communion with God presupposes the logical priority of the divine subject in
the divine-human relationship. This is the central idea that I will elaborate on in this section. By way of introduction, let us first explore the
discourse between people. In our daily interaction with other people,
we use many forms of discourse. When we make a statement such as "It
is raining today," that statement is either true or false. We may make
another kind of statement that is directive rather than factual, such as
making a request or giving an order: "Could you please pass me the
sugar" or "Close the door!" or "You're not going out tonight." In addition, there are statements that carry a commitment from the speaker
herself: "I guarantee that everything will turn out well" or "I promise
you I will come tomorrow." This commitment may also carry a negative
connotation: "Don't think I'll fall for that again." Statements with a
strong expressive character reveal something about the mood of the
speaker: "Thanks for your kind words" or "my sincere condolences" or
"I feel sad." However, these facets of speech don't usually occur in isolation in what we say in everyday situations. We are dealing with various
dimensions that may be distinguished in our speaking.[2]

Speaking as interaction is a lively event in that the personality of
the speaker finds expression. Every form of speaking is expressive,
manifesting something about the emotions of the speaker but also
about the aims and outcomes he has in mind. The speaker always expresses a particular intentionality. But he also makes a statement about
something, about the physical and social reality in which we live. In our
speaking we relate to that reality.

What is the crucial element in the structure of making a promise?
It is the trustworthiness of the speaker. The making of a promise creates a relationship between the speaker and the one who is addressed.
The strange thing is that the promise is not fulfilled by the one to
whom it is addressed, because it is not within his or her power. It depends on the speaker. In a successful communication the addressee
will react, and the reaction may have been intended by the speaker; for

---

2. Cf. Searle, *Mind, Language and Society*, pp. 146-52; see also Vincent Brümmer, *Theology and Philosophical Inquiry: An Introduction* (London, 1981).

example, the addressee will trust the statement, consider the speaker trustworthy, and expect the promise to be fulfilled. But the reaction is not a constitutive element in the making of the promise. The speaker determines the conditions on which the promise is to be based. It has to do with (1) the intention of the speaker, (2) the link between intention and promise, (3) the honesty and trustworthiness of the speaker, and (4) whether or not the speaker is able to fulfill the promise. The weight of the matter lies with the speaker and his control over the conditions in actual reality; in any event, it does not lie with the addressee. A promise is a promise because of the simple fact that the speaker makes the promise. Of course, making a promise also has its consequences for the addressee. If someone makes a promise to me, I may decide to trust that promise and base my actions on it. The making of promises and the fact that someone trusts these promises is a central nerve of social life. Things will go badly wrong if we can no longer trust each other. When we promise a lot of things but refuse to take responsibility for those promises or prove to be utterly unable to fulfill them, those promises become empty and meaningless, and life ends in chaos and confusion. Trustworthiness, responsibility, and the ability to act accordingly are important notions when we make promises.

God's Promise

In Protestant theology, the discourse between God and human beings is often defined by concepts that relate to the idea of promise. We have seen in Chapter 7 that, according to Martin Luther, God encounters us in the word of promise. This places the emphasis on the divine initiative. We meet this same structure in covenant theology. The relationship between God and man is rooted in the promises of the covenant: "The special relationship which God has initiated between himself and Abraham, Israel, his church, is expressed as a promise. The covenant cannot be thought of without the promise. The Scriptures use the words 'covenant' and 'promise' interchangeably."[3] The promising God meets humans and enters into a covenant with them. Thiemann suggests that the Word of God,

---

3. J. G. Woelderink, *Verbond en bevinding,* intro. by C. van der Wal (Amsterdam, 1974), pp. 50, 51.

understood as promise, is better suited to describe the relationship between God and humans than is the word "revelation": "Promise provides a category in which the notions of relation and priority can be held in dialectical balance."[4] The concept of promise implies that God's grace is prior to our faith. Promise and faith are correlate concepts, but the logical priority lies with the promise, and there remains a difference between divine initiative and human reception: God and humans do not stand next to each other as equals. This is deeply anchored in both Lutheran and Reformed theology. I will give two examples. We have seen (in Chapter 4) how, according to Calvin, the Spirit stimulates the human heart as the internal teacher. Remarkably enough, this happens when we direct our attention and affections toward God's promise. "Hence we must return," Calvin says, "to the point: that any promise whatsoever is a testimony of God's love toward us. . . . It follows that we should turn our eyes to him as often as any promise is offered to us."[5] Faith "ought to correspond to a simple and free promise."[6]

> We make the freely given promise of God the foundation of faith because upon it faith properly rests. Faith is certain that God is true in all things whether he command or forbid, whether he promise or threaten; and it also obediently receives his commandments, observes his prohibitions, heeds his threats. Nevertheless, faith properly begins with the promise, rests in it, and ends in it. For in God faith seeks life: a life that is not found in commandments or declarations of penalties, but in the promise of mercy, and only in a freely given promise.[7]

This quotation underscores the central role of "promise" in the concept of faith; but it also describes the discourse between God and humans, namely, the various forms of speaking.

We see the same line of thinking in the Lutheran tradition. Below is a statement from article IV of the *Apology of the Augsburg Confession*, attributed to Philipp Melanchthon. We hear God's promise in the Scriptures, namely when

4. Thiemann, *Revelation and Theology*, p. 151.
5. Calvin, *Institutes* III.2.32.
6. Calvin, *Institutes* III.2.38.
7. Calvin, *Institutes* III.2.29.

. . . it promises that the Messiah will come and because of Him promises forgiveness of sin, justification and eternal life, or when in the New Testament, the Christ who came, Himself promises the forgiveness of sin, justification and eternal life.[8]

The promise is here linked to forgiveness, justification, and eternal life. These are eschatological notions. The promise constantly directs us toward the future, toward victory and peace, just as in the Old Testament the promise points toward a land flowing with milk and honey. But the promise is always accompanied by a polar concept: the fulfillment. God not only promises but also fulfills his promises; and because of his trustworthiness we expect that fulfillment. The Christian faith confesses that the promises find their fulfillment in Jesus Christ: he is the content and guarantee of the salvation that has been promised. And because of this, Christ himself — as the quotation from the Confession says — now promises and distributes justification and eternal life. And the fulfillment in the Messiah evokes the promise of the final fulfillment. The New Testament testimony is filled with joy for the fulfillment of the promise. This is the gospel, Luther says, that the history of Christ is shared with us; in communion with him we share in the eschatological salvation. Christ embodies the salvation God has promised and involves us in it. Preaching plays an important role in this. "For the preaching of the gospel is nothing else than Christ coming to us or us being brought to Him."[9] Once again, in this relationship between Christ and the believer, the logical priority lies with Christ, who is God's gift to us.

> The most important aspect and foundation of the gospel is: before you can understand Christ as example, you must first accept and know Him as a gift that God has given you and is your possession. When you see Him or hear how He does something or suffers, you should not doubt that He Himself, Christ, is your possession in what He does and suffers. And you can trust this as if you had done it yourself, yes, as if you were this Christ.[10]

8. Quoted in Thiemann, *Revelation and Theology,* p. 97.

9. Martin Luther, *Ein kleiner Unterricht, was man in den Evangelien suchen und erwarten soll. Vorwort zur Kirchenpostille* (WA Band 10/1), pp. 8, 9.

10. Luther, *Ein kleiner Unterricht,* p. 11.

These words poignantly express that, in the relationship between Christ and the believer, the priority is with Christ. He is God's gift to us, but at the same time there is an intimate unity: the believer may trust that he is included in Christ. "That is the immense fire of God's love in us," Luther adds in this same passage, "which makes the heart and the conscience happy, certain and content. That is what is meant in the preaching of the gospel; that is why such preaching is called *evangelium,* which is translated as merry, good comforting news."

The promise comes to us in the structure of the discourse, that is, in the interaction of speaking *and* listening. The Word of promise is by definition existential: the Word of God is human-directed. The promise makes clear that salvation is fulfilled *pro nobis* and *in nobis,* in discipleship and indwelling. Luther made preaching into the central function of the praxis of faith. Nonetheless, it would be incorrect to define preaching as one-sided — only as a message coming from God. For it is also "the word that becomes history," which comes to human existence and touches it in its roots. Promise and fulfillment continue to be interrelated. In the Cross and Resurrection the promise is fulfilled and salvation is realized. But preaching is not simply a report on this state of affairs. For when that central act of God is proclaimed, it touches our existence, and the Word enters our life as liberation and renewal. And thus Christ and human existence are connected. J. T. Bakker comments on this aspect: "The connection with Christ cannot simply consist in the fact that we hear 'from a distance' a statement about his victory. With all the means he had at his disposal, Luther fought for the realization that this victory cannot reach me without drawing my life into a 'likeness of Christ.'"[11]

The Identity of the One Who Makes the Promise

I want to include two other, interconnected elements from the promise-structure of the Word in this discussion, namely, the role of the person who makes the promise and the future-directedness of the promise. Some relevant data from the biblical tradition come in the story of the calling of Abraham, an important event in the formation

11. J. T. Bakker, *Eschatologische prediking bij Luther* (Kampen, 1964), p. 40.

of Israel as God's people. God makes himself known as the God of the covenant; and he promises his blessing: a new country to live in and offspring. As history unfolds, this promise — and the ways it is threatened or delayed — remain the key. The remaining focus is on the certainty of the promise and on the faithfulness or faithlessness of the human partner. As part of this focus we see the word "faith" emerging: "Abraham believed God and he credited it to him as righteousness" (Gen. 15:6). Abraham put his trust in God; that is, he considered God's word trustworthy even though he could not as yet see the fulfillment (because of his childlessness). Therefore, the emptiness and deficiency on the human side do not put a halt to the faith relationship, but they result in the fact that certainty is found in the Other, that is, in the trustworthiness of the Other.

We see something similar in the well-known Emmanuel prophecy in Isaiah. King Ahaz and his people find themselves in a very precarious situation. The armies of Aram and Israel stand face to face before the walls of Jerusalem, and the heart of the king is filled with fear, as is also the heart of the people, "as the trees of the forest are shaken by the wind" (Isa. 7:2). Then the prophet Isaiah steps forward and says to the king, "Do not lose heart because of those two smoldering stubs." And then follows the well known statement: "If you do not stand firm in your faith, you will not stand at all" (Isa. 7:9). If you do not tie yourself to the promises of God, you will not make any progress. Without faith you will lose your position.[12] Faith does not find its stronghold and anchor in visible reality but in divine promises. The promising God is believed to be true and trustworthy, and this gives the believer the strength to endure and to continue. Faith is saying "amen" to what God speaks.

Thus everything depends on the identity of the speaker. The question is whether you dare to wait for God's answer, even when things seem to turn against you. Abraham was childless, and it seemed as though the promise would go unfulfilled. For him faith meant to be en-route-with-a-promise, but not without temptation and doubt: "You have given me no children" (Gen. 15:3). Everything depends on whether or not God has the kind of identity that ensures that he is absolutely trustworthy and will keep his word. In the Old and the New Testaments, this identity of God is illustrated in a long series of incidents,

12. Zimmerli, *Grundriss,* p. 129.

stories, prophecies, and hymns, in the history of the people of Israel and in the life, death, and resurrection of Jesus Christ. God's character is described in a multitude of ways. It is always about who God is, what God does, and what we may expect from God. He is a God with a name and a face: the God of Abraham, Isaac, and Jacob, the father of Jesus Christ. Faith completely depends on the identity of that name. Because divine speaking is characterized by promise, we must depend on the true identity of the promising divine person. "The justifiability of one's faith and hope in the trustworthiness of a promiser is never fully confirmed (or disconfirmed) until the promiser actually fulfills (or fails to fulfill) his/her promises. Until the moment of fulfillment the recipient must justify faith and hope on the basis of a judgment concerning the character of the promiser."[13]

As Christian community, therefore, we live between the giving of the promise and the ultimate fulfillment, of which Jesus Christ is the sign and the proof. His resurrection is the guarantee of our resurrection. But the New Testament is also clear that the full revelation of salvation in human existence is still in the future. For that reason, the key aspect of faith is the knowledge of God himself, the identity and trustworthiness of God's name. Salvation is often scarcely visible in the reality that surrounds us, in our own experience. Nonetheless, faith does not disappear in the midst of those temptations because we are directed toward God. Faith trusts the words of God, and that is why Scripture places such a strong emphasis on the true identity of God.

There is yet another faith characteristic that is embodied in the promise-structure: knowing about a different reality, about the kingdom of God. Just as Abraham, because of the promise, set out on his journey, and just as the Israelites left Egypt on their way to the promised land, so the Christian church sets out with the expectation of the glory of Christ. Faith in the risen Lord awakens new expectations. Paul refers to believers as fellow heirs of Christ; for, he writes, "if indeed we share in his suffering [it is] in order that we may also share in his glory" (Rom. 8:17), meaning that faith discerns more than the present reality. We walk by faith, the apostle says, and not by sight (2 Cor. 5:7); or, as the letter to the Hebrews formulates it, "Faith is being sure of what we hope for and certain of what we do not see" (Heb. 11:1). The expectation

13. Thiemann, *Revelation and Theology*, p. 154.

of the new reality is part and parcel of the Christian faith, since we identify God as the one who raised Jesus from the dead. Thus our expectation is also grounded in the identity of the revealed name.

The Referential Aspect of the Faith Relationship

In this next section I will address a number of preliminary theoretical questions about our speaking of God. I will try to explain the background and will indicate what the consequences are of the way we put the reality of God into words. The level of abstraction is inherent in this problem we are discussing. The main issue is the relationship between our human ability to know and perceive, on the one hand, and reality-as-such, on the other. It has to do with the fundamentals of the development of practical theological theory. I am not arguing that the theological positions and reconstructions regarding the praxis of faith are directly related to theoretical insights about human discourse, human knowledge, and the nature of reality; but there is reciprocity. Insights into the fundamentals of epistemology have their impact on the kind of theory we develop, and theological insights may influence theoretical points of departure as well. It is somewhat similar to playing with technical toys: you unscrew some parts to see how a gadget works, and then you try to put it together again. The same parts may allow you to build different vehicles.

The Kantian Paradigm

Our reflection on God-language takes place within some theoretical framework. It is embedded in a sum total of ideas about, for example, the nature of reality, the human ability to acquire knowledge, the interpersonal discourse, the relationship between language and reality, and so forth. In our practical theological reflection we cannot abstract from the broader theoretical framework. In Western theology, the intellectual climate of the Enlightenment has, to a large degree, determined the theoretical infrastructure of our speaking about God. For example, in order not to fall prey to the criticism of Kant, Schleiermacher localizes faith in the domain of feeling. He denies that God is a metaphysical being or an object of knowledge; we cannot speak of God in subject-object distinctions. However, the other side of the coin is that our affective life is seen as the place where our religion originates, and God can no longer be understood as the initiator of the faith relationship or as a speaking and acting subject. This means that we have to pay a theological price, and we are left with the question of whether the theoretical-philosophical argument that has led some Schleiermacher-influenced theologians to such a far-reaching conclusion is indeed defensible.

One cannot deny that certain of Kant's ideas have exercised an enormous influence on modern theology. This concerns particularly the belief that we always observe reality by means of the concepts and categories that spring from the human mind. The infrastructure of the human mind shapes the world that we observe, so we are told. Reality has a certain impact on us, but we ourselves construct from the raw materials the phenomena of the world. This implies that reality in itself *(an sich)* does not yet possess that structure. For instance, when we differentiate between substances and properties, we are the ones who make that distinction. We have no option but to think in terms of an object-property structure, because that's the way we format information. The concepts by which we format reality have their origin in the human self. Thus we can only speak of the world of phenomena: the phenomenal world and our concepts only apply in this world, and what lies behind these phenomena we cannot count as human knowledge. If we try to proceed beyond those limits, we move outside the sphere where humans can know. Therefore, since our concepts do not apply to the world beyond the phenomena, we cannot apply them to God. God is beyond the sphere of knowledge, but we can still speak of the world of religious experience and about religious phenomena. This leads theologians such as Tillich and Kaufman to their conclusion that our concepts cannot be applied to God, and this is, they say, the end of classical theism. The word "God" does not refer to anything in metaphysical reality; rather, it refers to something in human reality.

A Tentative Relativizing

Before I discuss this any further, I should point out that the Kantian approach is no longer common in analytical philosophy. And this is certainly not only by reason of religious motives, but it is so mainly on the grounds of philosophical arguments about realism and nominalism. Regarding the direction of Tillich and Kaufman, Alvin Plantinga, one of the most prominent analytical philosophers, remarks that this kind of thinking

> . . . begins in a pious and commendable concern for God's greatness and majesty and augustness; but it ends in agnosticism and in incoherence.[14]

Eleonore Stump and Norman Kretzman express their astonishment that theologians such as Kaufman blame the academic philosophers for still occupying themselves with the philosophical questions of classical theism. In a 1989 article in *Faith and Philosophy*, Kaufman suggested that the concept of "God" should be radically reconstructed. No more cognitive claims about a personal God, God's properties, his omnipresence, about God as Creator, and so forth — only the recognition that God is pure mystery. When we say the word "God," we speak of the ultimate ground of our being, the ultimate trust. But this God is beyond our knowledge and understanding.[15] Thus we must recognize, says Kaufman, that we are ignorant with respect to God. But Stump and Kretzman argue in reaction that Kaufman's agnostic position leads — as far as morality is concerned — to a disparaging attitude toward the adherents of world religions, and also that his position is untenable from the perspective of logical consistency.[16] Thus it is not a *sine qua non* that philosophical reflection on human knowledge and the reality of God leads automatically to a so-called modern understanding of God. There are numerous eminent philosophers (such as Plantinga, Kretzman, Nicholas Wolterstorff, Peter Geach, William Alston, and others) who defend a form of metaphysical realism and in fact strongly support theism.

14. Alvin Plantinga, *Does God Have a Nature?* (Milwaukee, 1980), p. 26.
15. Gordon D. Kaufman, "Evidentialism: A Theologian's Response," *Faith and Philosophy* 6 (1989): 43.
16. E. Stump and N. Kretzman, "Theologically Unfashionable Philosophy," *Faith and Philosophy* 7 (1990): 332.

Nonreferential Speaking of God

The Dutch theologian Gerrit Manenschijn has recently called anew for a nonreferential speaking about God in his study entitled *God is so great that he does not need to exist.*

> The unutterable is spoken of in metaphors, and the visible is shown in symbols. We use metaphors and symbols to construct a preliminary and refutable reality. No other reality is hidden behind this. . . . The reality of faith is not a miraculous reality which can only be experienced by believers; it is, in principle, accessible for all. It should, however, be noted that *the* reality does not exist. A particular view of reality provides us with an image of reality that fits with it. We have reason to believe that there is one undivided reality, but that we will never be able to observe, experience or comprehend that reality in its totality. We will have to be satisfied with images of reality and be content with what it provides in terms of reality-value. . . . With respect to the reality of faith we must recognize that we only have metaphors and symbols at our disposal; we will not get any further. . . . The consequence is a radical relativizing of theological attempts to say anything about God and Christ, and that includes my attempt.[17]

There are quite a number of presuppositions in that quotation. (1) There is an undivided reality — not a polarity between God as Creator and the human world as creature. Is Manenschijn trying to say that we cannot make any differentiation in our ontology, that there is no question of distinct species, and that, for example, we cannot differentiate between abstract and concrete entities, between necessary and contingent existence, between God and man? (2) Even though reality is accessible to all, according to Manenschijn, *the* reality does not exist. He probably wishes to say that we cannot have an all-inclusive image of it, that we obviously know only a segment of reality. But that is not what Manenschijn actually says. Our knowing is always a matter of a view of reality, an image that we ourselves construct. He doesn't want to emphasize that our knowledge always remains fragmentary but rather

---

17. Gerrit Manenschijn, *God is zo groot dat Hij niet hoeft te bestaan. Over narratieve constructies van de geloofswerkelijkheid* (Baarn, 2001), pp. 242, 243.

that our knowledge is always only a view of reality, an interpretation. (3) This opens the way to say that faith is also merely *a* view of this self-same reality. And the nature of this faith perspective is such that it can only be expressed in metaphors and symbols. To have faith in God is not, so it seems, to have faith in a divine reality but rather a religious interpretation of that one undivided reality. Faith is not a matter of a relationship with a divine subject, which has its own autonomy, but the human image of life's religious dimension. In any case, the result is that humanity and not God becomes the *locus* of religion.

What, ultimately, *is* the referent of the word or the name "God"? Manenschijn believes that this referent is to be found in the human world and not in something "above us." To what does faith refer?

> The point of reference of religion remains something that is situated in humanity: guilt, suffering, death, insecurity. This is religion as discovery. Based on this discovery man, in a sense, becomes the inventor of God as a person. This is what religion devises. The material of this creation is the age-old language of faith.[18]

What, then, do we say — ontologically speaking — about God? Are experiences of God not to be considered experiences of a divine reality. In other words, is there no relationship with an object? Indeed, Manenschijn believes that the referent of the faith experience is not to be found in the divine reality but in the religious feeling of the believer. However, he does suggest that the instruments of religious experience enable us to evoke a divine "reality"; but he means that it is created in the language of images. It is the conceptual world of the believer, for God does not exist independent of us humans. In terms of classical theology, there is no *aseitas Dei.* "Experiences of God do not refer directly to a divine reality, but indirectly, via uneradicable human feelings. For this we employ the metaphor 'heart.'"[19] Thus Manenschijn does not argue that God and the human heart relate to each other; rather, the human heart is the place where God is to be found, or, even more explicitly, the birthing place of God.

18. Manenschijn, *God is zo groot,* p. 257.
19. Manenschijn, *God is zo groot,* p. 263.

What Are Concepts?

We have already noted that a similar line of thinking is found in Schleiermacher (Chapter 6) and Kaufman (Chapter 10): "God" does not refer to a divine person but to a dimension of human and social-cultural reality. The idea behind this is that we have no access to God as the referent of "God"; for we happen to live in the world of phenomena, and even religion cannot penetrate beyond this. Let us turn toward humanity, says Schleiermacher, for there we find the substance of religion. But is there no alternative to this reasoning? Must we, from this time forward, consider the beliefs of a number of world religions concerning the existence of a divine person, who is merciful and just, as a human construct? Is every form of theism — the belief that God exists, that God is an intentional subject, has specific properties, and reveals himself in the lives of people — outdated? Is it true that "reasonable" people can no longer believe in God, that every reference to a divine person is an irrational act?

Plantinga believes that the Kantian thesis — that our concepts do not apply to God — is less than plausible. From a theistic perspective, he says, the idea is "totally untenable, both philosophically and theologically."[20] Plantinga is primarily concerned with philosophical argumentation; so, to avoid any ambiguity, he begins by explaining that we should not confuse the claim that our concepts do not apply to God with the claim that we have only a limited knowledge of God. True enough, what we can know of God is probably minuscule in comparison to what we do not know about God; and it is very well possible that there is much in God about which we have no idea. But this only means that God has properties of which we have no understanding. That is something entirely different from the proposition that our concepts do not apply to God.

But what is the issue in the Kantian thesis? What might it mean that our concepts are not applicable to God? In order to answer that question, we must first know what a concept is. If someone understands the concept "horse," it means that he or she understands the property of "being-a-horse." If someone understands the concept

20. Plantinga, *Does God Have a Nature?* p. 18; see also Plantinga, *Warranted Christian Belief* (New York/Oxford, 2000), pp. 3-63.

"prime number," he or she can understand the property of "being-a-prime-number," of what it means to be a prime number. Some properties, clearly enough, aren't understood or grasped by everyone; some people have concepts that others lack. Small children typically don't know what it is for a number to be prime; quite a few philosophers don't grasp such properties as, say, "being-a-quark." "We have concepts corresponding to those properties we grasp or apprehend. Furthermore, apprehending a property is a matter of degree. You and I may have some grasp of the property *being-a-quark;* a physicist, we hope, will have a better grasp."[21]

And what does it mean for one of my concepts to *apply* to something? Plantinga has a simple explanation: "I have the concept *horse* if I grasp the property of being a horse; and that concept *applies to* something, if that something is a horse, has the property of being a horse. Our concept *being a horse* applies to each thing that has the property of being a horse; my concept of prime number applies to all the prime numbers."[22]

Plantinga believes that it is a total confusion of tongues to say that a divine person or divine reality exists, and then to say that none of our concepts applies to that divine person. If our concepts cannot be applied to God, then God does not have such properties of being-merciful, being-Creator, and so forth. The concept of being-merciful is applicable to a person who is merciful. If our concepts do not apply to God, then such concepts as being-merciful, being-Creator, and providing-forgiveness would not apply to God. And that would mean that God in fact is not merciful, and so on. Plantinga argues that the Kantian argument does not make any sense. It is even impossible that there is anything to which none of our concepts would apply.

I can give only a simplified version of the argument here and cannot go into any depth about the logical and metaphysical backgrounds that play a role. The criticism by Plantinga and others does make clear that Kant's proposition that our concepts do not apply to God appears to be less obvious than is often thought. But the rather common opinion among theologians that God cannot himself be the referent of the word "God," and that our identifying descriptions of God do not refer

21. Plantinga, *Does God Have a Nature?* pp. 20, 21.
22. Plantinga, *Does God Have a Nature?* p. 22.

to God himself but rather to human reconstructions of God, happens to be based on Kant's proposition. One might expect this to be considered less obvious in the future.

The Absolutizing of the Transcendent

It seems justifiable to conclude that we speak of God in our religious discourse. We speak with God and about God, and we do actually say something about him, and we use all kinds of words and images that mean something to us. When we say that God is merciful and gracious, we have some notion of the meaning of those concepts and intend to say that God is like that. We ascribe certain meanings to God. When we pray, we ascribe certain properties to God, and we trust that God is like that and will manifest himself as such. How, then, is it possible that we are stuck with such an enormous gap between God and humanity? Why is it that, in the legacy of Schleiermacher and Tillich, statements about the reality of God are so bent that they become statements about human experiences of God. I believe it is caused by the absolutizing of the concept of transcendence through the influence of certain tendencies in contemporary Western thought. It is true that transcendence played a central role in the classical doctrine of God, but that was to emphasize the *aseitas* of God, the autonomous and independent existence of God.[23] In this mode of thinking, God is also separated from creaturely reality, but in the sense that he is the fullness of life and salvation *(actus purus)*, the origin of existence, and the guarantor of new life. This tradition does ascribe to God a concrete, creature-directed power because of his autonomous and independent existence. The transcendence does not detract from the fact that God is a subject and can be known. In the anthropological depiction of faith, the notion of the *aseitas Dei* has gradually been pushed to the background.

But we must be careful not to take the transcendence to the extreme, to the point where God disappears behind the horizon of the knowable. That would not accord with the praxis of faith. Christian faith communities claim to have knowledge: in the praxis of faith we speak in concrete terms about God and with God. Thus it would seem

23. See my *Divine Simplicity,* p. 27.

incorrect to me, when we speak of our faith, to detach our human understanding (as manifested in the subject functions of the human self) from the reality that is known, that is, from God. On this subject, Plantinga correctly remarks that our concepts constitute our understanding of properties that are part of reality. Our knowledge of God is thus a knowledge of *God,* and our experience of God is an experience of *God.* When I believe that God is merciful, I trust that he is indeed merciful, and that mercy is a characteristic — even an essential characteristic — of God. This also implies that in the process I, viewed subjectively, have certain images and certain experiences; the subjective experience and the objective existence do not exclude each other in any way. Humans have been given the possibility of living with intentionality (as I have argued in Chapter 1); we possess an intellectual infrastructure. We are able to know, experience, and enjoy everyday reality. Apparently, we have been endowed with numerous intellectual and spiritual capabilities that have been designed just for that purpose. Therefore, if we think that we can know and serve God, it is with the presupposition that our human functions enable us to do so.

External Realism

The practical theological reflection on our speaking of God forces us also to reflect on the nature of human discourse, for we are dealing with people who speak of God. Clearly, various and diverse theories have been developed about the human praxis of speaking, communicating, and knowing. The core questions return again and again in these various theories, albeit with differing solutions. One of the key issues is the relationship between our ability to know and to perceive, on the one hand, and reality as such, on the other. Do we genuinely know and comprehend external reality, or should we rather think in terms of gaining impressions and subjective experiences? In the first case, our human self directs itself toward reality. Searle refers to this as "external realism." This approach is usually accompanied by a referential view of thinking and language.[24] In the second case, reality conforms to the human mind, and human consciousness is the bearer of

24. Searle, *Mind, Language and Society,* p. 15.

RECONSTRUCTIONS OF PRAXIS

what we experience. It concerns the "imprint" that we receive from phenomena, and in our communication we transfer these to the other.

It should not surprise us that these theoretical backgrounds play a role in our speaking of God; for religious discourse is embedded in human discourse. For that reason we must, in our practical theological reflection, take into account the consequences of theoretical analyses. What are the implications of a particular construct, derived from the human sciences, for our speaking of God? Within the spectrum of views about the relationship between our ability to know and external reality, Plantinga, in criticizing the Kantian paradigm, undoubtedly stands at one end of the spectrum, namely in the tradition of a modern metaphysical realism. But other theories are possible. Nowadays, at the other end of the spectrum we find not so much classical Kantianism as a more postmodern approach — expressed, for example, in social constructionism. Adherents of this view believe that concepts, values, and truths are based on social conventions and have no anchor in any external reality, nor in the human subject functions.

What does metaphysical realism look like? The key idea is that what we express through our concepts refers to an autonomous existence, independent from the human self. We might call it a modern form of Platonism.[25] Representatives of this school of thought consider properties as abstract entities that have an existence independent of the human mind. Properties, propositions, and so forth are not seen as mental images, for if that were the case, they would depend for their existence on human beings. Even if there were no human beings, there would still be the properties of greenness, redness, roundness, and so on. These entities exist in their own particular way and must, moreover, be distinguished from such concrete objects as trees, mountains, and people. Concrete things or subjects may manifest a certain characteristic (have a certain property), but we are able to understand and observe this property detached from its concrete manifestation. Properties, so the thinking goes, have a particular existence as abstract entities and must be distinguished, as to their mode of existence, from concrete things. Properties are neither intellectual nor linguistic, nor are they material. "They belong to an 'independent world,'" according to Bertrand Russell, "which thought comprehends but does not cre-

25. See my *Divine Simplicity*, pp. 39-43.

ate."[26] When the human self develops a concept of something, it directs itself toward that independent reality. In contrast to what we find in neo-Kantian approaches, concepts are not mind-dependent or mind-made.

Metaphysical realism does not concern itself merely with the idea of a concrete world of individuals and things that exist independent of the human mind. This is implied, but the main issue is the way in which properties exist. Perhaps the easiest way to explain this is to refer to the difference in a statement between subject-term and predicate-term: the subject-term refers to the thing about which or the individual about whom we speak, while the predicate-term points to a property.[27] For example, the statement "John is blond" informs us that the subject-term, a certain individual named John, has the property of blondness, which is expressed by the predicate-term. Note the difference between the subject and the predicate: they do not share the same logical order. A subject-predicate phrase has the structure "$x = F$," where x stands for a concrete individual or thing, while F expresses the property that x possesses. By using the predicate F, we make a statement about the subject x. We must remember that the individual concrete things (the x's) should, as to their mode of being, be distinguished from their properties (the F's). In our use of language we refer to concrete individuals by using proper names such as "John," by using descriptive definitions such as "the son of Klaas and Thea," "the brother of Casey," "the brightest kid in the class," and so forth. As far as the x's are concerned, there is a referential relationship between the term and the concrete subject (the referent). But what about the predicate "is blond"? The term itself is a linguistic entity, which is not true of the property of "blondness" that the term expresses. Properties are not in themselves linguistic entities, even though they are expressed through language — for example, in predicate phrases.

The particular nature of properties in relationship to human comprehension has been the subject of discussion through the ages (from Plato to Plantinga). What do we, in fact, "grasp" when we com-

26. Bertrand Russell, "The Problems of Philosophy," reprinted in *Universals and Particulars,* ed. Michael J. Loux (Notre Dame, 1976), p. 30.

27. For a more detailed treatment of this problem, see my *Divine Simplicity,* pp. 36-73.

prehend a property? The fact is that several individual things may share the same property. The property of being-a-person is applied to more than one individual, namely to all people — indicating a property that is held in common. What do we comprehend when we understand this common property? Plato said that predicates are assigned to several things, since they share in the same common nature (the so-called *universalia*). What all just causes have in common is the Idea of justice; if several people are just, they share in the property of justice. And our minds know and understand that concept. But modern realists consider properties to be abstract entities: they exist abstractly, detached from concrete things. And the human self is able to think of these properties and to bring them to mind, detached from where they fit into concrete reality. They are part of an independent world to which the mind must direct itself. Properties are known by human beings, and in that sense they exist in the human mind, but they are more than just a mental act. They are, in fact, the object of the mental act.

In analytical philosophy, and certainly in the case of Plantinga, we find a whole world of thinking and argumentation behind this. In one of his major works, *The Nature of Necessity,* he deals primarily with modal distinctions, such as necessary being and essences. He argues that we should not localize the notion of necessity in our manner of observing, thinking, or speaking. It doesn't depend on the way we think, and most certainly not on the way we use language.[28] Objects, he says, may possess properties essentially, regardless of the way we describe them or refer to them. This approach has given notions such as "essence," "essential existence," "necessary existence," "logical impossibility," and so forth, a new actuality in analytical philosophy. But how can Plantinga, from his theistic perspective, give a place to this entire Platonic pantheon? By following in the footsteps of Augustine, Anselm, Thomas Aquinas, and many others, he claims that these necessary entities can best be comprehended as existing *in mente divina.*

Isn't all of this a bit far-fetched? We have to realize that we are primarily dealing with theoretical frameworks and mental structures here. But we cannot avoid touching on them in our reflection on the praxis of faith. For faith is a living relationship with God, and in practical theology we reflect on the establishment and actualization of that

28. Alvin Plantinga, *The Nature of Necessity* (Oxford, 1974), p. 27.

communion. In reflecting on the nature of that communion, we cannot avoid touching on anthropological and metaphysical questions (Chapter 1). The discussion above deals with the question of the relationship between our conceptual and linguistic abilities, on the one hand, and external reality, on the other. This does not impinge on theological convictions. But from the very moment we begin to argue as theologians about the nature of communion with God, we do meet these theoretical constructs. The analyses of Plantinga and other philosophers from the analytical tradition are purely philosophical in nature; but they do have consequences in the domain of theology. They have raised critical questions regarding the self-evidence of certain views from the Enlightenment, particularly regarding the Kantian paradigm, which has had an enormous influence on modern theology. Again, these questions are raised not only by philosophers who are theists but also by agnostics such as Searle.

Is it a far-fetched subject? Not if we reflect on the relationship between our conceptual abilities and external reality. Admittedly, at first glance this approach flies in the face of some theoretical paradigms that are at the core of many current theologies. But there are similarities with other points of view, since this approach concerns both our human comprehension and reality. The question is, what is the relationship between the mode of being of things and human comprehension? This issue has a long history, as is often the case with principal problems. We might also ask, where is the *locus veritatis?* Is the truth of a particular statement about reality in the statement itself (in language), or in the world of things (in objects), or in human knowledge or observation (in subjective judgment)? The fact that the question is answered in many different ways does not mean that there is no connection to the underlying theme.

Alternatives

When I discussed the communication of faith above (Chapter 5), I briefly referred to a few ideas of Paul Ricoeur. Ricoeur is interesting in that he links the ideas of the continental hermeneutical tradition — which, because of the influence of Kant and existentialism, placed a stronger emphasis on human subjectivity — with a more Anglo-Saxon analytical philosophical approach. In his comments on interpersonal communication, and particularly on the role of the spoken word and texts, Ricoeur tends to distance notions such as meaning and truth from the human subject to a certain degree. The human subject continues to play a key role in his understanding of reality, but the importance of the "I" is, on the other hand, somewhat reduced by the attention to various collective structures, such as language, thinking, and social conduct. In addition, we find in Ricoeur an awareness that the focus is not just on the human-to-human relationship, but particularly on the intentional relationship between humans and their world, the I-in-the-world, which precedes every relationship grounded in knowledge.

In a short note on Heidegger, Ricoeur says that the knowing subject should not make himself the norm by which things are to be measured. "What we must now regain from that pretense is the condition that man first of all is the inhabitant of this world and that this circumstance brings situation, understanding and interpretation. . . . First one has to be somewhere, to be somewhere and feel in a certain way, before there is any question of orientation."[29] This being-in-the-world precedes comprehension, which is expressed in the subject-object relationship. Here again, ontology precedes epistemology, and this ontology has its own status, which is independent of knowledge and interpretation. But there remains a major difference when we compare this to metaphysical realism. For in metaphysical realism the human self takes its cue from objective reality, while Ricoeur emphasizes that every understanding and every meaning is always preceded by a concrete and specific being-in-the-world. In metaphysical realism, comprehension means that one grasps a fact, while for Ricoeur comprehension relates to insight in a possible mode of being. But in both instances existence has logical priority over knowledge.

There is another area of similarity. Ricoeur says that in discourse the meaning is detached from the concrete linguistic expression, and that the listener comprehends this meaning in a noetic act. Moreover, this meaning is expressed in illocution and has a propositional content. This is the *what* of the statement, that which we understand. Ricoeur further argues that this illocutionary content is not a psycho-

29. Ricoeur, *Interpretation Theory*, p. 36.

logical entity and must not be equated with the inner condition of the speaker. It is not the private experience but the meaning that is communicated. When I understand what someone says, it does not mean that I understand the other person — only that I understand what she has said. But in order to avoid falling into the traps of Romanticism, Ricoeur inclines toward an objectivizing and abstracting of what has been stated in the linguistic expression. This, he indicates, is what makes communication possible. "What can be communicated is first of all the propositional content of discourse. . . . Because the sense of a sentence is, so to speak, 'external' to the sentence, it can be transferred; this exteriority of discourse to itself . . . *opens* discourse to the other. The message has the ground of its communicability in the structure of its meaning."[30] And this noetic content may be understood and appropriated by different people at different times and places. This implies that the propositional content receives its own ideal mode of existence, detached from the human subject and concrete linguistic expression.

It is precisely for this reason that Ricoeur insists that the discourse is not only concerned with the *what-is-said* but also with the *what-it-is-said-about,* between sense and reference. Otherwise, the propositional content would be detached from every concrete reference and would, as a result, be able to adopt any new meaning. In our use of language, he says, we always refer to something. In this way Ricoeur distances himself from any ideology of the "absolute text." The *what-it-is-said-about* always has to do with the linkage to the world; but, remarkably enough, this reference is routed via the speaker. The speaker is in-the-world-in-a-particular-way and can refer to a specific situation. Ricoeur assumes that this reference is always *deiktic* (from *deiknumi:* to point to; to show), or situational. But — and this is a crucial aspect — this *deiktic* reference is annulled when the statement is put into writing. So in this case we also find a distancing from the *what-it-is-said-about,* and we might well ask the question, to what, then, does the text refer? Apparently, no longer to a concrete reality. The reference is to a world that is designed; there is, at most, an indirect reference: "The effacement of the ostensive and descriptive reference liberates a power of reference to aspects of our being in the world that cannot be said in a direct descriptive way, but only alluded to, thanks

30. Ricoeur, *Interpretation Theory,* p. 16.

to the referential values of metaphoric and, in general, symbolic expressions."[31] It appears that there is still a reference to reality — but
this reality is not directly accessible. In that sense, Ricoeur inclines
back toward the continental hermeneutical tradition. He anchors his
ontology in the person of the "discourser," who is in the world in a
particular way, while external realism places the priority in actual reality, in what actually is the case.

Postmodern social constructionists explain this relationship between our conceptualizing and the world in which we live in a completely different way. In their approach, concepts and meanings do not
refer to a so-called external reality, and neither are they formed in the
human self. Concepts and meanings are social conventions, products
of historically and culturally determined interactions between people;
they are social artifacts.[32] Whereas Kant's view was that phenomenal
reality has its structure imposed on it by the (universal) human mind,
in social constructionism this structure is based on arbitrary conventions. Meanings, values, and truths are constructed by communities of
people, depending on the circumstances, and have no fixed point of
reference in external reality, nor in any inner psychological order.[33]

It is noteworthy that this approach assigns logical primacy to interpersonal discourse. Neither external reality (as would be the case in
metaphysical realism) nor the human subject forms the basis for any
conceptualizing. The discourse is explained on the basis of a network
of relationships and interactions, while no substance whatsoever is attributed to the psyche or to external reality. Likewise, mental states
such as emotion or fear do not presuppose a subject who is emotional
or fearful, but must be explained on the basis of an ongoing process of
relationships. Thus there is no independent human self (no subject of
understanding, will, or thought), nor any objective reality. The moment we say that something is this or that, we are dealing with a constructed reality. This means that the referential aspect of language
hardly plays a role, for we cannot refer to a reality, since we are always
dealing with a constructed reality. If we think we can find an adequate

31. Ricoeur, *Interpretation Theory*, p. 37.

32. Kenneth Gergen, *Realities and Relationships: Soundings in Social Construction*
(Cambridge/London, 1994), p. 49.

33. Kenneth Gergen, *An Invitation to Social Construction* (London/Thousand Oaks,
1999), p. 42.

term to describe "reality as it is," we are wrong, for we are always faced with "local convention."[34] There is always the possibility of fashioning a different construct; and, according to Kenneth Gergen, meanings and concepts are constantly negotiable.

Our Human Understanding of God

From what has been said above, it has become clear that a variety of theories exists regarding questions about the way we conceptualize the discourse and about our knowledge of the world in which we live. Since faith is embedded in human life, and the reflection on our faith occurs in a setting where we already find different theories about the reality we live in, it is not surprising that there is wide divergence in the views about how we might speak of God. In Plantinga's approach, we can refer to God, we can know God, and our concepts are applicable to God. However, Plantinga does not say that we cannot deny that God exists. Many people do just that. In fact, they will say that our concepts do not apply to God simply because God does not exist. Nevertheless, our concepts and images could also be projections. What Plantinga does say is that it would be nonsensical to believe that God does exist but that our concepts cannot be applied to him. That, he says, is logically impossible.

The structure of the faith relationship, as I have described it, implies that God is the subject of speaking and acting. God is an intentional subject that directs itself toward humans; at the same time, humans direct themselves toward God and know God. There is reciprocity as well as asymmetry. God is the Holy One and is entitled to priority in communion with him. God is not a human projection but an independent divine person. this means that the word "God" does not find its referent in the human being but points to the divine subject. When we say that God is merciful, we ascribe having mercy to God. Thus he is both the subject of the predicate and an identifiable referent. The first point implies that God has properties that are characteristic of him, and the second point implies that a possible response may be given to the question "Whom are you talking about?" We are talking about the God of Abraham, Isaac, and Jacob, the God who has made himself

---

34. Gergen, *Realities and Relationships,* p. 73.

known in his interaction with the people of Israel, and who has raised Jesus from the dead.

In practical theology's reflection on faith in God, the difference between the concept and the referent of the subject-term is important: they do not coincide. Our understanding of God is not the same as the referent of the word "God." God himself is the referent of the word "God," while our comprehension of God consists of a collection of properties and attributes that we hold to be characteristic of God. Therefore, our comprehension of a concept always has a subjective connotation; our human understanding is expressed in the concept. However, this does not mean that a concept is nothing more than purely human understanding, for our concepts enable us to understand external reality. If "being merciful" is an aspect of our God-concept, we comprehend God's being merciful. Our concepts provide the link with the external reality. But it remains *our* understanding, since our ability to understand plays an active role.

But we must not confuse this with the referent of the subject-term in a predicate-phrase. When we use predicative sentences, such as "God is merciful," "God" remains the logical subject of that statement. The term "God" in that statement refers to the person who is God. God is the referent; God is the person who answers to that term. This is clearest in our use of proper names, which are to be distinguished from generic names since they clearly mark the person's independence and distinction from others. In the sentence "Peter is a nuisance," the name "Peter" refers to a person called Peter: the person in question is identified in a unique way. Proper names are not the only uniquely identifying expressions. We may also think of descriptions that name a person: for example, instead of identifying the person with the name "Peter," we can call him "the second son of Case and Thea." When we speak of God, we use the name "God," but we use other expressions as well, such as "the Creator of heaven and earth," "the father of Jesus Christ," or "the one who revealed himself to Moses." These are ways of naming God and of referring to him. Philosophers have endlessly discussed the question how the word "God" is to be understood. Is it a proper name or a title?[35] The theology of revelation explicitly points to the name of God as the unique identification: YHWH (I am that I am).

---

35. I. U. Dalferth, *Religiöse Rede von Gott* (Munich, 1981), p. 577.

The distinction between a concept and a referent is important in the faith relationship between God and the human world. It provides a possibility to deal creatively with the tension between the object-side and the subject-side of the faith relationship. We can indeed speak about our concept of God. I prefer not to speak about "images of God" because this suggests too strongly that concepts are no more than mental constructs; in actual fact, concepts establish connections with external realities. They are links. When I conceptualize something, I comprehend it. When I have a concept of God, I understand something of God. We express a conglomerate of insights, experiences, and opinions in a concept. Thus, forming concepts presupposes the activity of the human consciousness, and in that sense it is subjective: it is linked to the mental activity of the human subject. But it is not subjective in the sense that it is purely a mental process, for it consists in knowledge and comprehension of an external reality.

Finally, I want to point to two aspects of this concept formation that are important to us. In the first place, our concept of God consists of a series of properties or characteristics. This collection of properties will only very partially coincide with the properties and characteristics God really has; that is, there is a difference between our concept of God and the referent of "God." Our concept of God develops and changes over time. Of course, that doesn't mean that God himself also changes. Our concept of God may also be inadequate to a smaller or larger degree. It may include ideas and opinions that are incorrect because God may be just a little different from what we think he is. In the second place, our human concepts are characterized by a certain gradation: I may have some understanding of the concept of justice or mercy, but my awareness of it may increase or decrease; our experiences may lead us to deeper insights; and the intensity of a certain concept may change.

The distinction between the concept and the referent of God is crucial in the communication of our faith. The way we conceive of God has a subjective and a social dimension, but not in the sense that our concept of God is merely a subjective construct. Our concept of God does truly have to do with a relationship with God himself. But it is a relationship in which the subject functions fully participate. Our ideas of God are partial and imperfect; yet, at the same time, in the living encounter of religious discourse we are constantly nurtured by God himself. Via interpersonal discourse we identify God and point toward him by using stories from the history of revelation, as we read and tell of the life, death, and resurrection of Jesus Christ. This is what God is like, and this is how God has made himself accessible. God meets us and has an impact on our lives in that concrete encounter; the person in that encounter is the referent God himself, not our concept of him. And during such encounters our concept may be intensified and adjusted.

The considerations of this chapter have their influence on the way we shape our theories. Though it is not a matter of a one-to-one relationship, there should be a connection between the theoretical fundamentals and the way we develop our theological theory. That does not mean that the one is simply the result of the other, but there is a constant interaction.

Theoretical arguments in the discussion about fundamentals have their influence on our reflection about the praxis of faith, something we have to deal with in our practical theological discourse. For practical theology is an interdisciplinary domain of study, and we are in constant dialogue with nontheological reflection on religious praxis. In this evaluation of insights and convictions we must always pursue the further questions of axioms and presuppositions that influence the ways we build our theories. Practical theological professionals should be able to come to a relatively independent judgment, without arbitrarily jumping on the bandwagon of one particular current of thought. Moreover, in practical theology we should also be able explicitly to identify our theological presuppositions. For theological reflection possesses a unique weight in the analysis of praxis. This chapter may be seen as a plea for a renewed focus on the fundamentals of practical theology.

CHAPTER 12

The Life of Faith

The Faith Relationship

If we want to live in the expectation of salvation, we must constantly be reminded of who the God of salvation is. For that reason, ecclesial praxis carefully searches for an adequate identification of God. Who is this God to whom we pray, in whose name we act, and whose kingdom we expect? The church confesses that revelation history provides a decisive criterion by which to pursue this identity. It offers us identifying descriptions, plus words and acts that reveal God's identity. God reveals his salvation in the words he speaks and the acts he performs. God's salvation and the name of God are indissolubly tied together.

In this study I have tried to explain the meaning and significance of the fact that God is the other party in the faith relationship. We have seen how that aspect is included in the ideas of Word and promise. But this does not exclude us humans; in fact, it activates us. The Word of God touches us in our concrete existence; it is understood and receives its meaning in daily life; it is a Word that offers orientation and provides direction. The human self absorbs the Word, and this has its influence on the praxis of life. This impact on our lives is not something secondary. The Word of God aims for that relationship — the communion. This focus on the human being, and the intention of not only being understood but also of awakening consent and response, is a unique characteristic of the Word. Therefore, there is a linkage between Word and Spirit. The Spirit evokes consent, change, and renewal. This is why the position of Thurneysen and Barth (as I have outlined in Chapter 9) must be corrected. The rupture of God's judgment over our lives does not only consist of an external judgment but also implies a concrete self-understanding: an insight into our own self from the perspective of our communion with God. As a result, the ruptures in our own lives may become points of departure in the discourse about God and God's promises. That is not to say that our own self-understanding coincides with God's judgment over our lives, but in this context God's Word becomes concrete and comprehensible. In that sense, the theology of the Word generates attention for humankind.

Nonetheless, the *a priori* character of the Word remains important. God's promises include more than our faith. Our concrete existence cannot fathom salvation in its fullness, at least not in this earthly life. Our human minds cannot grasp the fullness of grace and love. There is nothing that can, as it were, contain divine salvation; it is always greater and richer than we think or imagine. Christ is more than the Christian, revelation is superior to our faith, and salvation exceeds sanctification. For that reason the name of God and the Word of God must continue to be proclaimed, and salvation must continue to be heralded. It must be announced to us in some divine way, for otherwise we would reduce the scope and greatness of salvation. The life that God reveals is more than a response to our needs; the glory of God's kingdom is more than our desires. The atonement in Christ surpasses the forgiveness of our guilt: God "reconciled the world to himself in Christ" (2 Cor. 5:19); even the "thrones and powers" are subjected to Christ (Col. 1:16). This kerygma is of divine origin and does not evolve from the human self, and that is why we see the constant movement from God toward us as humans.

Faith as It Is Experienced

Faith is a relationship in which the human being faces God. Thus faith consists of a concrete involvement, interaction, and communion — words that point to a dynamic relationship. These words imply a degree of reciprocity: God speaks and we listen, we pray and call, and God manifests his presence. This is how faith may be characterized as a living faith. The Other is presupposed and allows himself to be known, but never as a matter of course or by force. The Other might also be absent, or stay in hiding, or remain deaf. God's salvation is not always experienced, and at times God's voice is not heard or understood. In such instances God remains hidden to us: we search, but we do not find. In the meantime, though, faith and trust may still be there in our consciousness — in our personal as well as our collective consciousness. For there is a continuity in the subject functions. Even if God happens to be absent, we may still remember God; and, in that sense, faith may be described as a habit of the heart.

Nor is communion a matter of course when seen from God's perspective. The Bible portrays God as a speaking and acting subject who initiates communion. We discover this in the calling of Abraham, the exodus from Egypt, the return from captivity, and the coming of the Messiah. But how often does God have to conclude that the people have been unfaithful, have lost their way, and have rejected him? The intended communion is not realized. This causes a tremendous commotion in heaven: "I am grieved that I have made Saul king, because he has turned away from me" (1 Sam. 15:11). But God remains true to himself, to his inner compassion, and to his salvation for the world: "I have swept away your offenses like a cloud, your sins like the morning mist. Return to me for I have redeemed you" (Isa. 44:22).

Faith experience and piety find their origin in this relationship between God and humans. God's Word and his salvation do not remain external; they are tested and experienced. Humans appropriate Word and salvation to themselves in the act of faith, through the activities of the mind. Grace and love become actual in the forgiveness of one's own guilt. We experience the judgment concerning sin in our own shortcomings. We feel joy because of the gift of life, gratitude because of the goodness we encounter. These states of mind are born in the awareness that God is good and is not going to let us down. The ground under our feet is not life itself, but the God of our life is. The hope and expectation we cherish is not anchored in our indestructible ideals but in the identity of him (YHWH) who has given his promise.

It is characteristic of piety in the Reformed tradition that humans themselves are important and that they throw themselves fully on God's mercy. The important thing is that Christ's salvation is truly lived in our own existence and our own walk through life. Dying and rising with Christ, as symbolized in baptism, cuts its own trail through the self and the praxis of life. Yet this does not mean that therefore the point of gravity is found in human subjectivity. For it is the constant concentration on God, on his person and being, that is the ultimate certainty in the life of faith. Characteristic of the experience of God, Van Ruler says, is "that one must be focused on God himself. Not on something that belongs to God; not even on his grace; and certainly not on a higher world — but *in* all this on God the Lord himself."[1]

In this way human beings remain in a state of facing God. The human recognition of God's glory and majesty are part of this. God is God, and as long as people recognize that boundary, there remains a place for wonderment and worship.[2] God is majestic and grand; nonetheless, his voice is understood by the human mind. Indeed, we can say that we know him and commune with him. The human self is enlightened through the presence of the Spirit, and God is no longer distant and strange. The distant God is, simultaneously, very close. There is reverence and humility, but also joy, gratitude, and commitment. Life is lived in the context of that relationship: in the struggle between the "old man" who has died with Christ and the new person who has risen with him, in the struggle for participation in salvation. Besides the rapprochement between God and humanity there is always distancing and alienation; besides attraction there is abandonment; besides love there is anger; and besides joy contrition.

Communicating Our Faith

In the kerygmatic reconstruction of faith praxis, the divine speaking and acting is assigned the logical priority in the relationship between God and humanity. For interpersonal communication this implies that the reference to and the naming of God is crucial. Church praxis is qualified by the service to the Word of God; the continuation of the prophetic word and the apostolic witness are at stake. This implies a linkage to salvation history, for there we find the identifying descriptions of and stories about God. For that reason the Bible plays a major role in many of the activities of the church. The close linkage with sal-

---

1. A. A. van Ruler, *Theologisch werk,* vol. 3, p. 83.
2. M. J. A. de Vrijer, *Het ingekeerde leven* (Leiden, 1938), pp. 23-47.

vation history is explicitly expressed in the liturgy, the order of the church calendar, and the administering of the sacraments.

But this priority of God regarding humans does not mean that humans are of little significance, because the relationship between God and people is a human as well as a divine affair. It is the intention that men and women will come to have faith and trust in God, and that is what happens. People begin to understand, to commit themselves, to seek communion with Christ, to enter into discipleship. The Word of God receives substance in our intellectual functions and in our praxis of life. We understand aspects of the Word of God and appropriate these. This means that, as believers, we ourselves gain insights into matters of faith, of salvation history, of Christ and of God; and we are ourselves the subjects of that insight.[3] In this process of religious appropriation, the human mind turns toward the Word as God's truth, and thus we may declare that the Word of God becomes truth in the human mind. It no longer exists outside of us, but it has become something that is part of us. And this results in our being held personally accountable for it. This is particularly important in interpersonal communication — in two directions. I may be held responsible for my share in the communication, and I cannot and should not deny my personal involvement. When I speak about the promises and faithfulness of God, I am speaking about its meaning for myself.

Thus the human being has major significance in the relationship. In this regard, dialectical theology has somewhat disturbed the balance. Reacting to the identification in liberal theology of the Word of God with the experience of the religious personality, dialectical theology is so suspicious of humanity that it also considers all human religiosity, *a priori*, to be suspect. It says that the human subject must withdraw for the sake of the Word of God, and it views all piety with great misgiving. For example, Thurneysen fears that piety as humanity's own work (in Pietism, for example) will receive equal standing with God's work in Christ.[4] And Barth worries that attention to the testifier (the preacher) reduces attention to the testimony.[5]

---

3. H. Bavinck, *Gereformeerde dogmatiek,* vol. 1 (Kampen, 1928), p. 556.
4. Thurneysen, *Die Lehre,* p. 63.
5. Manfred Josuttis, *Praxis des Evangeliums zwischen Politik und Religion. Grundprobleme der Praktischen Theologie* (Munich, 1974), pp. 70, 94.

These views lead to an unnecessary and undesirable elimination of human subjectivity. The core element of the relationship between God and human beings is that humans accept and appropriate the Word of God. For we are not merely concerned with the imputation but also with the indwelling of salvation. Faith is an attitude, a habit of the heart, a way of life. But we need to be specific here. Barth and Thurneysen are afraid that faith becomes a human-centered knowledge that is no longer directed toward the Word of God as a critical "over and against." Thus Barth speaks of the *nachher* (what comes after) of the human subject. But should we throw out the baby with the bathwater?

What is at stake? Regarding the functioning of the human subject, I believe that two conditions must be met. First, the key issue in the faith relationship should be that the human subject be directed toward the Word and the promise of God. God addresses us. Second, even in the act of faith, the functions of the human mind operate in such a way that the person enters into a relationship with an external reality, namely, with the reality of Christ and with the reality of the Word of God. That is, faith has to do with knowing and experiencing God. Meeting these conditions will ensure that we avoid an anthropologizing of our faith while we are continuing to do justice to the role of the human subject. People recognize and affirm the Word of God as truth; as a result, people are filled with God. Gunning says that we "acquire spiritual knowledge of God's Word"; we become familiar with it; and we enter into a relationship with God himself.[6] God becomes known by women and men, and this is the real indwelling. There is not only a chasm between God and humans, but there is also an intimate link that can be found in the human assent to God, the acceptance of his grace, and the knowledge of God himself in Christ.

With these observations in mind, we can look back at the practical disciplines of homiletics and pastoral care (as discussed in Chapters 9 and 10). I have explained in Part III how interpersonal communication plays an important role in the exercise of our faith. But what is the role of the human subject in that communication?

That is not an easy question to answer. We may say that the human subject is involved. But how? Not simply as a technical instru-

6. Gunning, *Blikken in de Openbaring,* vol. 1, p. 179.

ment. The entire human being makes his appearance in this communication. For, as I have said in Chapter I, our intentionality is expressed in the interaction between people. This is also true for the communication of faith, where intentionality is a key issue, not only in our involvement with the concrete world of everyday life but also in our engagement with the Word of God.[7] Neither of these two dimensions remains external to the subject; the subject participates in the interaction as a believing subject. We cannot detach the subject from this. But what are its implications for homiletics and pastoral care? I cannot go into any great detail in this concluding chapter because that subject would require a separate book. But I want to sketch an outline and point to some developments that may free us from the contrasts between the revelationary model and the anthropocentric model.

The Sermon as Public Address

The sermon provides interpersonal communication in the form of a public address by which the preacher engages in contact with the congregation with the intention of being heard and understood, and with the desire to accomplish something. Thus it is hardly surprising that rhetoric has always played a significant role in homiletics. Rhetoric deals with, among other things, the art of speaking correctly — that is, of speaking in such a way that one is heard and understood. This often means that the preacher wants to convince the hearers of something, that she hopes for their assent or wishes to encourage them toward a certain behavior or activity. Unfortunately, rhetoric has a somewhat negative reputation within homiletics: it has been said that it only serves as a means of convincing the hearers. But that is only half true. We might also argue that rhetoric is an instrument we can use to bring people together, conquer the division of spirits, and create community.[8]

The sermon as public address implies that speaker and hearer are closely related in the interaction. While rhetoric reflects on the role of

7. J. Firet, *Het agogisch moment in het pastoraal optreden* (Kampen, 1968), p. 300.
8. Lucy Lind Hogan, "Rethinking Persuasion: Developing an Incarnational Theology of Preaching," *Homiletic* 24:2 (1999): 6-7.

the speaker, there is always an interaction with the hearers. Both speaker and hearers form important foci of attention. The speaker must be aware of her own role and responsibility by asking some questions: What is my position? What is my relationship to my hearers? Am I conscious of the context within which I speak? Do I know the world in which my hearers live?

The process of understanding, the reception of what was said, and the realization in the lives of the hearers are also important components of preaching. From that perspective, contact with the hearers is of paramount importance for the success of the address. Thus a great deal of attention in more recent homiletics has been focused on the hearer. In what way does the interaction take place? How is the situation of the hearers taken into account? How is the sermon understood? How do the hearers apply the message in their own lives?

When we consider the sermon as a form of public address, we are dealing with the interaction between speaker and hearer. The speaker not only intends to say something, but he also wants to evoke some reaction from the hearer as he is, for example, giving comfort, creating hope, encouraging certain actions, or providing new insights. And even if we see the sermon exclusively as proclamation, this proclamation still implicitly wishes to achieve something. The hearers are brought into a situation of *Entscheidung,* the existential decision to respond to the Word. What I want to emphasize is that the person of the preacher plays an essential role in this interaction, and, because of the performative effect of the address, the reciprocity with the hearer is of crucial importance for the success of the sermon. The personal and existential involvement is not a minor matter, and it does not detract from the aim to speak about God.

The involvement of the speaker is already included in the notion of intentionality. When I speak, it is not just a matter of saying something; I say something with a clear intention. I am aiming at something, and I am involved with my hearers in some special way, which leads me to use a particular kind of language. I may have the intention of simply stating something, and this may take the form of a proposition. But I may also intend to make a request, to give an order, or to encourage people. Intentions are expressed in the linguistic act, and this is an interesting phenomenon precisely in the area of preaching, for the rhetorical form often reveals the particular systematic theological content. The form of the sermon — and the kinds of linguistic acts that take place — determine whether a sermon is experienced as liberating, exhortative, or instructive.[9]

The notion of intentionality is not restricted to the subjective involvement of the speaker; it also includes the focus on the hearer. In preaching, we hope that the hearers will understand us, recognize our intention, and act accordingly. Thus, as soon as we speak, we are already involved with the hearer. In our preparation we not only think about what we want to say, but we consider what our words may do in the lives of the hearers. We are dealing with things that have a high existential value: we are dealing with a reality that awakens emotions, determines the attitudes of people, and puts a stamp on their lives. For that reason, in homiletics we focus on the performative impact of preaching. Thomas Long, for instance, differentiates in the preparatory phase between a "focus statement" and a "function statement": the first term refers to a short formulation of the message, while the second refers to the possible reaction on the part of the hearers.[10] In other words, we not only ask ourselves, "What do I want to say?" but also "What do I want to accomplish?" Henning Luther emphasizes that respect for the freedom of the hearer is of crucial importance for the performative effect of the sermon. There should be no trace of power or force; the hearer must come to insight and assent voluntarily. The sermon is not a matter of putting pressure on the hearer, but of a *Verständiging mit dem Hörer* (being on the same wavelength with the hearer).[11]

This means that the preacher is involved as person and as believer in the act of preaching, and that the hearers are existentially involved with the preacher through this constant interaction regarding the life of faith and daily experience. This implies that human subjectivity is part of that interaction, and preaching does not remain outside of this human particularity. But does this mean that we automatically return to an expressive communication model, where the kerygma disappears under the canopy of communicating about the self and is determined by the needs and problems of the hearer? I do not believe that this will

9. Jan Hermelink, "Predigt in der Werkstatt," *Berliner Theologische Zeitschrift* 12 (1995): 49.

10. Thomas G. Long, *The Witness of Preaching* (Louisville, 1989), pp. 78-91.

11. Henning Luther, "Predigt als Handlung," *Zeitschrift für Theologie und Kirche* 80 (1983): 234.

be the case, on one condition: that we actually speak about God. By this I mean that we actually refer to and name God.

Clearly, then, the sermon has an existential and expressive dimension. The Word of God addresses us and touches us in the praxis of life; the preacher recognizes this and enters into a dialogue with the hearers. But does this still pose the risk that the sermon becomes a statement about our life experience and our subjective ideas about faith? Or that we simply try to put into words what we experience in our lives? Is it, in the end, merely an expression of our faith experience, where the movement of God toward man is no longer a point of discussion, and where the priority of God in the faith relationship is obscured? That very concern creates a desire in dialectical theology to keep the human "I" away from the pulpit. Only the Word of God may be heard. As a result, rhetoric is suspect, and the person of the preacher must remain in the background — must remain, in fact, completely unimportant. And even the faith of the preacher must not be an issue.

But that approach lacks balance. The sermon is a public address, and the interaction between people plays an important role. The person, the opinions, and the competence of the preacher are factors to be considered; but we should not forget that the preacher has an ecclesial responsibility and does not operate as a private person. This ecclesial character also determines the contextuality of the address. The sermon is embedded in a liturgical framework, in the setting of a specific congregation, and in a social context. This in itself places some restrictions on the personal nature of the address. Faith is not a private matter, and the sermon is not an individual expression. The sermon has a communal and a public character, and the preacher must be conscious of that fact.[12]

Still, there is another argument. When is it that we have no defense against the pulling power of the sermon as self-expression? When we no longer position God as "over and against" humankind, when we no longer refer to the external source of the Word and to salvation history. Indeed, then we are in danger of having the person and faith of the preacher become paramount elements of preaching (albeit in relation to that of the congregation). Then God would no longer be con-

12. Richard Lischer, *A Theology of Preaching: The Dynamics of the Gospel* (Durham, NC, 1992), pp. 76-92.

sidered the subject of speaking and acting. However, as I have indicated above (in Chapters 10 and 11), I do not see any inescapable reasons for following this line of thinking. Likewise, there is no need to follow dialectical theology in minimizing the role of the preacher.

Theologians of the past have been more flexible in dealing with this problem. The nineteenth-century Dutch theologian J. J. van Oosterzee argued that the sermon, as a form of public address, should conform to all the requirements that apply to any civilized public speech. He says, "The source of eloquence is hidden in the heart, where the fountains of life are found."[13] The sermon "presupposes the value and the possibility of the word to gain access to the mind and the heart of those who hear."[14] In other words, the sermon must also be seen as a speech in which the personality of the speaker and the situation of the hearers are of importance and have to be taken into account. Van Oosterzee says that all homiletical rules can be reduced to one: "Be yourself, or in other words: try to be truly human, a true Christian, a true theologian, and then speak, after having prepared yourself as widely and harmoniously, in the way your sanctified individuality, in view of the nature of the matter under consideration and the needs of the moment, demands."[15]

The discussion of this issue in the field of homiletics continues. In a recent article in the American journal *Homiletic,* Lucy Hogan argues in favor of a positive appraisal of rhetoric in homiletics. She takes her point of departure from the notion of the persuasive power that characterizes a speech, and she defends the idea that pastors also need to convince people: "To speak is to persuade."[16] If the intention of persuading others is indissolubly attached to the role of the speaker in a public address, perhaps we should pay closer attention to this notion in preaching so that we can investigate the elements of power that come into play. Communication is not a neutral exchange of ideas in which interests play no role. When we address other people, we have some kind of interest in others and in wanting to share something with them.

13. J. J. van Oosterzee, *Practische Theologie. Een handboek voor jeugdige godgeleerden,* vol. 1 (Utrecht, n.d.), p. 219.
14. Van Oosterzee, *Practische Theologie,* vol. 1, p. 212.
15. Van Oosterzee, *Practische Theologie,* vol. 1, p. 84.
16. Hogan, "Rethinking Persuasion," p. 5.

That same issue of *Homiletic* indicates that the classic debate about the value of rhetoric in homiletics is far from being resolved. The sermon, Richard Lischer says, is primarily a Word-event and can only be defined in theological categories. The notion of persuasion is derived from rhetoric, and Lischer believes that that road does not lead to the actual nature of the sermon. Moreover, he says, there is the immediate risk that the emphasis is shifted toward the personal experience of the preacher and to the technique of interpersonal discourse.[17]

Pastoral Care as Existential Faith Conversation

In the work of the pastor, interpersonal communication — as opposed to the sermon — takes place in the form of conversation, an encounter between concrete persons. What is characteristic of this kind of conversation as a form of interpersonal communication in the context of pastoral care? There are all kinds of conversations that, despite their similarities, we would not refer to as "pastoral" conversations. Let me first list some kinds of conversations. The informal visit is one obvious example: we talk a lot when we visit people, and this small talk is often entertaining in character. We are interested in what other people are doing, and we share experiences from the workplace or other parts of our private lives. We may also discuss political or social topics — or the weather. There is a degree of familiarity as we talk about things that are part of daily life, and these social conversations are usually unstructured and largely determine whether or not we find the visit pleasant. A conversation between friends usually has a higher degree of intimacy; they know they can trust each other, and this allows them to share more than they would otherwise feel comfortable doing. Trust brings a high degree of reciprocity and gives existential depth to the conversation. In these one-to-one conversations, which can be intimate and precious, or sometimes even sharp and accusatory, people learn more about each other, and they share something of their own walk through life. That's why we say that we need to "update" each other.

There are other kinds of conversations: business talks in the context of meetings at work to discuss progress, strategic planning, and so

17. Richard Lischer, "Why I Am Not Persuasive," *Homiletic* 24 (1999): 13-16.

forth; or sales talks, where we try to sell something to someone; diagnostic and therapeutic conversations in a doctor's office, where we tell the doctor where we feel pain or what troubles us. In that last kind of conversation we try to indicate as precisely as we can what we think is wrong, hoping that the doctor can give us a diagnosis.

How does the pastoral conversation compare with these various kinds of conversations? What is the uniqueness of the pastoral conversation? There are several elements from the descriptions above that are also part of the pastoral conversation. For example, just as anything from daily life may enter into the conversation during a visit with a friend, everything that occupies our minds in daily life may be a topic for the pastoral conversation. But this does not make the pastoral conversation a social visit. The pastoral conversation usually acquires existential depth, even though it is not a conversation between friends. And the pastoral conversation will explore how the various questions interconnect; but this is not the same as giving a diagnosis. The pastoral conversation is an encounter in which aspects of real life are discussed. The special nature and the setting of the conversation evoke a specific dimension of life. When the progress of a project at the office is discussed, the focus is primarily on work; in a doctor's room, health complaints are at issue; in a therapeutic conversation, psychosocial problems form the topic.

What is the nature of the pastoral conversation? This kind of conversation centers on faith and life in their reciprocal relationship. Everyday life is discussed, both in its personal and social dimension. The pastoral conversation is about the situation in which people find themselves, about their life story and their journey of faith, that is, about life as it is lived and faith as it is lived. This may include controversies and tensions between faith and daily life. It may also mean that, for the time being, only one of these poles is talked about. But the pastor may be questioned about the dimension of this faith as it is lived, and she brings a certain degree of expertise to the table. This not only consists of knowledge regarding the tradition of faith, but also insights into the ways in which faith functions in the concrete praxis of life. Thus pastoral care demands expertise in the area of religion and requires personal involvement.

Seen from this perspective, both the kerygmatic and the therapeutic pastorate contain a core of truth. Faith can and may be discussed in the pastoral conversation. And when the topic of faith is introduced, it is done within the context of a faith tradition, at least that's the presupposition under which pastoral care operates. Pastoral care is embedded in the pastoral and diaconal calling and responsibility of the church. Therefore, talking about faith has a legitimate place in a conversation about someone's journey through life. When we talk about faith, God's salvation will be on the agenda. The fact that pastoral work often takes place at the fringe, or even beyond the fringe, of the faith community does not necessarily imply that the inherent value of pastoral care — as given in the Christian view of faith — will be absent. But I believe that it is an overreaction to suggest, as Thurneysen does, that talking about faith must always end in some form of proclamation. Behind that is the idea that the pastoral conversation should lead to a kind of auricular confession, to be followed by an explicit acquittal. Confession of guilt and proclamation of grace do indeed belong together, and they happen under the canopy of God's grace. But that doesn't necessarily mean that they should be made explicit in a formal word of acquittal or a ritual.

Moreover, the idea of proclamation suggests too strongly that God's Word is only an external announcement and promise. For the Word also assumes form in human life, arousing humility, hope, endurance, and joy. A conversation about this does not imply a discontinuity with real life but connects to life as it is lived. When we speak of God, it includes the dimension of an appeal. We are encouraged by the Word of God. We are given a new direction, and as a result we find that new perspectives and other values open themselves to us. But this happens, in effect, as we give a name to God's promise and his salvation. To refer specifically and by name to the faith reality does not disrupt the conversation as such.

The pastoral conversation is about daily life. The therapeutic pastorate has given us more insight into the complexity of spiritual life and the human psyche, and we have become more aware of the psychosocial mechanisms that also manifest themselves in the life of faith. But pastoral care deals not just with emergencies and crises but also with the everyday nitty-gritty of professional life, social life, family life, and leisure life. With the therapeutic angle, however, the emphasis has shifted very pointedly to the broken life. Eberhard Hauschildt has introduced the term *Alltagsseelsorge* (everyday pastoral care) in an effort to correct an overly therapeutic approach.[18] It is hardly surprising that the pastoral conversation often leads to the fault lines in a parishioner's biography, and to dramatic transitions in a life's history. That is all part of the human journey through life and will inevitably come up in an existential conversation. But a pastor must always be conscious of certain boundaries. The history of someone's personal life is also a history of social interaction. The person we have become is not detached from either the positive or negative experiences we have had in our encounters with others. For that reason, the pastor must constantly analyze his own role in the interaction during the pastoral conversation. A pastoral conversation is not a form of therapy, and the pastor must always recognize that he may find himself — at some point in the interaction — in a situation of transference and countertransference.[19] Pastoral training and supervision can help us recognize these pitfalls.

From what perspective do we speak about the things of life? Therapy-oriented pastoral care is mainly concerned with help in a time of crisis. In the recognition that God's salvation has to do with healing life, this form of care sees the pastoral conversation as an instrument for providing people with guidance and help in times of crisis. It is true that the pastoral conversation will often cover the history of the person's private life and the individual's biography. When we speak about our life of faith, it will often happen by reviewing moments of disappointment and hope, sickness and health, death and life. We are always confronted with human beings in their *condition humaine*, which is what is at issue in the pastoral conversation. Because of the connectedness between faith and life, it would be incorrect to make help in crisis situations and help aimed at strengthening faith into antagonists. The crisis-help that the pastor is able to offer is of a specific kind: the pastor helps the person in need to understand the concrete *condition humaine* from the perspective of the revelation of salvation. This is not a denial of tangible help in crisis, but it is help from a particular perspective, for it means that the journey of life is connected to the salvific word of God.

18. Eberhard Hauschildt, *Alltagsseelsorge. Eine sozio-linguistische Analyse des pastoralen Geburtstagsbesuches* (Göttingen, 1996).

19. Gerben Heitink, *Pastorale Zorg. Theology, differentiatie, praktijk* (Kampen, 1998), p. 239.

It is at this point that the pastor recognizes that interpersonal interaction as an instrument in the pastoral conversation has its limits. The understanding of salvation and the significance of God's promise in the concrete life of the layperson are not within the reach of the pastor to effectuate; that is, the pastor may speak of God's salvation, but she cannot bring it about.[20] Here we find the main limitations of the pastoral conversation: on the one hand, it is essential that the freedom and personal responsibility of the layperson be guaranteed at all times; on the other hand, it must be clear that the pastor cannot act as a negotiator and must not present herself as a mediator. Compared with a therapist, the pastor plays a more modest role in the conversation technique. Nonetheless, personal engagement may be intense, and the layperson may appeal to the personal convictions of the pastor.

In the development of pastoral care, the hermeneutical school in particular has noted the unique impact of the gospel. Heitink, an authoritative representative of this school, believes that "in, with, and under the interpersonal encounter something of the encounter with God may be experienced, as a gift."[21] The interpersonal encounter, he says, becomes the vehicle of something that is beyond ourselves — that is, the work of the Spirit. Yet Heitink prefers to speak in terms of tradition and experience, leaving the dimension of revelation somewhat in the background. The following quotation, I think, accurately portrays how the faith dimension is dealt with in the hermeneutical pastorate, without losing the psychological dimension of the therapeutic pastorate.

> Someone's complaint may be clarified psychologically or therapeutically, but at a given moment the question of meaning is posed: "How will you cope with this?" This implies a switching from the pole of experience to that of the faith tradition. But the reverse may also happen. In a conversation about faith we might turn to the level of human experience. "How do you experience this yourself?" As a result, the experiential dimension is evoked and psychology enters the fray. This reciprocity determines the unique character of hermeneutical pastoral care.[22]

20. Helmut Tacke, *Mit dem Müden*, p. 112.
21. Gerben Heitink, *Pastorale Zorg*, p. 71.
22. Heitink, *Pastorale Zorg*, p. 72.

Heitink indicates that doing justice to both poles — that is, to the faith tradition as well as to experience — is not simple. One may err too much in either direction. The term "tradition," particularly, may be somewhat nebulous, which may result in an insufficient emphasis on the "otherness" of the Word as direct pronouncement from God.

How God Works in the Human Mind

After describing the faith relationship between God and humanity and discussing the subject of communicating our faith in this concluding chapter, I return to the human subject. Humans are engaged in the everyday world and live "over against" God. These two dimensions continue to play an important role in faith communication. Against this backdrop I want to say a few things about the impact of faith on everyday life. In the praxis of life we see reciprocity between communion with God and the experiences we have in everyday life. That reciprocity, I believe, is channeled through the human mind, via the human consciousness; for it is a human characteristic to be involved in reality through the mental faculties. And this involvement has to do with human life in the world, in the "here and now," but also with the world of God and his salvation. It is within this reciprocity that the believer lives his life.

The world in which we live presents itself to us in a particular way. All kinds of facts and circumstances determine the way we live, but these are not bare facts that surround us expressionlessly. We live our lives as subjects, that is, we are intentionally engaged in the world where we find ourselves. We know and experience the world in a specific way, and we form a judgment about the world. This includes an affective and an emotional dimension. We may think of something as beautiful or ugly, as good or bad. We are not machines but living persons who have entered into a relationship with the world and with people around us.

The concrete world in which we conduct everyday life is genuinely and intensely present in the functions of the human mind. This is, according to Berger and Luckmann, the *realissimum* of our consciousness.[23] We are constantly involved with this reality of daily existence,

---

23. Berger and Luckmann, eds., *The Social Construction of Reality*, p. 22.

but we're able to discriminate to some degree: we do not experience everything as equally important and intense. We can decide to prioritize certain things and to put other things on the back burner; we make distinctions between the center and the periphery. According to Searle, the intensity of our involvement and the attention we pay to different matters varies, but the reality of the everyday remains the given reality where we find ourselves.[24] And this not only concerns our involvement with a particular state of affairs, events, or processes, but also involves our intersubjective involvements, interpersonal encounters, and social relationships. We are involved with our fellow humans, and thus other people are present in our consciousness — along with their social context.

There is another presence in the life of the believer and of the faith community that is no less explicit and intense: God and his salvation, which is a presence in the functions of the human mind — in other words, in our consciousness. I am not saying that religion is locked into human consciousness, nor that human consciousness is the source of religious life. It is more of an "if . . . then" statement: if there is a subjective involvement with God and with his promise of salvation, then there is indeed a particular layer in our consciousness that is involved and certain functions of the human mind are affected. In saying this, I do not in any way wish to detract from the logical priority in the divine-human relationship. But if revelation is effective, then there is also human faith, and human faith is located in the human subject. Thus may we speak of the presence of God and his salvation in our consciousness. And that presence is an *ens realissimum,* an utterly existential reality that determines the climate of our daily lives. It is a knowing, a feeling, and a direction of the will that is as close to us as the immediate situations in which we live. Faith is an immediate insight and a direct perception: the believer experiences the Word of God as truth and experiences the reality of forgiveness and grace. It is a state of mind that allows for the impact of God's salvation on the human mind. The human mind absorbs it as knowledge, insight, and experience: a knowledge that arises from one's own experience and an experience that needs no further foundation.

This is how we may also imagine the *unio mystica* between Christ

24. Searle, *Mind, Language and Society,* p. 78.

and the believer. We are dealing with a knowledge that is acquired through experience, a knowledge that allows us to experience forgiveness and salvation, a knowledge that produces change and conversion. It is thus an act of the human mind that expresses an intimate bond with God and has an impact on the way we feel and act. This is how we may understand the *applicatio salutis:* God's Spirit becomes operative in the human heart.

Doumergue, in his study of Calvin, points out that Calvin gives an important place to the mystical moment. He uses numerous metaphors to indicate that we are united with Christ to the extent that his power overflows into us. Christ lives in us, and we must clothe ourselves with him. It is a communion, a unity, a holy matrimony that makes us into flesh of his flesh and bone of his bone — one with him. In another metaphor, it is a grafting: we are grafted into Christ.[25] Our spiritual relationship with God and his salvation has an intersubjective structure, including a personal encounter in which we sense that we are addressed by God. God comes to us in his own person, and we may speak of the presence of God in the human mind because of that. The Holy Spirit affects the operations of our mind and adds its voice in our experiences of salvation and doom, in the choices we make, and in the expectations we cherish. But the presence of God in our consciousness always remains a presence of *God.*

Both our involvement in everyday life and our relationship with God and his salvation present themselves in the human mind. I believe that it is theologically incorrect to deny the presence of God in our consciousness; but it is of crucial importance to underscore the intersubjective character of that presence. It is a relationship and a communion that is characterized by a movement from the divine Other toward us. God is the subject of speaking and acting, and God addresses us with his salvific word in our human consciousness. If we want to do full justice to the presence of God in human consciousness, we must give full weight to the *aseitas* of God and to *gratia preveniens;* otherwise, we will run the risk of reducing God to "our awareness of God." Over and against the pull of our spiritual experience Barth rightly poses the *unferfügbarkeit Gottes* (the impossibility of manipulat-

---

25. Em. Doumergue, *Calvijn als mensch en hervormer,* Dutch translation by Helena C. Pos (Amsterdam, n.d.), p. 70.

ing God). He is correct in the sense that God should be assigned priority in the divine-human relationship; but he is incorrect in his suggestion that the *unferfügbarkeit Gottes* implies that divine reality and
salvation cannot be experienced by the human subject. The presence of
the divine reality in the human mind makes it possible that our faith
has meaning for our journey through life.

Now that we have given this presence of God in the human consciousness its rightful place in the understanding of faith, subjective
engagement stands out clearly: we become engaged with God and his
salvation while we live our concrete lives, and those concrete, everyday
lives remain present in our minds. We cannot detach ourselves from
them. The palpable joy that is ours, the expectations we cherish, but
also the tragedies we bear and the disappointments we have had to
face — all these we carry along with us, consciously or subconsciously.
And these things tend to occupy us. Our minds can be so full of the
things that touch us directly that there is hardly space for anything
else.

But there is a similar involvement and intensity regarding the
Word of God, God's promises and commandments, God's word of
grace and salvation. It touches us as a presence-of-God, as a word that
comes uniquely to us from God and penetrates our inner selves, our
consciousnesses. The word of grace — as *iustificatio,* as a word of compassion and love, as a token of kindness and affection, as a sign of resurrection and renewal, of salvation and hope — sounds from close by.
The Spirit of God pronounces it in our minds so that our minds will
consciously focus on it. We are united with Christ, and thus God's
word of grace turns into a known and lived reality. Forgiveness, love,
hope, and all benevolent things that belong to God become part of our
lives.

There remains a tension between our "life experience" and our
"faith experience." At the very least, that tension cannot be excluded,
because human life is characterized by a thoroughgoing obstinacy: life
and faith do not automatically coincide. There is discontinuity as well
as continuity. And because of our connection with God and his salvation, we may have to be critical about the reality of the "here and now."
We have seen that this is inherent in *iustificatio* and is also symbolized in
baptism: we must lay down the "old man" and take on the new person.
On the other hand, our "faith experience" may keep us going and it

does give us courage. Our lives and joys receive a new ring and a new color in our relationship with God. For the sting of death has been removed. The threat of destruction and meaninglessness has been conquered because Christ is alive! Therefore, we face life with trust and expectation.

Bibliography

Achelis, E. Chr. *Praktische Theologie.* Edited by L. W. Bakhuizen van den Brink. Utrecht, 1906.

Bakker, J. T. *Eschatologische prediking bij Luther.* Kampen, 1964.

Barth, Karl. *Der Römerbrief.* 2nd ed. Munich, 1933.

———. *Church Dogmatics.* Edinburgh, 1956-75.

———. *Fides quaerens intellectum. Anselms Beweis der Existenz Gottes im Zusammenhang seines theologische Programms.* 2nd ed. Zurich, 1958.

———. "Die Gemeindemäszigkeit der Predigt." In *Aufgabe der Predigt,* ed. Gert Hummel. Darmstadt, 1971.

———. *Homiletik. Wesen und Vorbereitung der Predigt.* Zurich, 1966.

———. *Die protestantische Theologie im 19. Jahrhundert.* Volume 2. Hamburg, 1975.

Bavinck, H. *Gereformeerde dogmatiek.* Volumes 1-4. Kampen, 1928-30.

Beker, J. Christiaan. *Paul the Apostle: The Triumph of God in Life and Thought.* Edinburgh, 1980.

Berg, J. H. van den. "Psychologie en theologische antropologie." In *Van gisteren tot heden. Godsdienstpsychologie in Nederland,* ed. J. A. van Belzen. Volume 1. Kampen, 1999.

Berger, Peter L. *A Far Glory: The Quest for Faith in an Age of Credulity.* New York, 1992.

———. *The Sacred Canopy: Elements of a Sociological Theory of Religion.* New York, 1969.

Berger, Peter L., and Thomas Luckmann. *The Social Construction of Reality: A Treatise in the Sociology of Knowledge.* New York/London, 1966.

Berkhof, H. *Christelijk geloof.* 5th ed. Nijkerk, 1985.

———. *Christian Faith: An Introduction to the Study of the Faith.* Revised ed. Grand Rapids, 1986.

Berkouwer, G. C. *Dogmatische Studiën. Geloof en rechtvaardiging.* Kampen, 1949.

Beutel, Albrecht. "Sprache und Religion." *Pastoraltheologie* 83 (1994).

Bohren, Rudolf. *Das Gott schön werde*. Munich, 1975.

————. *Predigtlehre*. 5th ed. Munich, 1986.

————. *In der Tiefe der Zisterne. Erfahrungen met der Schwermut*. Munich, 1990.

Browning, Don. *A Fundamental Practical Theology: Descriptive and Strategic Proposals*. Minneapolis, 1991.

Brümmer, Vincent. *Theology and Philosophical Inquiry: An Introduction*. London, 1981.

————. *Wijsgerige begripsanalyse. Een inleiding voor theologen en andere belangstellenden*. Kampen, 1975.

Burke, Kenneth. *A Rhetoric of Motives*. Berkeley, 1969.

Buttrick, David. *Homiletic: Moves and Structures*. London, 1987.

Calvin, John. *Institutes of the Christian Religion*. Philadelphia, 1960.

Canons, Ratified in the National Synod of the Reformed Church, Held at Dordrecht, in the Years 1618 and 1619.

Clinebell, Howard. *Basic Types of Pastoral Care and Counseling*. Nashville, 1991.

Dalferth, I. U. *Religiöse Rede von Gott*. Munich, 1981.

Davidson, Donald, and Gilbert Harman, eds. *Semantics of Natural Language*. Dordrecht/Boston, 1972.

Dekker, G. *Godsdienst en samenleving. Inleiding tot de studie van de godsdienstsociologie*. Kampen, 1993.

Dekker, Gerard. *Zodat de wereld verandert. Over de toekomst van de kerk*. Baarn, 2000.

Dingemans, G. D. J. *Manieren van doen. Inleiding tot de studie van de praktische theologie*. Kampen, 1996.

————. "Normativiteit in de praktische theologie." In *Lijden en belijden. Over de Derde Gestalte van het Antwoord*, ed. J. H. van de Bank and R. Brouwer. Zoetermeer, 1993.

————. "Practical Theology in the Academy: A Contemporary Overview." *Journal of Religion* 76:1 (1996).

Donagan, Alan. "Universals and Metaphysical Realism." In *Universals and Particulars: Readings in Ontology*, ed. Michael J. Loux. Notre Dame, 1976.

Donnellan, Keith S. "Proper Names and Identifying Descriptions." In *Semantics of Natural Language*, ed. Donald Davidson and Gilbert Harman. Dordrecht/Boston, 1972.

Doumergue, Em. *Calvijn als mensch en hervormer*. Dutch translation by Helena C. Pos. Amsterdam, n.d.

Dulk, Maarten den. *Heren van de praxis. Karl Barth en de praktische theologie*. Zoetermeer, 1996.

Edwards, Jonathan. *The Religious Affections*. First published in 1746; reprinted Edinburgh, 1997.

Ehrensperger, Alfred. *Gottesdienst. Visionen, Erfahrungen, Schmerzstellen.* Zurich, 1972.

Fackre, Gabriel. *The Doctrine of Revelation: A Narrative Interpretation.* Edinburgh/ Grand Rapids, 1997.

Failing, Wolf-Eckart, and Hans Günther Heimbrock. *Gelebte Religion wahrnehmen. Lebenswelt — Alltagskultur — Religionspraxis.* Stuttgart/Berlin, 1998.

Firet, J. *Het agogisch moment in het pastoraal optreden.* Kampen, 1968.

————. *Spreken als een leerling. Praktisch-theologische opstellen.* Kampen, 1987.

Friedrich, Gerhard. "Kerusso." In *Theologisches Wörterbuch zum Neuen Testament,* ed. Gerhard Kittel. Volume 3. Stuttgart, 1938.

Fries, Paul Roy. *Religion and the Hope for a Truly Human Existence: An Inquiry into the Theology of F. D. E. Schleiermacher and A. A. Van Ruler with Questions for America.* 1979.

Gergen, Kenneth. *An Invitation to Social Construction.* London/Thousand Oaks, 1999.

————. *Realities and Relationships: Soundings in Social Construction.* Cambridge/ London, 1994.

Gräb, Wilhelm. *Lebensgeschichten, Lebensentwürfe, Sinndeutungen. Eine Praktische Theologie gelebter Religion.* Gütersloh, 1998.

————. *Predigt als Mitteilung des Glaubens. Studien zu einer prinzipiellen Homiletik in praktischer Absicht.* Gütersloh, 1988.

Grözinger, Albrecht. *Praktische Theologie als Kunst der Wahrnehmung.* Gütersloh, 1995.

————. "Eduard Thurneysen." In *Geschichte der Seelsorge in Einzelporträts,* ed. Christian Möller. Volume 3. Göttingen/Zurich, 1996.

————. "Praktische Theologie als Kunst der Wahrnehmung." In *Gelebte Religion. Im Brennpunkt praktisch-theologischen Denkens und Handelns,* ed. Albrecht Grözinger and Jürgen Lott. Festschrift for Gert Otto. Rheinbach, 1997.

Grözinger, Albrecht, and Jürgen Lott, eds. *Gelebte Religion. Im Brennpunkt praktisch-theologischen Denkens uns Handelns.* Rheinbach, 1997.

Gunning, J. H., Jr. *Blikken in de Openbaring.* Volumes 1-3. Rotterdam, 1929.

Harskamp, Anton van. *Het nieuw-religieuze verlangen.* Kampen, 2000.

Hauschildt, Eberhard. *Alltagsseelsorge. Eine sozio-linguistische Analyse des pastoralen Geburtstagsbesuches.* Göttingen, 1996.

Heering, G. J. *Geloof en Openbaring.* Volume 1. Arnhem, 1935.

Heiler, Friedrich. *Das Gebet. Eine religionsgeschichtliche und religionspsychologische Untersuchung.* 5th ed. Munich, 1923.

Heitink, Gerben. *Pastorale zorg. Theology, differentiatie, praktijk.* Kampen, 1998.

————. *Practical Theology: History, Theory, Action Domains.* Grand Rapids, 1999.

————. *Praktische Theologie. Geschiedenis, theorie, handelingsvelden.* Kampen, 1993.

Hellemans, G. A. F., M. A. G. T. Kloppenburg, H. J. Tieleman, eds. *De moderniteit van religie.* Zoetermeer, 2001.

Heppe, H., and E. Bizer, eds. *Die Dogmatik der evangelisch-reformierten Kirche.* Neukirchen, 1958.

Hermans, C. A. M., and G. Immink, eds. *Social Constructionism and Theology.* Leiden/Boston, 2002.

Hermelink, Jan. "Predigt in der Werkstatt." *Berliner Theologische Zeitschrift* 12 (1995).

Hick, John. *Faith and Knowledge.* 2nd ed. London/Ithaca, NY, 1970.

———. *Philosophy of Religion.* Englewood Cliffs, NJ, 1973.

Hiltner, Sewart. *Preface to Pastoral Theology: The Ministry and Theory of Shepherding.* Nashville, 1958.

Hogan, Lucy Lind. "Rethinking Persuasion: Developing an Incarnational Theology of Preaching." In *Homiletic* 24:2 (1999).

Hoitenga, Dewey J. *Faith and Reason from Plato to Plantinga.* Albany, 1991.

Immink, F. G. *Divine Simplicity.* Kampen, 1987.

———. "Human Discourse and Preaching." In *Social Constructionism and Theology,* ed. C. A. M. Hermans, G. Immink, et al. Leiden/Boston, 2002.

———. "Theism and Christian Worship." In *Christian Faith and Philosophical Theology,* ed. Gijsbert van den Brink et al. Kampen, 1992.

Josuttis, Manfred. *Die Einführung in das Leben. Pastoraltheologie zwischen Phaenomenologie und Spiritualität.* Gütersloh, 1996.

———. *Praxis des Evangeliums zwischen Politik und Religion. Grundprobleme der Praktischen Theologie.* Munich, 1974.

———. *Segenskräfte. Potentiale einer energetischen Seelsorge.* Gütersloh, 2000.

Jüngel, Eberhard. *Das Evangelium von der Rechtfertigung des Gottlosen als Zentrum des christlichen Glaubens. Eine theologische Studie in ökumenischer Absicht.* Tübingen, 1999.

———. *Gottes Sein ist im Werden.* 4th ed. Tübingen, 1986.

Kant, Immanuel. *Kritik der reinen Vernunft (The Critique of Pure Reason).* Wilhelm Weischedel/Wissenschaftliche Buchgesellschaft edition. *Kant Werke,* vol. 4. Darmstadt, 1975.

Kaufman, Gordon D. "Evidentialism: A Theologian's Response." In *Faith and Philosophy* 6 (1989).

———. *God the Problem.* Cambridge, 1972.

———. *Theology for a Nuclear Age.* Manchester/Philadelphia, 1985.

Klostermann, Ferdinand, and Rolf Zerfasz, eds. *Praktische Theologie Heute.* Munich, 1974.

Knippenberg, Tjeu van. *Tussen Naam en Identiteit. Ontwerp van een model voor geestelijke begeleiding.* Kampen, 1998.

Kolk, Herman. *Actief en passief bewustzijn. Korte voorgeschiedenis van de cognitieve psychologie.* 2nd ed. Rotterdam, 2000.

Kraemer, H. *Communicatie. Een tijdvraag.* The Hague, 1957.

Krause, Gerhard, ed. *Praktische Theologie. Texte zum werden und Selbstverständnis der praktischen Disziplin der evangelischen Theologie.* Darmstadt, 1972.

Kuitert, H. M. *Over religie. Aan de liejhebbers onder haar beoefenaars.* Baarn, 2000.

————. *Wat heel geloven?* Baarn, 1977.

Kuyper, A. *Het Werk van den Heiligen Geest.* Volume 3. Amsterdam, 1889.

Lämmermann, Godwin. *Einleitung in die Praktische Theologie. Handlungstheorien und Handlungsfelder.* Stuttgart, 2001.

Leeuw, G. van der. *Liturgiek.* Nijkerk, 1946.

Liebner, Theodor Albert. "Begriff, Gegenstand und Einteilung der praktischen Theologie." In *Praktische Theologie. Texte zum Werden und Selbstverständnis der praktischen Disziplin der Evangelischen Theologie,* ed. Gerhard Krause. Darmstadt, 1972.

Lindbeck, George A. *The Nature of Doctrine: Religion and Theology in a Postliberal Age.* Philadelphia, 1984.

Lischer, Richard. *A Theology of Preaching: The Dynamics of the Gospel.* Durham, NC, 1992.

————. "Why I Am Not Persuasive." *Homiletic* 24 (1999).

Long, Thomas G. *The Witness of Preaching.* Louisville, 1989.

Loux, Michael J., ed. *Universals and Particulars: Readings in Ontology.* Notre Dame, 1976.

Luther, Henning. "Predigt als Handlung." *Zeitschrift für Theologie und Kirche* 80 (1983).

————. *Religion und Alltag. Bausteine zu einer Praktische Theologie des Subjects.* Stuttgart, 1992.

Luther, Martin. *De babylonische gevangenschap van de kerk; Brief aan Paus Leo X; De vrijheid van een christen.* Dutch translation by C. N. Impeta; introduction by W. J. Kooiman. Kampen, 1959.

————. *Ein kleiner Unterricht, was man in den Evangelien suchen und erwarten soll. Vorwort zur Kirchenpostille.* WA Band 10/1.

McFague, Sallie. *Models of God: Theology for an Ecological, Nuclear Age.* London, 1987.

Manenschijn, Gerrit. *God is zo groot dat Hij niet hoeft te bestaan. Over narratieve constructies van de geloofswerkelijkheid.* Baarn, 2001.

Meiden, Anne van der. *De markt van geloven. Ontsokkeling, vernieuwing en verandering in geloofsgemeenschappen.* Baarn, 1999.

Miedema, Siebren, ed. *Pedagogiek in meervoud. Wegen in het denken van opvoeding en onderwijs.* Houten, 1997.

Migliore, Daniel L. *Faith Seeking Understanding: An Introduction to Christian Theology.* Grand Rapids, 1991.

Molen, I. J. van der. *Opvoedingstheorie en opvoedingspraktijk.* Groningen, 1994.

Möller, Christian, ed. *Geschichte der Seelsorge in Einzelporträts.* Volume 3. Göttingen/Zurich, 1996.

Müller, Alfred Dedo. *Grundriss der praktischen Theologie.* Gütersloh, 1950.

Müller, Alois. "Praktische Theologie zwischen Kirche und Gesellschaft." In *Praktische Theologie Heute,* ed. Ferdinand Klostermann and Rolf Zerfasz. Munich, 1974.

Nembach, Ulrich. *Predigt des Evangeliums.* Neukirchen, 1972.

Newman, J. H. *Grammar of Assent.* Garden City, NY, 1955.

Nicol, Martin. *Gespräch als Seelsorge. Theologische Fragmenten zu einer Kultur des Gesprächs.* Göttingen, 1990.

Niebergall, Friedrich. "Die moderne Predigt." In *Aufgabe der Predigt,* ed. Gert Hummel. Darmstadt, 1971.

———. "Wissenschaftliche Grundlagen der Praktischen Theologie." In *Praktische Theologie. Texte zum werden und Selbstverständnis der praktischen Disziplin der evangelischen Theologie,* ed. Gerhard Krause. Darmstadt, 1972.

Niebuhr, H. Richard. *Faith on Earth: An Inquiry into the Structure of Human Faith.* New Haven/London, 1989.

Nipkow, Karl Ernst. "Practical Theology and Contemporary Culture." In *Practical Theology: International Perspectives,* ed. Friedrich Schweitzer and Johannes A. van der Ven. Frankfurt am Main/Berlin, 1999.

Noordmans, O. *Liturgie.* Amsterdam, 1939.

———. *Verzamelde werken.* Volume 2. Kampen, 1979.

———. *Verzamelde werken.* Volume 3. Kampen, 1981.

Oosterzee, J. J. van. *Practische Theologie. Een handboek voor jeugdige godgeleerden.* Volume 1. Utrecht, n.d.

Osmer, Richard R. "Practical Theology as Argument, Rhetoric, and Conversation." *The Princeton Seminary Bulletin* 18:1 (1997).

Otto, Gert. *Grundlegung der Praktische Theologie.* Munich, 1986.

Otto, Rudolf. *The Idea of the Holy.* London/Oxford, 1972.

Plantinga, Alvin. *Does God Have a Nature?* Milwaukee, 1980.

———. *The Nature of Necessity.* Oxford, 1974.

———. "Reason and Belief in God." In *Faith and Rationality,* ed. Alvin Plantinga and Nicholas Wolterstorff. Notre Dame, 1983.

———. *The Twin Pillars of Christian Scholarship.* Grand Rapids, 1990.

———. *Warranted Christian Belief.* New York/Oxford, 2000.

Plantinga, Alvin, and Nicholas Wolterstorff, eds. *Faith and Rationality.* Notre Dame, 1983.

Plantinga, Cornelius, Jr. *Not the Way It's Supposed to Be: A Breviary of Sin.* Grand Rapids, 1995.

Poling, James N., and Donald E. Miller. *Foundations for a Practical Theology of Ministry.* Nashville, 1985.

Ricoeur, Paul. "Contribution d'une réflexion sur le langage à une théologie de la Parole." *Revue de Théologie et de Philosophie* 18 (1968).

———. *Interpretation Theory: Discourse and the Surplus of Meaning.* Fort Worth, 1976.

———. *Tekst en betekenis. Opstellen over de interpretatie van literatuur.* Baarn, 1991.

———. *Wegen van de filosofie. Structuralisme, psycholanalyse, hermeneutiek.* Essays of Paul Ricoeur, selected and introduced by Ad Peperzak. Bilthoven, 1970.

Ridderbos, Herman. *Paulus. Ontwerp van zijn theologie.* Kampen, 1971.

Rössler, Dietrich. *Grundrisz der Praktischen Theologie.* Berlin/New York, 1986.

Ruler, A. A. van. *De vervulling van de wet. Een dogmatische studie over de verhouding van openbaring en existentie.* 2nd ed. Nijkerk, 1974.

———. *Theologisch werk.* Volumes 1-5. Nijkerk, 1969-72.

Russell, Bertrand. "The Problems of Philosophy." Reprinted in *Universals and Particulars,* ed. Michael J. Loux. Notre Dame, 1976.

Scharfenberg, Joachim. *Seelsorge als Gespräch.* Göttingen, 1974.

Schleiermacher, Friedrich. *Der christliche Glaube.* Halle, 1830.

———. *Die praktische Theologie nach den Grundsätzen der evangelischen Kirche im Zusammenhang dargestellt.* Edited by Jacob Frerich. Berlin, 1850; reprinted New York, 1983.

———. *On Religion: Speeches to Its Cultured Despisers.* Translated by Richard Crouter. Cambridge, 1988. First published Berlin, 1799.

———. *Kurze Darstellung.* Edited by Heinrich Scholz. Darmstadt, 1993.

Schweitzer, Friedrich. "Gelehrte, gelernte, gelebte Religion." In *Gelebte Religion. Im Brennpunkt praktisch-theologischen Denkens und Handelns,* ed. Albrecht Grözinger and Jürgen Lott. Festschrift for Gert Otto. Rheinbach, 1997.

———. "Practical Theology, Contemporary Culture, and the Social Sciences: Interdisciplinary Relationships and the Unity of Practical Theology as a Discipline." In *Practical Theology: International Perspectives,* ed. Friedrich Schweitzer and Johannes A. van der Ven. Frankfurt am Main/Berlin, 1999.

———. "Praktische Theologie und Hermeneutik." In *Paradigmenentwicklung in der Praktischen Theologie,* ed. Johannes A. van der Ven and Hans Georg Zieberz. Kampen/Weinheim, 1993.

Schweitzer, Friedrich, and Johannes A. van der Ven, eds. *Practical Theology: International Perspectives.* Frankfurt am Main/Berlin, 1999.

Schweitzer, J. *Zur Ordnung des Gottesdienstes.* Zurich, 1944.

Bibliography

Searle, John R. *Mind, Language and Society: Philosophy in the Real World.* New York, 1999.

Spiegel, Yorick. "Praktische Theologie als empirische Theologie." In *Praktische Theologie Heute,* ed. Ferdinand Klostermann and Rolf Zerfasz. Munich, 1974.

Strawson, P. F. *Subject and Predicate in Logic and Grammar.* London, 1974.

Stump, E., and N. Kretzman. "Theologically Unfashionable Philosophy." *Faith and Philosophy* 7 (1990).

Tacke, Helmut. *Mit dem Müden zur rechten Zeit zu reden. Beiträge zu einer bibelorientierten Seelsorge.* Neukirchen-Vluyn, 1989.

Taylor, Charles. *Sources of the Self: The Making of the Modern Identity.* Cambridge, 1989.

Thiemann, Ronald F. *Revelation and Theology: The Gospel as Narrated Promise.* Notre Dame, 1985.

Thurneysen, Eduard. "Die Aufgabe der Predigt." In *Aufgabe der Predigt,* ed. Gert Hummel. Darmstadt, 1971.

———. *Die Lehre von der Seelsorge.* Zurich, 1946.

Tillich, Paul. *The Courage to Be.* London, 1955.

———. *De moed om te zijn.* Utrecht, 1969.

———. *Dynamics of Faith.* New York, 1957.

———. *Perspectief op de protestantse theologie van de 19ᵉ en 20ᵉ Eeuw.* Utrecht, 1967.

———. *Systematic Theology.* Volume 1. Nisbet, 1968.

Tracy, David. *Blessed Rage for Order: The New Pluralism in Theology.* Chicago/London, 1996.

Ven, Johannes A. van der. *Ecclesiology in Context.* Grand Rapids, 1993.

———. *Entwurf einer empirischen Theologie.* Kampen/Weinheim, 1990.

———. "Pastorale protocolanalyse I. Pastoraat in vernieuwing." *Praktische Theologie* 5 (1993).

———. "Pastorale protocolanalyse II. Pastoraat in maat en getal." *Praktische Theologie* 1 (1994).

———. "Pastorale protocolanalyse III. Pastoraat naar zin en betekenis." *Praktische Theologie* 1 (1994).

———. *Practical Theology: An Empirical Approach.* Kampen, 1993.

Ven, Johannes A. van der, and Hans Georg Ziebertz, eds. *Paradigmenentwicklung in der Praktischen Theologie.* Kampen/Weinheim, 1993.

Voetius, Gijsbertus. *De praktijk der godzaligheid.* Edited with introduction, translation, and commentary by C. A. de Niet. Utrecht, 1996.

Vriezen, Th. C. *Hoofdlijnen der theologie van het Oude Testament.* Wageningen, 1966.

Vrijer, M. J. A. de. *Het ingekeerde leven.* Leiden, 1938.

Waals, D. B. van der. *Het Heilig Communiceren.* Kampen, 1990.

Woelderink, J. G. *Verbond en bevinding.* Introduction by C. van der Wal. Amsterdam, 1974.

Wolterstorff, Nicholas. *Divine Discourse: Philosophical Reflections on the Claim that God Speaks.* Cambridge, 1995.

————. "Is It Possible and Desirable for Theologians to Recover from Kant?" *Modern Theology* 14:1 (January 1998).

————. *Reason within the Bounds of Religion.* Grand Rapids, 1976.

Zerfasz, Rolf. "Praktische Theologie als Handlungswissenschaft." In *Praktische Theologie Heute,* ed. Ferdinand Klostermann and Rolf Zerfasz. Munich, 1974.

Ziebertz, Hans-Georg. *Religie in een tijd zonder religie?* Utrecht, 1996.

Zijlstra, W. *Klinisch pastorale vorming. Een voorlopige analyse van het leer-en groepsproces van zeven cursussen.* Assen, 1969.

Zimmerli, W. *Grundriss der alttestamentlichen Theologie.* Stuttgart, 1972.

Index of Names and Subjects